5·95

THE DEBATE ON
THE ENGLISH
REVOLUTION

BY THE SAME AUTHOR

Puritanism in North-West England: a regional study of the diocese of Chester to 1642 (Manchester University Press, 1972).

(with W.H. Chaloner) *British Economic and Social History: a bibliographical guide* (Manchester University Press, 1976).

THE DEBATE ON
THE ENGLISH REVOLUTION

R. C. Richardson

Methuen & Co Ltd
London

First published in 1977
by Methuen & Co Ltd
11 New Fetter Lane, London EC4P 4EE

Copyright © 1977 R C Richardson

Photoset by Red Lion Setters, London
Printed and bound in Great Britain by
Richard Clay (The Chaucer Press) Ltd.,
Bungay, Suffolk

ISBN 0 416 81750 5 (Hardbound)
ISBN 0 416 81760 2 (Paperback)

FOR
JOAN THIRSK
IN FRIENDSHIP AND GRATITUDE

Contents

Preface

History, E.H. Carr reminded his readers, is 'an unending dialogue between the present and the past'. 'When you read a work of history', he went on, 'always listen out for the buzzing. If you can detect none, either you are deaf or your historian is a dull dog.'

> Before you study the history study the historian ... Before you study the historian study his historical and social environment. The historian, being an individual, is also a product of history and of society; and it is in this two-fold light that the student of history must learn to regard him.[1]

The increasing attention given to historiography in first-degree courses in universities and colleges presumably rests partly on a growing agreement with the kind of precept which Carr laid down. It rests also, of course, on the belief that history's own past needs to be explored, and that the very latest books and articles on a given subject are not the only ones worth reading. 'Exciting new techniques', it has been observed, 'can imprison the mind as surely as old prejudices. Reading old history can help one escape the tyranny of new, and be a useful cerebral hygiene.'[2]

Arguably one of the most realistic and fruitful approaches to historiography is by way of case studies, a number of which are now conveniently available. On the British industrial revolution, for example, there is *Capitalism and the Historians* (Chicago, University Press, 1954), a collection of essays edited by F.A. Hayek, and more recently A.J. Taylor's volume on *The Standard of Living in Britain in the Industrial Revolution* (London, Methuen, 1975). On political history, there is Sir Herbert Butterfield's skilful investigation of

George III and the Historians (London, Collins, 1957), and Hedva Ben-Israel's study of *English Historians and the French Revolution* (Cambridge, C.U.P., 1968). The Trinidad premier, Eric Williams, wrote an interesting account of *British Historians and the West Indies* (London, Deutsch, 1966).

But the classic historiographical case study is *Napoleon For and Against* (London, Cape, 1949) by the great Dutch historian Pieter Geyl (1887-1966). The book superbly illustrates the author's general contention that the study of history is 'an argument without end'.

> The lack of finality strikes me as both unavoidable and natural ... As soon as there is a question of explanation, of interpretation, of appreciation, though the special method of the historian remains valuable, the personal element can no longer be ruled out, that point of view which is determined by the circumstances of his time and by his own preconceptions. Every historical narrative is dependent upon explanation, interpretation, appreciation. In other words we cannot see the past in a single, communicable picture except from a point of view, which implies a choice, a personal perspective. It is impossible that two historians living in different periods, should see any historical personality in the same light. The greater the political importance of an historical character the more impossible this is.[3]

This book adds the English Revolution of the mid-seventeenth century to the list of available historiographical case studies.[4] Let it be said at once, however, that the present work makes no claim to completeness; it presupposes some basic knowledge of the historical events themselves. What follows is no more than a modest contribution to the history of a vast subject which still awaits a large-scale treatment. All that a short study of this kind can hope to do is to provide an introduction to the historiography of the English Revolution, to identify the main areas of debate, the context in which they took place, and to explore some of the principal tendencies in research and writing on the subject. It is designed as an aid to further reading, not as a substitute for it. As such it is hoped that students in universities and colleges will find it helpful and that they will want to go on to look at more of the texts on which it is based and at other works on the development of history.

The book has arisen out of a course which I have been teaching at Thames Polytechnic for the last six years; I have gained enormously from the experience of planning and running it and from discussions with colleagues and with past and present students. Many historians have helped me in various ways during the period of writing. Dr J.T. Cliffe, Dr Mary Finch, Anthony Fletcher, Dr Christopher Hill, Dr Derek Hirst, Dr Clive Holmes, Professor Roger Howell, Dr H.A. Lloyd, Dr J.S. Morrill, Dr Valerie Pearl, Ross Terrill and Professor George Yule kindly supplied information on specific points. Dr Brian Manning generously made available to me the page proofs of his book on *The English People and the English Revolution 1640-1649* prior to its publication. The enthusiasm for this project shown by John Naylor of Methuen was a constant support. I am grateful to my colleague Paul Stigant for reading the book in typescript and for his constructive suggestions. Peter Oxlade nobly helped in checking the proofs. Joan Thirsk added to the many kindnesses she has shown to me over the years by reading the whole work in typescript and by suggesting a number of improvements. It is to her that I dedicate this book.

The spelling and punctuation in quotations from seventeenth- and eighteenth-century works have occasionally been modernized where this seemed necessary in the interests of clarity. The notes are collected together at the end of the book.

July 1976

Chapter 1

Introduction: the context of the debate

The final, dispassionate, authoritative history of the Civil Wars cannot be written until the problems have ceased to matter; by that time it will not be worth writing. (C.V. Wedgwood, *The King's Peace 1637-1641* (London, Collins, 1955), p.14.)

The English Revolution of the mid-seventeenth century — that complex period which involved the downfall of Charles I's government, civil wars, social upheaval, and the creation of a republic — has long attracted the attention of historians, and the available literature on the subject is now formidably large and indigestible. This book does not set out to provide another 'straight' history of the original events, either in the form of a general survey or of a monograph on a particular aspect. Its concern is, in fact, not so much with the mid-seventeenth century itself but with the posthumous history of that period, with the ways in which it has been interpreted and analysed by successive generations of historians. Following a chronological sequence, chapters 2-4 look at writings on the English Revolution in the seventeenth, eighteenth and nineteenth centuries respectively. Chapters 5-9 deal with various aspects of the twentieth-century historiography of the subject. The book as a whole is designed as a sustained attempt to answer two distinct but closely related questions:

(1) Why has the English Revolution remained such a controversial subject for historians?

(2) How have historians approached and explained it?

The explanation of the continuing importance attached to the English Revolution rests partly, of course, on the undoubted impact of the original events themselves. Civil wars and revolutions are by their nature divisive. They divide between those who support, oppose, or hold aloof from the struggle. They divide between those who win and those who lose, between those who benefit from, and those who simply suffer as a result of, political upheaval or social and economic change. The English Revolution produced just this range of contemporary responses and results. It was inherently controversial. Its events were momentous and far-reaching. 'If in time, as in place,' wrote Thomas Hobbes (see pp.21-4), 'there were degrees of high and low, I verily believe that the highest of time would be that which passed between the years of 1640 and 1660.' Civil wars in themselves were not new in England; there were several medieval precedents. But in the seventeenth century for the first time a defeated king was put on trial in the name of his people, found guilty and publicly executed. The traditional hierarchies of the monarchical state and the Anglican Church were systematically dismantled. The institutions of government were restructured, the House of Lords was abolished, feudal tenures were ended, bishops were dispossessed, a standing army came into existence. For the first, and only, time in English history the country became a republic. Though the monarchy was restored in 1660 there could be no question of putting back the clock to where it had stood before the Civil War.

The events themselves, then, were inherently divisive and controversial; there could be no general agreement among contemporary historians about the causes and significance of what had taken place. How far back in time did they need to go to discover the origins? Were the real causes to be found in the immediate past? (Clarendon). Was rebellion the perverse product of a period of peace and plenty?

> The first and general cause was the Sins of the People, who (taking a surfeit of ease, plenty and pleasure) and growing wanton thereby, gazed after novelty (that magnetical attraction of the plebeian rout) and as discontented with their present condition, sought felicity in things they wanted, and were still unsatisfied even in the accomplishment thereof: whence is occasioned the hatred of tranquillity, the desire of motion, the loathing of present things, and seeking after future.[1]

So wrote the anonymous author of *Britania Triumphalis; a brief history of the Warres* in 1654. Clement Walker agreed (see p.13). Or did the Civil War represent the avenging hand of God at work? (Thomas May). And where in fact should historians look for an explanation? Did responsibility rest squarely with the King's dark designs and political ineptitude? (Thomas May, Joshua Sprigge, John Vicars). Or was it Parliament's ambition that was to blame? (Thomas Hobbes, John Nalson, William Dugdale). Was the rebellion the work of a subversive conspiracy? (Hobbes, Nalson). Could the upheavals be explained in purely political terms or was it necessary to take into account changes in society and the distribution of wealth? (James Harrington). What part did religion play? Could one agree with Peter Heylyn (see p.9) when he discussed the Scottish rebellion 'that though Liturgy and Episcopacy were made the occasions, yet they were not the causes of this war, religion being but the vizard to disguise that business, which covetousness, sacrilege, and rapine had the greatest hand in'?[2] What was the role of individual actors in the drama such as Charles I and Cromwell?

The kind of explanations which were put forward by the earliest historians of the Revolution reflected, of course, the differences in the range of sources which they had at their disposal. As their own personal experiences — the controlling factor — contrasted sharply these differences were in fact greater than at any later point in the historiography of this subject. In other words, seventeenth-century historians of the Civil War could not make use of a common body of evidence. The different explanations they put forward also reflected changes in the prevailing political situation. Could a Royalist speak freely before 1660, and conversely could a Parliamentarian historian really speak his mind in the uncongenial period 1660-88?

But the explanations which they offered were also bound up with the state of history at that time and the kind of expectations that were entertained about its political and moral utility. In the sixteenth and seventeenth centuries, the study of history was undergoing a number of important changes; one writer, indeed, has spoken of a 'revolution' in historical writing and thought taking place in this period.[3] It is true that the older moral purposes of history were not abandoned, and the growth of puritanism lent added weight to historical explanations based on notions of divine intervention. But in general, the study of history in post-Reformation England became noticeably more secularized. Its writers and its audience were no longer — as in the Middle Ages — drawn largely from the clergy. Historians now catered increasingly for the varied interests of a lay audience, and as a subject history began to play an important part in the political and social education of the gentry and middle classes.[4] History, it was increasingly believed, taught patriotism, political wisdom and true religion. Francis Bacon granted history an important place in his schemes for the advancement of learning. Harrington's political philosophy was historically based. The antiquarian researches of lawyers and others in the public records placed history at the service of politics.[5] The Civil War, in fact, re-emphasized the importance of history; both sides in the war ransacked the past for historical precedents with which to buttress themselves. In the Civil War, then, there emerged not simply opposing parties and opposing armies, but opposing theories of history[6] (see pp.11-12, 19).

The impact of the English Revolution and its effects on historical study long outlived their original context. The political and religious dimensions of the seventeenth-century crisis remained intensely relevant and controversial far beyond 1660. They became, in fact, part of the very substance of eighteenth-century political life and religious disagreements. In the eighteenth century the history of the English Revolution became inseparably bound up with the party political rivalries of Whigs and Tories and with the mutual animosities of Anglicans and Dissenters. Historical objectivity, even if it was aimed at, was unlikely to be respected. It was the readers, the users of history as much as the writers who created Whig and Tory versions of the past in the eighteenth century. (The 'philosophical' history which emerged in the eighteenth century should be seen partly as the historian's bid for political independence). Histories of the seventeenth-century crisis were far too valuable as political ammunition to be left in the hands of scholars. The eighteenth-century historiography of the English Revolution, then, was a series of contests. The works of Clarendon and Echard, which appeared in the first two decades of the century, were denounced as Tory propaganda by a succession of Whig writers (Oldmixon, Rapin). In the second half of the century Hume's anti-Whig *History* was proclaimed as a moderate Toryism and as such held the field until it was itself displaced from popularity in the nineteenth-century Whig revival (Brodie, Hallam, Macaulay).

The English Revolution continued to be politically relevant in the nineteenth century; one has only to study political attitudes to Oliver Cromwell to appreciate that.[7] Radicals like Godwin extolled the neglected virtues of England's seventeenth-century republic and extracted predictable lessons from the past for their own contemporaries. Mainstream Whigs, and Macaulay above all, with a new nationalism around them and the Romantic Movement behind them, re-emphasized the glorious achievements of the parliamentary struggle against Charles I for the political and religious liberty of the English people. Macaulay's *History of England* rapidly became one of the great Victorian classics. Published at a time when upper- and middle-class Englishmen were congratulating themselves that their country had escaped the 1848 revolutions in Europe, its agreeable political message was communicated in unforgettable prose style. This was history at the peak of its popularity, and the subject matter of Macaulay's seventeenth-century narrative became as familiar to his readers as the plot of a novel by Dickens or Thackeray.

The same could not be said of the work of those so-called 'scientific' historians in the second half of the nineteenth century who set out, by the application of a rigorous methodology, to achieve a truer, and more objective view of the English past. Macaulay's *History* was a best-seller; the first instalment of S.R. Gardiner's great work of meticulous scholarship proved quite unsaleable and was ignominiously pulped. But scientific history did not destroy the Whig interpretation of history; it merely diluted it. [8] The *Cambridge Modern History*, planned by Lord Acton as a great monument to objective history and published in the early years of the twentieth century, was recognizable as the swan-song of Victorian liberalism. Gardiner's mammoth history of seventeenth-century England, despite all its scholarly moderation and its unyielding adherence to chronology, was still Whig history of a kind, inferentially displaying the author's own political sympathies and present-mindedness.

The main novelty in historical scholarship in the later nineteenth century lay not in any total break with the complacent, present-based Whig interpretation of the English past, but in the emergence of the historian's profession. The major historians of the later nineteenth century were not, as earlier, gentlemen amateurs or political party hacks. They were professionals, men with university appointments, proud of their academic status and of their research methods, and always at pains to stress the great difficulties of the work they undertook. Under their influence history left the open political arena, and historians themselves — now in sole charge of their subject — busily made new rules for the game. That the new historical product still bore some resemblance to the one which it aimed at replacing, we now see as being fundamentally inevitable. A historian, even one who claimed to be a detached academic, is always a part of his own society, and consciously or unconsciously will use the present in his approach to the past. The main difference between Macaulay and Gardiner was that the first historian openly and proudly approached the seventeenth-century crisis from a nineteenth-century Whig standpoint, while the second did something similar despite himself.

The historical study of the English Revolution has been closely bound up with political and social change. In a real sense, as Croce's famous dictum has it, 'all history is contemporary history'. The real break with the nineteenth-century Whig interpretation came not in the late nineteenth century, but in the harsher, less bracing climate prevailing after the two World Wars. It is true, of course, that the Marxist alternative to the liberal version of determinism dates back to the nineteenth century. But before the inter-war period the historical work of Marx and Engels on economic inevitability, on the place of class struggle in the general pattern of social and economic change, and on the role of the proletariat, had made a negligible impact in England. Christopher Hill's earliest articles and the book on the English Revolution which he edited in 1940 were deliberately designed to publicize what was still for most English historians of the seventeenth century, reared on Gardiner, Firth, and Trevelyan, a new and alarmingly radical way of looking at the past. (See pp.100-1.)

Partly under the influence of Marxist ideas — both directly and indirectly (in attempts to counter and disprove the dangerous heresy) — and partly due to the influential work of R.H. Tawney (see pp.85-97), historians of the English Revolution began to unfix their gaze on seventeenth-century constitutional struggles and to look instead at the relatively uncharted territory of the society and the economy out of which the crisis had emerged. The gentry controversy (see pp.89-93) was one rather spectacular and noisy example of this new-found interest in the social and economic. But it demonstrated the ease with which alluringly plausible hypotheses could outrun the research needed to support them, and hinted at the potential dangers of constructing a separate social and economic interpretation which did not take full count of political divisions, regional differences, and the conservatism of many parliamentarians. Hence one of the most recent stages in the historiography of the English Revolution has been a revival of interest in political events, processes, participation, and machinery — a revisiting of the region explored by Gardiner but with the aid of new maps, new travelling aids provided by the twentieth-century economic, social and regional historians. Political historians of the English Revolution are now mindful that they must place government and administration within a broader context and recognize that a narrow view of the popular politics of the 'revolution from below' is impossible. Increasingly, too, historians of the English Revolution are realizing the necessity of looking at the seventeenth century as a whole. But historians continue to disagree about the causes and consequences of the English Revolution; on this subject there is no generally accepted historical orthodoxy. New research sometimes takes on a dual function, on the one hand of undermining old myths and on the other of reinforcing old prejudices.[9]

Although specifically concerned with the historiography of the English Revolution, this book is also a case study of the development of historical research and writing in England in the last three centuries. It reveals the historian at work in his capacity as a demolition expert. History as a subject is a means of questioning the past, but as society itself changes and history with it, no two generations are likely to agree about the kind of questions that need asking nor are they necessarily satisfied with each other's answers. History, said the nineteenth-century Swiss historian Jacob Burckhardt, 'is on every occasion the record of what one age finds worthy of note in another'.[10] This book examines changes in the historical perception of the English Revolution in the light of Burckhardt's judgement.

Chapter 2

The seventeenth century: the debate begins

Happy those English historians who wrote some sixty years since before our civil distempers were born or conceived, seeing then there was a general right understanding betwixt the nation. But alas! such as wrote in or since our civil wars are seldom apprehended truly and candidly save of such of their own persuasion. (Thomas Fuller, *An Appeal of Injured Innocence* (1659), p.1.)

The historical debate on the English Revolution began, of course, in the seventeenth century and itself formed part of the contemporary struggles. The first historians of the Revolution — Clarendon, May, Hobbes, Harrington, and the others discussed in this chapter — were participants in or observers of the events they described, and what they wrote was in the full sense of the term *contemporary* history. History of this sort has obvious dangers and pitfalls as well as a particular value, a fact which the church historian Thomas Fuller (1608-61) entirely appreciated. Fuller firmly believed that 'the most informative histories to posterity and such as are most highly prized by the judicious are such as were written by the eye-witnesses thereof, as Thucydides the reporter of the Peloponnesian War'. But equally he recognized that, in writing contemporary history,

... I must tread tenderly because I go not, as before, on men's graves, but am ready to touch the quick of some yet alive. I know how dangerous it is to follow truth too near to the heels; yet better it is that the teeth of a historian be struck out of his head for writing the truth than that they remain still and rot in his jaws by feeding too much on the sweetmeats of flattery.[1]

Fuller's apprehensions about writing on recent events proved well founded, and his *Church History of Britain* published in 1655, despite its moderate tone and ostensibly non-political subject, did not save its author from savage attacks. Chief of his opponents was the Laudian Peter Heylyn (1600-62), whose *Life of Archbishop Laud* was published posthumously in 1668. But before this date Heylyn had already set out his objections to the bias of Fuller's *Church History*. Far from being neutral, Fuller's work, said Heylyn, offered unmistakable evidence of the author's puritan sympathies.

> All things pass on smoothly for the Presbyterians, whom he chiefly acts for ... No professed Puritan, no cunning Nonconformist or open Separatist comes upon the stage whom he follows not with plaudits and some fair commends ... [Whereas] the Fathers of the Church and conformable children of it are sent off commonly in silence and sometimes with censure.[2]

The question of puritanism, like that of the strictly political issues at stake in the English Revolution, was exceedingly controversial, and by discussing this subject Fuller had put his hand into a wasps' nest.[3]

But in the seventeenth century the historical controversy over the English Revolution was primarily political and constitutional. With the Civil Wars still fresh in their minds, contemporaries on both sides of the political fence vigorously debated the issues which had been defended and fought over in the 1630s and 1640s. Royalists and Parliamentarians both found their historians, who based their rival accounts on the abundant pamphlet literature of the period, on party manifestoes and reports of parliamentary speeches, on newspaper evidence, and last but by no means least on their own personal experience and prejudice.[4]

One of the first contemporary writers to give an account of the politics of the English Revolution was Thomas May (1595-1650), who in 1647 produced the officially commissioned *History of the Parliament of England*, following it three years later with *A Breviary of the History of the Parliament of England*. Although he recognized that the subject of the Civil War was extremely contentious, May pleaded with his readers in the preface to the first of his two books that what he was offering to them was the truth, a plain, naked narrative and explanation of events. May's position, however, as one of the Long Parliament's secretaries made such an objective history impossible, and in practice he wrote from the biased standpoint of the King's opponents; the 1647 book was designed as an apology for Parliament itself, while its companion, which was published after the second Civil War and the execution of the King, was written to praise the army and the Independents. Clarendon, who had once been May's confederate, bluntly dismissed him once 'he fell from his duty and all his former friends and prostituted himself to the vile office of celebrating the infamous acts of those who were in rebellion against the King; which he did so meanly that he seemed to all men to have lost his wits when he left his honesty; and so shortly afterwards died, miserable and neglected and deserved to be forgotten'.[5]

Clarendon was perhaps too severe. May at least made some effort to be fair to the Royalists and took no delight in the hostilities between King and Parliament ('this unnatural war', 'the unhappy distractions of these kingdoms'). But ultimately it was Parliament's case which Thomas May put forward, believing that,

the Parliament of England ... was more misunderstood in England that at Rome; and that there was a greater need to remind our own countrymen than to inform strangers of what was past, so much ... have they seemed to forget both the things themselves and their own former notions concerning them.

And it was Parliament's case from both his own situation and political preferences that May was best qualified to present.

My residence hath been during these wars in the quarters and under the protection of the Parliament; and whatsoever is briefly related of the soldiery ... is according to the light which I discerned there — If in this discourse more particulars are set down concerning the actions of those men who defended the Parliament than of those who warred against it, it was because my conversation gave me more light on that side.[6]

May's Parliamentarian history of the English Revolution, not surprisingly, stressed the untrustworthiness of James I and Charles I, their disregard of Parliament's rights and liberties, their illegal and inept actions, and their apparent abandonment of the Protestant cause. James I, May lamented, although he had some good qualities, showed too much favour towards the papists. Moreover, his relations with his Parliaments deteriorated, 'projects against the laws were found out to supply the King's expenses, which were not small', and government increasingly devolved into the grasping, unscrupulous hands of the Duke of Buckingham. All this, as May pointedly reminded his readers, stood in marked contrast to the actions of Queen Elizabeth 'of glorious memory' who had made 'the right use of her subjects' hearts, hands and purses in a parliamentary way' and during whose reign 'the prosperity of England seemed at the height ...'[7]

Under Charles I, grievances multiplied as the situation went rapidly from bad to worse.

> Forty years old was King Charles, and fifteen years had he reigned when this Parliament was called [i.e. in 1640]; so long had the laws been violated ... the liberties of the people invaded and the authority of Parliament, by which laws and liberties are supported, trodden under foot: which had by degrees much discontented the English nation.[8]

The King's acceptance of the Petition of Right was quickly forgotten, peace was made with Spain without Parliament's consent, titles and offices were sold freely to the highest bidder, 'multitudes of monopolies were granted by the King', the judiciary was interfered with, and from 1629 Parliament was dispensed with altogether. The ambitions and crimes of Strafford and Laud ('an English Pope') were rehearsed, and May lost no opportunity of emphasizing the Queen's popish preferences and her influence over the court. 'The countenancing of looseness and irreligion was no doubt a good preparative to the introducing of another religion, and the power of godliness being beaten down, popery might more easily by degrees enter.' No wonder, then, that Civil War finally erupted in England; all such causes worked relentlessly in this direction.

> It cannot but be thought, by all wise and honest men, that the sins of England were at a great height, that the injustice of governors and vices of private men were very great, which have since called down from Almighty God so sharp a judgement, and drawn on by degrees so calamitous and consuming a war.[9]

Thomas May's two publications, issued in 1647 and 1650, occupy a prominent place in what was in fact a growing Parliamentarian historical literature on the Civil War. The Parliamentarian cause indeed, more so than that of the King, was based on historical foundations. It had to be! Not to proclaim themselves as defenders of tradition would have been for Parliamentarians to admit that they were rebels. To deny the importance of Parliament in the past was implicitly to minimize its significance in the present. And what the Parliamentarians were defending, as they saw it, was the ancient constitution, the common law which had existed (so Coke said) since time immemorial, and the rights and liberties of all free-born Englishmen which Levellers and other radicals believed had been subverted by the Norman Conquest.[10]

Joshua Sprigge (1618-84) in his *Anglia Rediva* (1647), for example, presented the contemporary struggles as a necessary defence of Parliament, laws and liberties, and dedicated his work to all true Englishmen 'that have with bleeding hearts and distilling eyes been spectators of and common sufferers under the insulting paces of arbitrary power and unlimited prerogative'.[11] Also in the 1640s John Vicars (1580?-1652) was busily engaged in bringing out the three parts of his fiercely puritan *England's Parliamentarie Chronicle* (1644-6). The work was dedicated to the members of the Long Parliament, 'the most renowned reformers, breach repairers, and revivers of a despised, distressed, and almost destroyed Church and State'. The M.P.s' virtues appeared all the more obvious in Vicars' eyes when contrasted with the Royalists: 'the most boisterous and rebellious rout of atheistical and papistical philistines and viperous malignants who would have maliciously immured, damned, yea dried up and destroyed the precious wells of our Bethlem ...' Vicars went on in the course of his enthusiastic text to applaud Parliament's action in taking away 'that state staggering Star Chamber Court [and continuing in the same spirit] dissolved and dissipated into smoke the crushing courts of the President and Council of the North, and limited and confined the unlimited bounds of business at the Council table', The King's advisers in general Vicars contemptuously dismissed as 'living grievances', 'stinking channels of wrong and oppression'. But his bitterest spleen was reserved for Strafford and Laud.

> That insulting arch-traitor the Earl of Strafford who as he had well nigh stabbed the state to the heart by his deep and most dangerous plots both abroad and at home, so the stroke of justice retaliated with blood [for] his most bold and bloody designs ...
> That lamb-skinned wolf the Archprelate of Canterbury who had so long and so craftily and cruelly worried Christ's innocent lambs ...

To the same 1640s vintage belongs the hostile *History of Independency* (1648) by Clement Walker (d. 1651), a stubborn and quarrelsome M.P. excluded by Pride's Purge and imprisoned on account of his historical work. It was Walker who provided an extremely explicit statement of the seventeenth-century view that rebellion in England was the unlooked-for product of a corrupting period of peace and plenty.

A long Peace begat Plenty, Plenty begat Pride, and her sister Riot, Pride begat Ambition, Ambition begat Faction, Faction begat Civil War: and if our evils be not incurable ... our War will beget Poverty, Poverty Humility, Humility Peace again ... The declining spoke of the wheel will rise again. But we are not yet sufficiently humbled ...
[12]

In the 1650s came two works of a very different kind, the one a work of political theory and the other a valuable and extensive collection of contemporary source material. The first, published in 1656, was *The Commonwealth of Oceana* by James Harrington (1611-77). Properly speaking, Harrington was not a historian at all, and his later influence, too, in France and America to a greater extent than in England, was mainly in the sphere of political ideas. But his place in the historiography of the English Revolution is assured on two counts. First, Harrington believed in the importance of history and offered a general theory of historical development.

No man can be a politician except he be first a historian or a traveller, for except he can see what must be or what may be he is no politician. Nor if he has no knowledge in history he cannot tell what is; but he that neither knows what has been nor what is can never tell what must be nor what may be.[13]

Second, Harrington's analysis has come to occupy an important position in twentieth-century debates on the origins of the Civil War. On the first count Professor Zagorin goes so far as to claim that Harrington 'rose to a degree of sophistication in his historical thinking that makes even the greatest historical work of his time seem primitive by comparison'.[14] For the insights he offers into the nature and causes of the English Revolution Harrington is rated by Zagorin more highly than Clarendon. Certainly, Harrington's work lies at the centre of modern historical controversies such as that over the rise of the gentry. (See pp.89-93). Both sides in the debate, of course, have used Harrington, who arguably was more concerned with the decline of the aristocracy than with the rise of the gentry, in different ways. Other historians — surprisingly, since Harrington did not think in terms of a class struggle — have seen in *Oceana* a prototype of the Marxist critique. Another writer has found in Harrington's book the blueprint of an 'opportunity state' while, such is the diversity of opinion on the subject, Professor Pocock has argued that Harrington 'was primarily a historian of feudalism and only in a most rudimentary sense an observer of contemporary social processes'. [15]

Despite the expedient use of fictitious names — Oceana (England), Marpesia (Scotland), Emporium (London), Parthenia (Elizabeth I), Morpheus (James I), Olphaus Megaletor (Oliver Cromwell), Leviathan (Thomas Hobbes), and so on — Harrington's republican tract was firmly grounded in the harsh, but promising reality of mid-seventeenth-century England. The political system outlined in *Oceana* was not an impracticable Utopia. Given the situation in England at the time, and the redistribution of power which had already occurred, Oceana, as Harrington conceived it, was the logical, indeed necessary, outcome. *Oceana* was intended to place the English Revolution in historical perspective, to show that there had been an irreversible drift towards republicanism, and that in the circumstances Harrington's settlement was the only one possible.[16] Harrington was convinced that the main key to events in the seventeenth century was the economic one. (R.H. Tawney's famous essay on 'Harrington's Interpretation of His Age' was an elaboration of this point.[17]) Civil War took place in England because the political structure had ceased to correspond with economic reality.

> The dissolution of the late monarchy was as natural as the death of a man ... Oceana, or any other nation of no greater extent must have a competent nobility, or is altogether incapable of monarchy: for where there is equality of estates, there must be equality of power; and where there is equality of power there can be no monarchy ...
>
> Nor was there anything now wanting unto the destruction of the throne but that the people not apt to see their own strength should be put to feel it; when a prince, as stiff in disputes as the nerve of monarchy was grown slack, received that unhappy encouragement from his clergy which became his utter ruin, while trusting more unto their logick than the rough philosophy of his Parliament, it came unto an irreparable breach; for the house of Peers which alone had stood in this gap, now sinking down between the King and the Commons, showed that Crassus was dead and Isthmus broken. But a monarchy divested of her nobility hath no refuge under heaven but an army. Wherefore the dissolution of this Government caused the War, not the War the dissolution of this government.[18]

Harrington's prescription for England's troubles was the political system outlined in *Oceana*, with the Agrarian Law designed to provide a stable economic base for the government and to prevent excessive concentrations of wealth.[19]

The other major work in this field to appear in the 1650s was the first volume of the *Historical Collections* of John Rushworth (1612?-90). Published in 1659 and dedicated to Richard Cromwell, Rushworth's work was as provocative in the short term as it has proved valuable in the long term to subsequent historians.[20] The preface which Rushworth supplied to Volume One declared his objectives and expounded his conception of historical method; it is worth quoting at length on both counts.

> Yet certainly of some use it may be to us, and of concernment also to those that may come after us ... to consider indifferently how we came to fall out among our selves and so to learn the true causes, the rises and growths of our late miseries, the strange alterations and revolutions with the characters of divers eminent persons, the mutability of councils, the remarkableness of actions, the subtilty of pretensions, and the drifts of several interests. From such premisses the best deduction which can be made is to look up to and acknowledge God who only is unchangeable and to admire His wisdom and providence even in human miscarriages. For empires, and kingdoms and commonwealths everywhere in the world have their periods, but the histories thereof remain and live for the instruction of men and glory of God...
>
> I began early to take in characters, speeches, and passages at conferences in Parliament and from the King's own mouth when he spake to both the Houses, and have been upon stage continually and an eye and ear witness of the greatest transactions; employed as an agent in and entrusted with affairs of weightiest concernment; privy also both to the debates in Parliament and to the most secret results of councils of war in times of action: which I mention without ostentation only to qualify me to report to posterity what will rather be their wonder at first than their belief. It is a pity they should altogether be deprived of the advantages which they may reap from our misfortunes. Hereafter they will hear that every man almost in this generation durst fight for what either was or pretended to be Truth. They should also know that some durst write the Truth, whilst other men's fancies were more busie than their

hands forging relations, building and battering castles in the air, publishing speeches as spoken in Parliament which were never spoken there, printing declarations which were never passed, relating battles that were never fought, and victories which were never obtained, dispersing letters which were never writ by the authors, together with many such contrivances to abet a party or interest ... Such practices and the experience I had thereof and the impossibility for any man in after ages to ground a true history by relying on the printed pamphlets in our days which passed the Press whilst it was without control, obliged to all the pains and charge I have been at for many years together to make a great collection; and whilst things were fresh in memory to separate truth from falsehood, things real from things fictitious or imaginary. Whereof I shall not at all repent if I may but prove an ordinary instrument to undeceive those that come after us....

I allow and accept it as a good memento which I meet with in a late Author: that most writers nowadays appear in public, not crook-backed (as it is reported of the Jews) but crook-sided, warped and bowed to the right or to the left. For I have heartily studied to declare myself unbiassed and to give an instance, that it is possible for an ingenuous man to be of party and yet not partial.

I pretend only in this work to a bare narrative of matter of fact digested in order of time, not interposing my own opinion or interpretation of actions. I infuse neither vinegar nor gall into my ink ... If I speak of any transactions which I myself did not see or hear I do so with all the caution imaginable, having first consulted records, conferred with persons of unquestionable esteem interested in the very actions or perused their known handwritings of those times. And where I make mention of any letters or passages scattered in print I first well weighed the same and out of whose closets they came and found many of them concredited before I inserted them....

As I never did approve so neither could I persuade myself to tread in their steps, who intermingle their passion with their stories and are not content to write of unless they write also for a party or to serve an interest, and so declare themselves far better Advocates than Historians. I profess that in singleness of heart I aim at Truth which to me has always seemed hugely amiable, even without the attires and advantages of wit and eloquence.

Rushworth's theory of historical method, unfortunately, was more difficult to translate into practice than he imagined. Despite his professed impartiality, his career in the republic's civil service, in which for a time he was Cromwell's secretary, and his dedication of the book to the Protector's son, identified him with the King's opponents and so exposed him to attacks from the right in the Royalist-dominated period of historiography between the Restoration and 1688.[21]

The most polemical of these was John Nalson's *Impartial Collection of the Great Affairs of State from the Beginning of the Scotch Rebellion in the Year 1639 to the Murder of King Charles I* (2 vols, 1682-3). The contradictions in the title chosen by Nalson (1638?-86) announced where his own allegiances lay. Moreover the work enjoyed royal patronage, and the official records were made available to this preferment-seeking author who obsequiously dedicated the finished publication to Charles II. Nalson, none the less, described himself as a 'votary of truth' while indulging in the 'liberty of an historian to tie up the loose and scattered papers with the circumstances, causes and consequences of them ...'. It was Nalson's express aim:

> To manifest the innocence of the government and vindicate it from those notorious detractions and calumnies which some factious and turbulent spirits who have had all along a design to subvert the establishment both of Church and State persuading the nation of strange designs to introduce arbitrary government and re-establish popery, whereas the truth is and I doubt not to make it appear, that these popular bugbears were only the contrivance of the anti-monarchical and schismatical faction to draw in a party, thereby to enable them to carry on their own wicked designs of at least reducing the monarchy to an impotent Venetian seigniory, and utterly to extirpate the most apostolical government of episcopy and set up the anarchy of Toleration and Liberty of Conscience in the church.
>
> [I vigorously condemn those who] under the smooth surface of pretences to maintain Liberty, Property, Protestant religion, and Privileges of Parliament, betrayed us into the most deplorable shipwreck that ever England saw, even to the entire loss of all these valuable things which were pretended to be preserved ...

Rushworth's *Historical Collections* came in for special attack, its editor being roundly denounced for his sympathies with the

Parliamentarian rebels, for his distortions and suppression of the evidence.

> The truth is if Mr Rushworth leans apparently to one side I would attribute it to his having grown so long, even from his very first taking root in the world, under the influences of that whirlwind of Rebellion ... Mr Rushworth hath concealed Truth, endeavoured to vindicate the prevailing detractions of the late times as well as their barbarous actions and with a kind of re-bound libelled the government at secondhand ... His *Collections* are the malicious part of the transactions of public affairs, picked out of the whole mass and represented with all the disadvantages that can be found out to justify the actions of the late rebels ... [Rushworth seems] so wholly transported with partiality to a party that he has recorded little but what relates to the justification of those he favours and their proceedings ... I would render this preface a volume to trace this gentleman in all his omissions, mutilations, abridgements, and, I may justly fear, additions ... The truth is those speeches which were loyal he has generally omitted but those who have fallen upon the popular theme of grievances he has carefully indeed collected and displayed to insinuate into the credulous and unwary that the heavy complaints of grievances were vox populi and the universal and just cry of the nation, and by consequence that the King, his ministers and government were wholly unjust, oppressive, cruel and tyrannical ...

Having mercilessly exposed Rushworth's bias, Nalson then proceeded to set the record straight and, in what he deluded himself was a calm and objective manner, began to narrate 'those affairs which brought ruin upon this excellent government' of Charles I. Nalson continued,

> To palliate the horrid sin of Rebellion they [the Parliamentarians] endeavoured to render his Majesty the aggressor and themselves engaged in a defensive war for the liberty of the subject, the laws of the land, and the true Protestant religion ... They razed the very foundations of the government both civil and ecclesiastical and erected upon the ruins of this glorious and imperial monarchy the title of the Commonwealth of England.
>
> These were the men who pretended religion and a thorough Reformation and these were some of the arts by which they betrayed

the easy people into rebellion, and the nation into ruin. These were the fatal consequences and effects of these popular fears and groundless jealousies of popery and arbitrary government, and this the dismal period of that horrid Rebellion ...

As Nalson saw it, there was only one conclusion to be drawn from the wicked revolt against Charles I: 'that true loyalty to their prince is both their interest and their duty, as they are men, christians and Englishmen. And that without it the fairest pretences to religion and Reformation are the most pernicious vizards and covers of the most dangerous of all kinds of rebellion.'[22]

Nalson's account was the most polemical of the anti-Parliamentarian histories to appear after the Restoration, but it was not an isolated one. The Royalist version of English history in general as well as of the Civil War in particular, stressing the sovereign and paternal aspects of monarchy and utilizing Brady's and Spelman's ideas on feudalism, was rapidly developing in the more congenial climate of the later seventeenth century.[23] James Heath (1629-64), for instance, earlier a staunch supporter of the cause of the exiled Charles II, in 1661 published his *Chronicle of the late Intestine War in the Three Kingdoms*, and dedicated it to General Monck. And in 1681, the anti-puritan, anti-Parliamentarian William Dugdale (1605-86) brought out his *Short View of the Late Troubles in England*. Dugdale could find little good to say about 'that viperous brood which not long since hath so miserably infested these kingdoms' and who had contrived the 'nefarious murder of King Charles I'. To Dugdale, the real origin of the Civil War lay in the hypocritical and subversive religion of the Parliamentarian leaders.

That all rebellions did ever begin with the fairest pretences for reforming of somewhat amiss in the government, is a truth so clear that there needs thereof no manifestation from examples. Nor were they ever observed to have greater success than when the colours for religion did openly appear in the van of their armed forces; most men being desirous to have it really thought (how bad and vile soever their practices are) that zeal to God's glory is no small part of their aim. Which gilded bait hath been usually held forth to allure the vulgar, by those whose ends and designs were nothing else than to get into power, and so to possess themselves of the estates and fortunes of their more opulent neighbours.[24]

What had taken place in mid-seventeenth-century England could only be described as a rebellion against justly constituted authority. Contrasts were drawn between Charles I 'a most pious and gracious prince', 'the happy Restoration of Charles II', and 'that grand impostor Cromwell', and analogies made between the Civil War and the Baronial Wars of Henry III and the French Wars of Religion. Dugdale had been active on the King's side in the Civil War, and the first part of his history (covering the years up to 1646) was written in the Royalist stronghold of Oxford. At the root of the Civil War troubles were religious extremists whose 'fair and smooth pretences set forth in several declarations and remonstrances by which the too credulous people were miserably deluded and drawn from their due allegiance'. In Parliament they constantly and unreasonably obstructed the King, and in the country they curried favour 'by planting schismatical lectures in most corporate towns and populous places throughout the realm so to poison the people with anti-monarchical principles'.

> If the reflections on what is past are sometimes severe let it be imputed to the just indignation conceived against those men who under specious pretences masked the most black designs, and [to] an abhorrence of those proceedings which embroiled the nation in a civil war, perfidious in its rise, bloody in its prosecution, fatal in its end and which to this day proves mischievous in its consequences ...
>
> That the meeting of these members of Parliament from all parts of the realm (being many of them men of turbulent spirits, and principles totally anti-monarchical), gave opportunity for those contrivances which afterwards were put in action, there is nothing more sure. For in the first place, they took care to infuse fears and jealousies into the people everywhere that the government was designed to be arbitrary, and popery like to be introduced, to promote which scandals many seditious preachers took no small pains in their pulpits especially in and about London.

Dugdale's conclusion echoed the persistent message of his text: that the Parliamentarian leaders had wilfully misled the people, and, for no good reason, contrived the downfall of the monarchy.

> And the people of England may now see how by bracing them too far in the forbidden paths of a conceived liberty they not long since fell into the known slavery of the French peasant. A misery which

some of them felt but a little, when for fear of it they first petitioned to be put into a posture of defence, but justly brought upon themselves by those undue courses which they took to prevent it, God in his wisdom thinking it fit to punish this nation by a real slavery unto some of their own fellow subjects for fancying to themselves an imaginary [one], under their lawful sovereign as a ground to justify their rebellion when there was no cause for it.

The book ends by quoting Sir Edward Coke's *Institutes* on treason, thus turning Parliamentarian legal theory against the rebels.[25]

Dugdale's emphasis on the subversive role of religious extremists is similar in this respect to *Behemoth or the Long Parliament* by Thomas Hobbes (1586-1679), written in the 1660s and published in 1679 and 1682. But Hobbes's work had something in common, too, with Harrington's *Oceana*, since again this was not a historical study in the conventional sense. For as the student remarks to the doctor in the first dialogue of *Behemoth*,

> I suppose your purpose was to aquaint me with the history, not so much of those actions that passed in the time of the late troubles, as of their causes, and of the councils and artifice by which they were brought to pass. There be divers men that have written the history, out of which I might have learned what they did, and somewhat also of the contrivance; but I find little in them of what I would ask.[26]

Like Harrington, Hobbes was first and foremost a philosopher, and he turned to history largely to find a tool with which to test his own science of politics which he had already systematically expounded in *The Elements of Law* (1640), *De Cive* (1642), and in *Leviathan* (1651). As Professor Goldsmith says,

> *Behemoth* is more than a brief history of the Civil War. It is not only an attack on what Hobbes regarded as false and dangerous prevailing opinions, but also an attempt to show how Hobbes's science explains the historical phenomena of the Great Rebellion. Even more it is Hobbes's triumphant vindication of the doctrines he had expounded since 1640 and of his proposal that Hobbism should be established by authority.[27]

Hobbes, therefore, had a less exalted view than Harrington of the nature and value of history, and unlike Harrington his interpretation of the English Revolution was not primarily a materialist one. There were elements of such an interpretation, however, in Hobbes's analysis, and Professor Macpherson has highlighted them in his book on *The Political Theory of Possessive Individualism.* [28] According to Macpherson, Hobbes attributed the outbreak of the Civil War to the new strength of market morality and to market-made wealth. Hobbes, his argument goes on, saw the Civil War as an attempt to replace the old constitution with one which was more economically favourable to the middle classes. Hobbes believed that each man was 'so much master of whatsoever he possessed that it could not be taken from him upon any pretence of common safety without his own consent'. Presbyterianism took root because it was a comfortable religion which did not 'inveigh against the lucrative vices of men of trade or handicraft ... which was a great ease to the generality of citizens and the inhabitants of market towns'. 'The city of London and other great towns of trade, having in admiration the great prosperity of the Low Countries after they had revolted from their monarch, the King of Spain, were inclined to think that the like change of government here would to them produce the like prosperity.' The Parliamentary army was maintained by 'the great purse of the city of London and contributions of almost all the towns corporate in England'. The main grievance at the time was taxation 'to which citizens, that is merchants, whose profession is their private gain are naturally mortal enemies, their only glory being to grow excessively rich by the wisdom of buying and selling'.[29]

Such passages, however, should not be given an exaggerated importance. Unlike Harrington, Hobbes offered a mainly ideological rather than a materialist interpretation of the seventeenth-century crisis. To Hobbes, the Civil War was basically a struggle for sovereignty and, as in his works on political philosophy, he argued in *Behemoth* in favour of undivided rule. 'There can be no government', he repeated endlessly, 'where there is more than one sovereign.' The Parliamentarians, on the other hand, said Hobbes, at the beginning of the Civil War 'dreamt of a mixed power of the King and of the two Houses. That it was a divided power in which there could be no peace was above their understanding.' The Earl of Essex, the Parliamentarian commander, 'was carried away with the stream [in a manner] of the whole nation to think that England was not an absolute but a mixed monarchy: not considering that the supreme power must always be absolute whether it be in the King or the Parliament'.[30] As this

quotation makes clear, therefore, Hobbes's theory of undivided
sovereignty was inherently ambiguous, as he himself admitted in an
apology to Charles II in 1662. Hobbes begged the King not 'to think
the worse of me, if snatching up all the weapons to fight against your
enemies I lighted upon one that had a double edge'.[31]

So the Civil War, in Hobbes's view, was basically a struggle for
sovereignty, first between King and Parliament and later between
Cromwell and the army on the one hand and Parliament on the other.
And how did these struggles originate? To a large extent, argued
Hobbes, they were the outcome of a subversive conspiracy stemming
from the universities, 'the core of rebellion', breeding grounds for
advanced, extravagant and seditious ideas. 'The universities', Hobbes
declared in a striking phrase, 'have been to this nation as the wooden
horse was to the Trojans.' The corrupting influences nurtured in the
universities were of two kinds: lawyers, and above all, clergymen —
war-mongering Presbyterian divines.

> Had it not been much better that those seditious ministers, which
> were not perhaps 1000, had all been killed before they had
> preached? It had been (I confess) a great massacre; but the killing of
> 100,000 [in the Civil War] is a greater ... They that preached us
> into the rebellion ... will say they did it in obedience to God,
> inasmuch as they did believe it was according to the Scripture; out
> of which they will bring examples, perhaps of David and his
> adherents that resisted King Saul ... Besides you cannot doubt but
> that they, who in the pulpit did animate the people to take arms in
> the defence of the then Parliament, alleged Scripture, that is, the
> word of God, for it. If it be lawful then for subjects to resist the
> King, when he commands anything that is against the Scripture,
> that is, contrary to the command of God, and to be judge of the
> meaning of the Scripture, it is impossible that the life of any King,
> or the peace of any Christian kingdom can be long secure. It is this
> doctrine that divides a kingdom within itself, whatsoever the men
> be, loyal or rebels, that preach it publicly ...[32]

Although it was the Presbyterian clergy who came in for particular
denunciation, Hobbes had no great love for clergymen of any
persuasion, or indeed for any religious group; papists as well as
puritans were exposed and criticized in *Behemoth*. What Hobbes
favoured was the establishment of a single Erastian church in which
ecclesiastical doctrine and practice would be a matter of civil law.[33]

Given the situation which had finally erupted into Civil War, to Hobbes the message was obvious: restoration of stability to the commonwealth would mean that the independent powers of universities, lawyers, and clergy would all have to be drastically curtailed by a totalitarian state.

> The core of rebellion, as you have seen by this, and read of other rebellions, are the universities; which nevertheless are not to be cast away, but to be better disciplined; that is to say, that the politics there taught be made to be (as true politics should be) such as are fit to make men know, that it is their duty to obey all laws whatsoever that shall by the authority of the King be enacted till by the same authority they shall be repealed; such as are fit to make men understand that the civil laws are God's laws, as they that make them are by God appointed to make them; and to make men know, that the people and the Church are one thing and have but one head, the King; and that no man has title to govern under him that has it not from him; that the King owes his crown to God only, and to no man, ecclesiastic or other; and that the religion they teach there be a quiet waiting for the coming again of our blessed Saviour, and in the meantime a resolution to obey the King's laws (which also are God's laws); to injure no man, to be in charity with all men, to cherish the poor and sick, and to live soberly and free from scandal; without mingling our religion with points of natural philosophy, as freedom of will, incorporeal substance, everlasting nows, ubiquities, hypostases, which the people understand not, nor will ever care for. When the universities shall be thus disciplined, there will come out of them, from time to time, well-principled preachers, and they that are now ill-principled, from time to time fall away.[34]

Hobbes emphasized the supreme importance of what had taken place in the middle of the century.

> If in time, as in place, there were degrees of high and low, I verily believe that the highest of time would be that which passed between the years of 1640 and 1660. For he that thence, as from the Devil's Mountain, should have looked upon the world and observed the actions of men, especially in England, might have had a prospect of all kinds of injustice, and of all kinds of folly, that the world could afford, and how they were produced by their dams' hypocrisy and self-conceit, whereof the one is double iniquity, and the other double folly.[35]

Hobbes's political philosophy, his views on undivided sovereignty, aroused many opponents in the seventeenth century, but of all these for our purposes the most noteworthy was Edward Hyde, Earl of Clarendon (1609-74), constitutional Royalist and empirical theorist of mixed monarchy.[36] With Clarendon we move unmistakably from quasi-history to the real thing. His *History of the Rebellion and Civil Wars in England* was the first full-length, systematic treatment of events in the early seventeenth century, and has been described as 'epoch-making in the development of English historical writing'.[37] First published in 1702-04, and reissued in at least twelve subsequent editions in the next 150 years, Clarendon's work is indeed a historical classic.

Clarendon, of course, was a prominent participant in the events he described. In the early 1640s he emerged as the leading constitutional Royalist and was one of the chief architects responsible for the creation of the King's party. In eclipse during the period of fighting when his message of moderation lost its relevance, Clarendon re-emerged in the 1650s and honours were heaped upon him after the Restoration which, in a diplomatic sense, he more than anyone had helped to make possible. Yet by 1667 Clarendon was in disgrace, deprived of office, and banished from England by his royal master. His *History of the Rebellion* reflects the extreme vicissitudes of his career. A conflation of an earlier work written in the 1640s for the private instruction of the King and his counsellors, and of a self-justifying autobiography begun in exile in France twenty years later, Clarendon's *History* gives the most famous Royalist account of the English Revolution.[38] Clarendon, in fact, ranks much more highly as a historian than as a politician.

> Whatever his defects as a politician [Christopher Hill has observed] Clarendon was a great historian. His profound social insight, tempered by acute penetration in analyzing individual character; his lack of illusions, his scepticism, tempered by recognition of the fact of human progress even if he disliked the means which brought it about; all this fitted him to understand the conflicts of his age better than any contemporary and most later historians.[39]

Christopher Hill uses Clarendon's work to support his own social interpretation of the English Revolution. Whether Clarendon's *History* — which is basically a political narrative — contains such an

astute and extended analysis of the social causes and social nature of
the Civil War struggles, as Dr Hill would have us believe, is another
matter. Clarendon, however, was certainly well placed and well
qualified to write his *History of the Rebellion.*

> And as I may not be thought altogether an incompetent person for
> this communication, having been present as a member of parlia-
> ment in those councils before and till the breaking out of the
> rebellion, and having since had the honour to be near two great
> kings in some trust, so I shall perform the same with all faithfulness
> and ingenuity; with an equal observation of the faults and infirm-
> ities of both sides, with their defects and oversights in pursuing
> their own ends ... I know myself to be very free from any of those
> passions which naturally transport men with prejudice towards the
> persons whom they are obliged to mention, and whose actions they
> are at liberty to censure. There is not a man who acted the worst part
> in this ensuing year with whom I had ever the least difference or
> personal unkindness, or towards whom I had not much inclination
> of kindness, or from whom I did not receive all invitations of further
> endearments.[40]

To explain the outbreak of the mid-seventeenth-century troubles it
was not necessary to go very far back in time. (Here, as in other
respects, Clarendon was at odds with his former friend Thomas May.)

> That posterity may not be deceived, by the prosperous wickedness
> of these times, into an opinion, that less than a general combination,
> and universal apostasy in the whole nation from their religion and
> allegiance, could, in so short a time, have produced such a total and
> prodigious alteration and confusion over the whole kingdom; and
> so the memory of those few, who, out of duty and conscience, have
> opposed and resisted that torrent, which hath overwhelmed them,
> may lose the recompense due to their virtue; and, having under-
> gone the injuries and reproaches of this, may not find a vindication
> in a better age; it will not be unuseful, at least to the curiosity if not
> the conscience of men, to present to the world a full and clear
> narration of the grounds, circumstances, and artifices of this rebel-
> lion: not only from the time since the flame hath been visible in a
> civil war, but, looking further back, from those former passages,
> accidents, and actions, by which the seed-plots were made and
> framed, from whence these mischiefs have successively grown to the
> height they are now at ...

I shall not lead any man farther back in this journey, for the discovery of the entrance into these dark ways than the beginning of this king's reign. For I am not so sharp-sighted as those, who have discerned this rebellion contriving from (if not before) the death of Queen Elizabeth, and fomented by several princes and great ministers of state in Christendom, to the time that it brake out. Neither do I look so far back as believing the design to be so long since formed; (they who have observed the several accidents, not capable of being contrived to the several successes, and do know the persons who have been the grand instruments towards this change, of whom there have not been any four of familiarity and trust with each other, will easily absolve them from so much industry and foresight in their mischief;) but that by viewing the temper, disposition, and habit of that time, of the court and of the country, we may discern the minds of men prepared, of some to do, and of others to suffer, all that hath since happened; the pride of this man, and the popularity of that; the levity of one, and the morosity of another; the excess of the court in the greatest want, and the parsimony and retention of the country in the greatest plenty; the spirit of craft and subtlety in some, and the rude and unpolished integrity of others, too much despising craft or art; like so many atoms contributing jointly to this mass of confusion now before us.[41]

So Clarendon set out to produce a magisterially balanced and impartial account of English events in the first half of the seventeenth century, aiming 'to do justice to every man who hath fallen into the quarrel in which side soever'. The extent to which Clarendon actually achieved this aim can be gauged first by examining his treatment of individuals on the opposing sides, and then by looking at his more general comments on a force like puritanism and on a whole nation such as the Scots.

Clarendon, who before 1640 had been a reformer and moderate critic of Charles I, was faithful to his constitutional royalism when he dealt with the King's side in the war. He was not blind to the failings even of the King himself. In his estimate of Charles I Clarendon emphasized,

... how difficult it was for a prince, so unworthily reduced to those straits his majesty was in, to find ministers and instruments equal to the great work that was to be done; and how impossible it was for him to have better success under their conduct, whom it was then very proper for him to trust with it; and then, without my being over-solicitous to absolve him from those mistakes and weaknesses to which he was in truth sometimes liable, he will be found not only a prince of admirable virtue and piety, but of great parts of know-ledge, wisdom and judgment; and that the most signal parts of his misfortunes proceeded chiefly from the modesty of his nature, which kept him from trusting himself enough, and made him believe, that others discerned better, who were much inferior to him in those faculties; and so to depart often from his own reason, to follow the opinions of more unskilful men, whose affections he believed to be unquestionable to his service ...

His kingly virtues had some mixture and allay, that hindered them from shining in full lustre, and from producing those fruits they should have been attended with. He was not in his nature very bountiful ... and he paused too long in giving, which made those to whom he gave, less sensible of the benefit ... He was fearless in his person, but not very enterprising ...[42]

If his assessment of Charles I contained an element of 'white-washing', this is no doubt as much due to the sources of information available to him as to his personal proximity to the King. Clarendon was more outspoken in his comments on the Queen, Henrietta Maria, and on her meddling in politics.[43] On Thomas Wentworth, Earl of Strafford, the King's chief servant, Clarendon had this to say:

He was no doubt of great observation, and a piercing judgment, both into things and persons; but his too good skill in persons made him judge the worse of things ... discerning many defects in most men, he too much neglected what they said or did. Of all his passions, his pride was most predominant: which a moderate exercise of ill fortune might have corrected and reformed; and which was by the hand of Heaven strangely punished, by bringing his destruction upon him by two things he most despised, the people and Sir Harry Vane. In a word, the epitaph, which Plutarch records that Sylla wrote for himself, may not be unfitly applied to him; 'that no man did ever pass him, either in doing good to his friends, or in doing mischief to his enemies'; for his acts of both kinds were most exemplary and notorious.[44]

Archbishop Laud, in Clarendon's account, emerged as one more sinned against than sinning.

He was always maligned and persecuted by those who were of the Calvinist faction, which was then very powerful, and who, according to the useful maxim and practice, call every man they do not love, papist; and under this senseless appellation they created him many troubles and vexations ... No man was a greater or abler enemy to popery; no man a more resolute and devout son of the church of England ... Much hath been said of the person of this great prelate before, of his great endowments, and natural infirmities; to which shall be added no more in this place, (his memory deserving a particular celebration), than that his learning, piety, and virtue have been attained by very few, and the greatest of his infirmities are common to all, even to the best men.[45]

Strafford and Laud received from Clarendon's pen a charitable rather than an enthusiastic appraisal. But for Lucius Cary, Viscount Falkland, the King's secretary of state from 1641, a constitutional royalist like himself, who was killed at the Battle of Newbury, Clarendon's admiration scarcely knew any bounds.

If the celebrating the memory of eminent and extraordinary persons, and transmitting their great virtues, for the imitation of posterity, be one of the principal ends and duties of history, it will not be thought impertinent in this place, to remember a loss which no time will suffer to be forgotten, and no success or good fortune could repair. In this unhappy battle was slain the Lord Viscount Falkland, a person of such prodigious parts of learning and know- ledge, of that inimitable sweetness and delight in conversation, of so flowing and obliging a humanity and goodness to mankind, and of that primitive simplicity and integrity of life, that if there were no other brand upon this odious and accursed civil war, than that single loss, it must be most infamous and execrable to all posterity. [46]

When he came to the Parliamentarians, for obvious reasons, impartiality was much more difficult. Take, for example, Clarendon's pithy verdict on John Hampden.

Mr Hampden was a man of much greater cunning, and it may be of the most discerning spirit, and of the greatest address and insinua- tion to bring any thing to pass which he desired, of any man of that time, and who laid the design deepest ... He made so great a show of civility, and modesty, and humility, and always of mistrusting his own judgment, and of esteeming his with whom he conferred for the present, that he seemed to have no opinions or resolutions, but such as he contracted from the information and instruction he received upon the discourses of others, whom he had a wonderful art of governing, and leading into his principles and inclinations, whilst they believed that he wholly depended upon their counsel and advice. No man had ever a greater power over himself, or was less the man that he seemed to be, which shortly after appeared to everybody, when he cared less to keep on the mask ... His death was no less congratulated on the one party, than it was condoled in the other. In a word, what was said of Cinna might well be applied to him: 'he had a head to contrive, and a tongue to persuade, and a hand to execute any mischief'. His death, therefore, seemed to be a great deliverance to the nation.[47]

For Oliver Cromwell, Clarendon, despite himself, showed a certain reluctant admiration.

Cromwell, though the greatest dissembler living, always made his hypocrisy of singular use and benefit to him; and never did anything, how ungracious or imprudent soever it seemed to be, but what was necessary to the design ... He could never have done half that mischief without great parts of courage, industry and judgment. He must have had a wonderful understanding in the natures and humours of men, and as great a dexterity in applying them ... Without doubt, no man with more wickedness ever attempted anything, or brought to pass what he desired more wickedly, more in the face and contempt of religion, and moral honesty; yet wickedness as great as his could never have accomplished those trophies, without the assistance of a great spirit, an admirable circumspection and sagacity, and a most magnanimous resolution... To reduce three nations, which perfectly hated him, to an entire obedience, to all his dictates; to awe and govern those nations by an army that was indevoted to him, and wished his ruin, was an instance of a very prodigious address. But his greatness at home was but a shadow of the glory he had abroad ...

In a word, as he had all the wickedness against which damnation is denounced, and for which hell-fire is prepared, so he had some virtues which have caused the memory of some men in all ages to be celebrated; and he will be looked upon by posterity as a brave bad man.[48]

Turning from the portraits of individuals to his general observations on a whole people, the Scots, we find that Clarendon indulged his prejudices on a correspondingly grander scale. 'Vermin', 'that foreign contemned nation' are among the choice epithets which rushed from Clarendon's pen when he turned to social life, religion, and politics north of the border. With immense disdain he spoke of,

> ... the numerous proud and indigent nobility of Scotland (for of the common people, who are naturally slaves to the other, there can be no wonder) [who] concurred in the carrying on this rebellion; their strange condescension and submission to their ignorant and insolent clergy, who were to have great authority, because they were to inflame all sorts of men upon the oglibations of conscience; and in order thereunto, and to revenge a little indiscretion and ill manners of some of the bishops, had liberty to erect a tribunal the most tyrannical over all sorts of men, and in all the families of the kingdom.

He counted it one of Charles I's great weaknesses that 'he was always an immoderate lover of the Scottish nation, having not only been born there, but educated by that people, and besieged by them always'. Conversely, Clarendon considered Cromwell's conquest of Scotland to be one of his most admirable achievements.[49]

As for puritanism, understandably perhaps, Clarendon could only see it as a subversive fanaticism, socially harmful and politically disastrous. The puritan clergy, in his view — and it was similar to Hobbes's — had much to answer for; it was they, above all, who had raised the political temperature to such a height in the 1640s, rousing men's passions and goading them into action by their inflammatory preaching.

> I must not forget, though it cannot be remembered without much horror, that this strange wildfire among the people was not so much and so furiously kindled by the breath of the parliament, as of the clergy, who both administered fuel, and blowed the coals in the houses too. These men having creeped into, and at last driven all learned and orthodox men from the pulpits had, as is before remembered, from the beginning of this parliament, under the notion of reformation and extirpating of popery, infused seditious inclinations into the hearts of men against the present government of the church, with many libellous invectives against the state too ...

There are monuments enough in the seditious sermons at that

time printed, and in the memories of men, of others not printed, of such wresting and perverting of scripture to the odious purposes of the preacher, that pious men will not look over without trembling.

And indeed no good Christian can, without horror, think of those ministers of the church, who by their function being messengers of peace, were the only trumpets of war, and incendiaries towards rebellion ...[50]

Clearly, then, there is much that is lacking in Clarendon's estimate or puritanism, but when Sir Charles Firth (see pp.75-8) complained that Clarendon's *'History of the Rebellion* has the fundamental defect that it is a history of a religious revolution in which the religious element is omitted', it is important to remember that he was using a Victorian yardstick;[51] methods of measurement have changed since then. Clarendon did not achieve the impartiality at which he aimed, but this in any case was an impossible target which he set for himself. But given his own place in the events he was describing, Clarendon's survey of the period is remarkably broad in its sweep and fairly generous in its tone. The *History of the Rebellion* emphatically is not the work of a sycophantic party historian; Clarendon was in a different class altogether from such writers as John Vicars and John Nalson. 'Insular in his field, conservative in his outlook,' argues Professor Trevor-Roper, 'empirical in his method, he nevertheless has his place among the "philosophical historians".'[52] To Clarendon, like Bacon, history was a source of political wisdom, and he saw that a cool appraisal of the Civil Wars would contain many vital lessons for contemporaries and for posterity.

Chapter 3

The eighteenth century: the political uses of history

There are persons so over-run with prejudice, so involved or rather immersed in Party, that it is next to impossible that they should always distinguish between truth and falsehood. Men whose eyesights are thus darkened and contracted can never see far before them. The extremities of Parties are the scandals and excrescences of human nature ... (Laurence Echard, *Appendix to the History of England* (London, 1720), p.36.)

Clarendon occupies a special position in the historiography of the English Revolution. Chronologically, his *History of the Rebellion* belongs, as we have seen, to the seventeenth-century literature of the subject and to the active and commonly angry debate among contemporary observers and participants. But Clarendon has a place, too, in the eighteenth-century historiography of the Revolution, since although his work was written between the 1640s and 1670s, in line with the wishes of its author who advised a lengthy delay until passions had cooled, it was not actually *published* until 1702-4. It appeared, therefore, in the reign of Queen Anne, Clarendon's own grand-daughter, and was ushered into the world with a preface by Clarendon's son, the Earl of Rochester. Rochester presented his father's work 'rather as an instruction to the present age than a reproach upon the last'; its publication, in short, was designed to support Tory historical orthodoxy. The appearance of the *History of the Rebellion*, Rochester argued, could be delayed no longer.

In an age when so many memoirs, narratives, and pieces of history come out as it were on purpose to justify the taking up arms against that king,[1] and to blacken, revile, and ridicule the sacred majesty of an anointed head in distress; and when so much of the sense of religion to God, and of allegiance and duty to the crown is so defaced that it is already within little more than fifty years since the murder committed on that pious prince by some men made a mystery to judge on whose side was the right and on which the Rebellion is to be charged...

In the dedication to Queen Anne in Volume Three, Rochester, by now out of office and in opposition, drew a stark contrast between 'the peace and the plenty of this kingdom [under Charles I] and in so short a space of time the bloody desolation of it by a most wicked rebellion'. He went on to elaborate his disgust even more pointedly. Charles I was,

> ... brought by unaccountable administrations on the one hand and by vile contrivances on the other into the greatest difficulties and distresses throughout all his kingdoms; then left and abandoned by most of his servants whom he had himself raised to the greatest honours and preferments, thus reduced to have scarce one faithful, able counsellor about him to whom he could breathe his conscience and complaints, and from whom he might expect one honest, sound, disinterested advice; after this how he was obliged to take up arms and to contend with his own subjects in the field for his crown, the laws, his liberty, and life; there meeting with unequal fortune how he was drawn from one part of the kingdom and from one body of an army to another, till at last he was brought under the power of cruel and merciless men, imprisoned and arraigned, condemned and executed like a common malefactor.[2]

More of a Tory than his father, Rochester helped to ensure that Clarendon's more subtle masterpiece would be denounced by the Whigs as partisan, Tory history. The early eighteenth-century reception given to the publication of the *History of the Rebellion* showed, in fact, how controversial a subject the English Revolution still remained. The connections between politics and history were far too strong to allow Civil War studies to lapse into a mere academic debate. In Queen Anne's reign, Whig and Tory groupings acquired cohesion and greater political meaning, though not always with complete consistency or with uninterrupted continuity. One should be wary of using too rigid and mechanistic a model, but the party divisions, none the less, were there, and the study of history, and of seventeenth-century history above all, increasingly took on an explicit and pronounced present purpose. Whig and Tory interpretations of the English Revolution became an essential ingredient in the subject matter of eighteenth-century politics and eighteenth-century religious controversy. When writing about this period of history, noted Gibbon in 1762, 'every writer is expected to hang out a badge of party and is devoted to destruction by the opposite faction'.[3]

Take, for instance, the debate which raged in the early years of the eighteenth century between Edmund Calamy (1671-1732) and John Walker (1674-1747). The debate focused on one aspect of the religious history of the English Revolution, the respective fortunes of opposition clergy during the Interregnum and at the Restoration, and it indicates the importance of the two religious extremes of Whigs and Tories in maintaining the temperature of party strife. This particular debate was initiated between 1702 and 1713 when Calamy published his account of ejected and silenced divines. In this work Calamy, himself the son of an ejected minister, discussed those puritan clergy who had been removed from their livings after 1660. It was obvious where his Whig sympathies lay and the authors of the Restoration settlement were vigorously denounced for fatally undermining the unity and welfare of the Church. But this was seventeenth-century history with an eighteenth-century message, as Matthews reminds us in his commentary on Calamy's work.

> It was impossible for the publication of such opinions to pass unnoticed in an age so given to controversy as that of Queen Anne. Calamy had invaded the very storm centre of contemporary party politics. To reflect on the Settlement of 1662 was to reflect on the Church of 1702, and that in the eyes of the High Churchmen and Tories was to lay sacrilegious hands upon the ark of the covenant. A nonconformist apologist stood condemned not only as a Whig but also as one who still believed in the obligation of the Solemn League and Covenant and was therefore only waiting an opportunity to re-enact the persecution of the Interregnum. Churchmen were bound to reply to the challenge offered to them and their response was profuse and bitter.[4]

John Walker, a Tory high churchman, emerged as the conspicuous of Calamy's opponents, publishing in 1714 his *Sufferings of the Clergy*, a book which countered Calamy's evidence by documenting the deprivations of loyal Anglicans during the Interregnum. Like Calamy's account, Walker's book was specifically related to his own times. As Matthews says:

The events Walker wrote of could not be withdrawn from the heat of party politics into the cool atmosphere of detached historical study. Tory history was an inseparable part of Tory dogma and a primary factor in its creation. The ruling men of the Interregnum had foully outraged the two sanctities of the Tory creed, the Church and the Crown ... The historical writing that resulted from this outlook was of the pragmatic order, directed more to the making of history than to its impartial study.[5]

Tory political historiography, whose cause Rochester had been serving when he published Clarendon's *History*, was quickly reinforced by a *History of England* by Laurence Echard (1670?-1730), issued between 1707 and 1718. On James I, for example, Echard had this to say:

It is true there were some heats between him and his Parliaments about the prerogative, and it happened then, as it does in most feuds, things were carried to great extremities. Yet impartial writers think that considering his majesty's circumstances he was not well used, and that if the House had been freed from half a dozen popular and discontented members the disturbances would soon have ended.[6]

And when he came to the unhappy reign of Charles I, he made it clear how, in his view, the troubles had arisen.

On the other side, beside the disgusts and waverings of the nobility and great men, the people proceeded to unprecedented liberties which naturally led them into many errors and dangerous paths and precipices, so that they assumed to themselves a power of censuring and intermeddling with such matters of state and religion as were unquestionably above their sphere and capacity.[7]

Echard, like so many who contributed to the discussion of this period, saw himself as an entirely truthful, unbiased historian. 'While there are such things in the world as Truth and Honesty,' he wrote, 'undoubtedly there may be an impartial historian.' But in the contentious age in which he lived, Echard's professions of neutrality, even if they were true, were unlikely to be taken very seriously, and the well-meaning archdeacon provoked a storm of opposition from Whig and dissenting circles.

Edmund Calamy, Walker's adversary, for example, rallied to the defence of the reputation of the puritans which he believed had been sullied by Echard's harsh treatment.

> You are too severe upon the puritans who, when you have found all faults with them you can, were generally men of great piety and true to the interest of their country, and therefore favoured by our greatest patriots, though run down by zealous ecclesiastics, who thought allowing others to differ from them tended to their own diminution ... Methinks you more than once discover a great tenderness to the papists. They seem to pass for a harmless sort of people ...
>
> Arbitrary power, which is what so many in this reign [Charles I's] were so much afraid of, to you appears a mere bugbear, and the dreading it you represent as a great weakness.[8]

A more extensive and heated indictment of Echard's Toryism came from John Oldmixon (1673-1743) in his *Critical History of England*. His preface explicitly connected past history with present politics. 'What can be more necessary', Oldmixon asked, 'than to set people right in that which most concerns them, their religious and civil liberties, and justify the proceedings of the present age by those of the past?' Echard, according to Oldmixon, had maliciously misrepresented the Parliamentarians.

> [He] treats them as so many rebels, and vindicates or extenuates all King Charles I's invasions of the rights and liberties of the subject [as though] ... all our fathers and we had said and done for liberty spiritual and temporal was unsaid and undone and the statutes and ordinances of the Parliament in 1640 et seq and the Convention of 1688 represented as so many acts of sedition and rebellion ...[9]

Comparing the adjectives used to describe the opposing sides in the war, Oldmixon concluded that:

> The partiality is so strong that 'tis ridiculous, and there is not the like in History from that of Herodotus to Mr Echard's ... Mr Echard has one of the prettiest ways of softening things that I ever met with. Thus he melts down tyrannical proceedings into disobliging measures, and he can turn to the other hand when he pleases, and then impeachments and remonstrances are disturbers of parliament, the Rochellers rebels, the Book of Sports a pious intention, Bishop Juxon a wonderful treasurer, puritans cheats though not

whoremasters etc. Innumerable are the instances of this kind in him, too tedious and hateful to repeat. Yet he closes the chapter with saying 'Thus with all simplicity and fidelity we have gone so far'.

The reader will find so many panegyrics on Bishop Laud that if he had really been a saint and a martyr, as he represents him, he could not have said more of him; whereas there's nothing so certain in his character as Pride, Cruelty, Bigotry, and invincible Obstinacy. [10]

All Echard's sly attempts to disguise the fact that the English Revolution was a necessary defence of the ancient constitution and of the Englishman's civil and religious liberties were completely vain. The truth, Oldmixon persevered, still shone through the Tory shroud.

The laws and customs delivered down to us from our British and Saxon fathers, justified the practices of those brave English heroes who have always stood in the gap when our constitution has been in danger ...

It had been impossible for the Archdeacon to have run himself into so many mistakes and errors if before he began his history he had not listed himself on the side of ceremony and severity, arbitrary power and oppression, if he had not resolved to follow such blind guides as Heath, Nalson, etc ... 'Tis impossible by this writer's history to conceive any idea of these times. One would imagine by his writings that the republic consisted of a parcel of thieves, cowards, blockheads, atheists and scoundrels, that their power was tyranny and the people of England slaves in the very height of liberty; that in the midst of strict justice nothing was heard of but robberies and rapes, and in the strictest practice of religion, impiety and profaness everywhere triumphed; that at a time when trade was flourishing, poverty and beggary made the nation desolate, and when the English name and credit were the envy and dread of the world that the kingdoms and states around us looked upon us with contempt or detestation; in a word that the government of England was as much neglected and despised abroad as it had been in the reigns of King James and King Charles I. Why does he and his party invent things thus? But because they had not the power to plunder, persecute, torture and enslave their honest neighbours as in the days of Laud, Wren, Neile, etc ... [11]

Oldmixon dismissed the seventeenth-century sections of Echard's work as a warped and very imperfect copy of Clarendon's *History of the Rebellion* (partly in his view a forgery by its Tory editors), and he proceeded after the corrective exercise of the *Critical History*, to present his own view of the English Revolution in his *History of England during the Reigns of the Royal House of Stuart*. Published in 1730, it was dedicated to 'all true Englishmen, lovers of our present happy constitution' which in the previous century had been attacked by 'the tyranny of the High Commission court' and by all those who favoured 'the boundless prerogative of the crown, the slavish obedience of the subject, and the blessings of arbitrary power and servitude'. After looking at Oldmixon's own account, however, his readers would be able to see,

> ... the facts of the four Stuarts' reigns in a true light, that the glorious principles and practices of your ancestors might no longer lie under the reproach of rebellion ... It will appear plain enough by the history of the Stuart kings that they were continually making breaches in this constitution and endeavouring utterly to subvert it ... while their opponents were the only true sons of the Common-wealth, good Protestants and good Englishmen, adhering to their birthright, their religion, liberties and properties which those princes and their adherents in so many instances invaded and violated.[12]

Oldmixon ingeniously claimed that he himself was above party. He was a faithful servant and admirer of the constitution. The only 'Party' were the Tories who, in their efforts to undermine the constitution and justify absolutism, had in Queen Anne's reign brought forth the distorted and worthless histories of Clarendon and Echard.

> Perhaps I may myself be thought guilty of that passion and prejudice and be thought misled by the same weakness I condemn in others. It is therefore necessary to consider what is or ought to be understood by the word Party. And I wish what I have to say on that subject were worth the reader's attention, for if my conceptions are right, and I must think they are till I am better informed, I cannot justly be deemed a Party-man, or pass under that censure with men of reason and candour, however appearances may at first sight make against me....
> If this Constitution is founded in the Protestant religion, a due

and impartial execution of the laws, a just and equal administration of affairs, then all contrary courses are contrary to the Constitution, and he who adheres to it cannot be said to be of a Party because the Constitution is the whole, and those are only Party-men who divide from it by setting up an arbitrary, partial, unequal, illegal government, and interest separate from that of the public...[13]

Whether or not this period was one of such complete Whig supremacy in politics as older historians believed, Whiggish versions of history certainly predominated at this time, and Oldmixon's robust narrative coincided with the appearance of another like-minded but more moderate work. This was the *Impartial History of England* written by the émigré Huguenot supporter of William III Paul de Rapin Thoyras (1661-1725). Originally written in French for a European audience, the work appeared in Tindal's English translation between 1726 and 1731, and a further six editions demonstrated its popularity. Rapin's work was the most fashionable history of its vintage, and its author included discussion of the work of previous historians including Rushworth, who although invaluable for his documents was admittedly in his interpretation too disparaging of the King.

> He therefore that undertakes to write at this time the history of Charles I must endeavour to discover the truth in even the most partial historians and be extremely careful to avoid the continual snares they lay for their readers to favour the cause they maintain. One must know what was their design in writing, what system they followed, and the artifices they used to engage in their principles such as make but few reflections in reading a history and are apt to be easily drawn into the prejudices of the historian.[14]

Yet although Rapin frankly admitted that 'the King and the Parliament were both very much in the wrong, though not always nor on the same occasions', none the less it is his censures of Charles I which come through most clearly in his version of events.

> If it is not supposed that Charles I from the beginning of his reign to the time of this last parliament, had formed a design to establish in England an arbitrary government it will be almost impossible to understand his history, and particularly this second part. But upon this supposition, which to me appears incontestable, all difficulties vanish. It is not surprising to see the King's council, his ministers,

favourites, the Star chamber, High Commission, judges of the realm, in a word, all persons in public employment, intent upon one single point, I mean the stretching of the royal authority as far as lay in their power. It is not surprising to see the implacable hatred of the House of Commons to the King's ministers, and particularly to those who were most trusted by his Majesty, and believed the chief authors of the public evils...

[For the King] sincerity, as appears in his history was not his favourite virtue. He made frequent use of mental reservations, concealed in ambiguous terms and general expressions, of which he reserved the explication at a proper time and place. For this reason, the Parliament could never confide in his promises, wherein there was always either some ambiguous term, or some restriction that rendered them useless. This may be said to be one of the principal causes of his ruin, because giving thereby occasion of distrust, it was not possible to find any expedient for a peace with the Parliament. He was thought to act with so little sincerity in his engagements that it was believed there was no dependence on his word ...[15]

Certainly not uncritically Whiggish in interpretation, none the less it was as a Whig historian that Rapin was regarded, and it was as a Whig that he was attacked by the Jacobite Thomas Carte (1680-1754). Carte did this first of all in his *Defence of English History against the Misrepresentations of Mr Rapin de Thoyras* (London, 1734), and later, and at much greater length, in his *General History of England* (London, 1747-55). Rapin, declared Carte in an intermediate publication,

... writing his *History* abroad, had no opportunity either of consulting persons better versed in our antiquities than himself, or of searching into any of our records and repositories of public papers. Being likewise a foreigner unacquainted with our constitution he was in no respect qualified to give us the civil history of this nation.[16]

In contrast with this foreign meddler in English history, Carte proudly proclaimed himself on the title-page of his *General History* as an *Englishman*, and his preface advertised the laborious research which he had carried out. Carte's own picture of the early seventeenth century involved a denunciation of puritanism and of the unreasonableness of the parliamentary opposition to Charles I. Elizabeth, he

wrote, 'left that turbulent sect of men [the puritans] in a condition
that enabled them to distress her successor throughout all his reign
and in that of his son, to subvert the monarchy as well as the
episcopacy, liturgy, and the whole constitution of the Church of
England'.[17] Moving to Charles I's reign, his comments on the
Grand Remonstrance are indicative of his general approach to this
period.

> They had been for near a twelvemonth hammering out a
> Remonstrance of what they called that state of the kingdom,
> and the King having settled Scotland in quiet it was thought
> necessary to keep up jealousies in England by filling it with a
> bitter recapitulation of all the irregular or disagreeable steps taken
> since his Majesty's accession, absolutely false in some particulars,
> misrepresented in more, and exaggerated in all with the utmost
> virulence ... the whole was calculated to infuse jealousies into the
> people, for which purpose it was afterwards printed.[18]

As such rivalries make clear, Whigs and Tories clashed in the field of
historical interpretation as they did in the turmoil of party politics.
But one should not oversimplify. The parties themselves were not
fixed and monolithic; the disagreement between 'old' and 'new'
Whigs is a case in point. Nor do party labels neatly fit all historians of
this period. One such exception was White Kennett (1660-1728),
Bishop of Peterborough. Kennett contributed a volume covering the
period 1625-1702 to a *Complete History of England* which was
published in 1706. Accused of Whiggery in the eighteenth century —
and with some justification — his modern biographer is nevertheless
inclined to see him as a Tory historian whose 'historical writing often
became a mask to cover a commentary upon current events'.[19]
Kennett's volume was severely factual and chronological, it quoted
extensively from Clarendon, and was published anonymously; 'no
prudent writer would set a name to the history of his own times, for it
is impossible to please or to be thought impartial till posterity find out
his plain and honest dealing'. Kennett's attempts to apply scholarly
standards to his historical writing and his generous assessment of
Archbishop Laud, for example, make the conventional Whig label
seem inappropriate.

> Another popular outcry against Archbishop Laud and the bishops
> directed by him was innovation in matters of religion; few people

being willing to distinguish between arbitrary alterations and the restoring an antecedent decency and order, which latter was undoubtedly the good archbishop's meaning ... [Laud, faced with] such a heap of accusations, made such an admirable defence against them that the innocence of this prelate and the malice of his enemies are hardly to be matched in any account of the primitive persecutions ...[20]

Kennett had earlier (in 1704) vindicated Charles I's reputation in his sermon *A Compassionate Enquiry into the Causes of the Civil War*, a fascinating work which not only put forward Whig notions about the ancient constitution but also defended the King at the same time from all charges that he was attempting to subvert it.

The evil of this day we now deplore in fasting and mourning was an unnatural Civil War that overturned the best constitution in the world, that made our whole island an Aceldama, a field of blood, and through heaps of rapine and slaughter proceeded to the deplorable death of the martyr of this day, one of the most virtuous and most religious of our English princes. [We must try to discover] how and why this evil came upon us as it did this day that seeing and understanding the cursed causes of it we may be better able to atone for the past iniquities and the more careful to prevent the like fatal effects for the future.[21]

Kennett proceeded to lavish fulsome praise on English liberties and the ancient constitution, but argued that Charles I was unjustly suspected of attempting to overthrow them.

We of this happy nation have certainly the best constitution in the world, the sovereignty of the prince, the rights of the nobility, the liberties of the people, all so balanced and bearing upon one another that no government on this side Heaven can be more wisely contrived while it stands even upon its true balance ...

Far be it from any honest heart to think that [Charles I] out of ambition or sinister ends ever proposed to injure the birthright of his subjects or to alter the constitution received from his ancestors. No! his clemency and justice, his honour and conscience were upon too high a principle for such ill designs. But it is possible that the influence of others may bring a suspicion upon princes when they themselves are innocent and then in many cases a suspicion artfully improved shall work up as much mischief as the real guilt would do...

If we trace back the history of former ages we shall [all] along find that the body of the English people had the spirit of a free people; that they would not by any means put their necks into a yoke nor their feet into chains, nor would they bow down their backs to any illegal burden.[22]

As Kennett's example shows, Whig and Tory versions of the past were at times just as complicated as eighteenth-century political warfare and could, on occasions, take the same unexpected turns. In the 1730s, for instance, the political rivalry between Walpole and the Whigs and Bolingbroke and the Tories came to acquire a curious historiographical dimension, the long-term result of which was to reduce the partisan character of the feudal interpretation of the English past. Here in the 1730s we find Tory politicians espousing the basic tenets of Whig historiography, while in retaliation Whigs hurled back a hastily assimilated version of Tory historical principles![23]

At first glance astonishing and inexplicable, this intriguing episode in the political use of history makes sense when we appreciate that what the Tory Bolingbroke was doing was to use the Whig appeal to a free past as a weapon in his assault on the corrupting and enslaving efforts of Walpole's Whig administration. Turning Whig theories of history on their head, Bolingbroke was arguing in his *Remarks on the History of England* (London, 1730), that the present was not better than the past but *worse*. With Tories making such impertinently novel use of Whig propaganda, what was left to Walpole and the Whigs but to detach the Tory version of the past — Brady, Spelman and the rest — from Tory politics and proclaim it as their own modernized Whiggism? This they did, first as a religious argument in the Convocation controversy which raged for two decades after 1697, and then for strictly political purposes in the 1730s when faced with Bolingbroke's historiographical gymnastics. So, using Robert Brady's high-Tory arguments, Walpole the Whig countered the Tory Bolingbroke's Whig history by arguing that English liberties and freedoms were not ancient at all; they had not existed since time immemorial. They were recent, and were in fact the product only of the seventeenth-century constitutional and religious struggles. Walpole's administration, therefore, did not represent a retreat from the ancient constitution.

The very reverse is true of our government, which was bad in the beginning, made better by degrees and is brought to perfection at last ... To bring the government of England back to its first principles, is to bring the people back to absolute slavery; the primitive purity of our constitution was that the people had no share in the government, but were the villeins, vassals, or bondmen of the lords, a sort of cattle bought and sold with the land.[24]

Lord Hervey agreed in his essay *Ancient and Modern Liberty Stated and Compared* (London, 1734); not until the Glorious Revolution was liberty achieved and firmly guaranteed. No wonder then that such Whigs in politics but Tories in history should find Rapin — decidedly Whig in the usual sense — unacceptable and denounce him as a Tory.

It was, more accurately, as a Whig historian that Rapin was denounced in mid-century by the cosmopolitan Scot, David Hume (1711-76). Originally attracted by Rapin's historical method, his anti-clericalism and apparent detachment from party disputes, Hume's opinion changed. Greater familiarity bred contempt, and his *History of Great Britain* came, in fact, to be specifically directed against Rapin's Whig treatment, which he caricatured thus: 'Charles I was a tyrant, a papist and a contriver of the Irish massacre; the Church of England was relapsing fast into idolatry; puritanism was the only true religion, and the Covenant the favourite object of heavenly regard.'[25]

But, just as White Kennett had been unconventional in his combination of party and history, so Hume was not a Tory historian in the usual sense. 'Mr Hume in his *History*', wrote Voltaire, 'is neither Parliamentarian nor Royalist, nor Anglican nor Presbyterian: he is simply judicious.'[26] Hume saw himself as a philosopher/historian *above* party. In a sense it was largely by chance that he became a Tory historian, and the fact owed less to Hume himself than to the way his standpoint was distorted both by contemporary supporters and by later Whig opponents. Duncan Forbes has shown the complex combination of Whig and Tory elements which existed side by side in Hume's historical interpretation — an easier feat to accomplish at this point in the century than earlier, coming as it did after the historiographical confusions of the 1730s. Hume identified himself wholly with neither camp. Using a formula that would also describe White Kennett, Hume tried to claim that the bias of his book on the Stuarts, which was the first of his complete history to appear, was 'Tory as to persons and Whig as to things'. He observed that the publication of his work met with a chorus of opposition from all sides, from 'English, Scotch and Irish, Whig and Tory, churchman and sectary, freethinker and religionist, patriot and courtier. [All] united in their rage against the man who had presumed to shed a generous tear for the fate of Charles I and the Earl of Strafford.'[27] Faced with this general criticism, highly disconcerting in the short term, Hume could at least console himself with the thought that his impartiality had been widely recognized! Given its context, however, Hume's *History* is extremely moderate in tone; he wrote not in order to supply new Tory ammunition but, rather, as Dr Forbes suggests, to further 'the abolition of the "dangerous" distinction of Whig and Tory'.[28] The central theme in his *History* is that without authority, freedom cannot exist, and by stressing this axiom Hume sought to educate the Whigs in political moderation, and to teach them that government is established to provide justice and not liberty. Resistance to established authority could not be excused.

Hume tried to achieve this process of political re-education by arguing, contrary to the orthodox Whig view, that there simply was no clearly defined ancient constitution in seventeenth-century England, and that it was its very lack of precision which helped to cause the Civil War.

> The uncertain and undefined limits of prerogative and privilege had been eagerly disputed during that whole period; and in every controversy betwixt prince and people, the question, however doubtful, had always been decided by each party in favour of its own pretensions ... [Yet] nothing will tend more to abate the acrimony of party disputes than to show men that those events which they impute to their adversaries as the deepest crimes, were the natural, if not the necessary result of the situation in which the nation was placed during any period.[29]

A philosophical historian rather than blindly pro-Tory in the conventional sense, Hume none the less felt obliged to refute the extravagant claims made by uncritical exponents of the Whig interpretation of the seventeenth century.

> The Whig party for the course of near seventy years has almost without interruption enjoyed the whole authority of government, and no honours or offices could be obtained but by their countenance and protection. But this event which in some particulars has been advantageous to the state, has proved destructive to the truth

of history, and has established many gross falsehoods which it is unaccountable how any civilised nation could have embraced with regard to its domestic occurrences. Compositions the most despicable, both for style and matter, have been extolled and propagated and read as if they had equalled the most celebrated remains of antiquity (such as Rapin Thoyras, Locke, Sidney, Hoadley, etc.). And forgetting that a regard for liberty, though a laudable passion, ought commonly to be subordinate to a reverence for established government, the prevailing faction has celebrated only the partisans of the former who pursued as their object the perfection of civil society, and has extolled them at the expense of their antagonists who maintained those maxims that are essential to its very existence. But extremes of all kinds are to be avoided; and though no-one will ever please either faction by moderate opinions, it is there we are most likely to meet with truth and certainty. ... The more I advance in my undertaking [he had written earlier] the more I am convinced that the history of England has never yet been written, not only for style, which is notorious to all the world, but also for matter, such is the ignorance and partiality of our historians. Rapin, whom I had an esteem for, is totally despicable. [30]

Hume's political sympathies, then, were by no means completely clear-cut, but there was much in his interpretation which was Tory in standpoint. Cromwell was contemptuously written off as a mere 'fanatical hypocrite'. Hume's rationalist attitude to the doctrinal puritans, too, was extremely hostile, and although he recognized the constitutional importance of political puritans, in dealing with them he could never overcome his conviction that religious enthusiasm was only an expression of human weakness and a source of much discord and misery.

'Tis however probable, if not certain, that they were generally speaking the dupes of their own zeal ... So congenial to the human mind are religious sentiments that, where the temper is not guarded by a philosophical scepticism, the most cool and determined, it is impossible to counterfeit long these holy fervours without feeling some share of the assumed warmth. And on the other hand, so precarious and temporary is the operation of these supernatural views that the religious extasies, if constantly employed, must often be counterfeit, and must ever be warped by those more familiar motives of interest and ambition, which insensibly gain upon the mind. This indeed seems the key to most of the celebrated characters of that age. Equally full of fraud and ardour, these pious patriots talked perpetually of seeking the Lord, yet still pursued their own purposes; and have left a memorable lesson to posterity, how delusive, how destructive that principle is by which they were animated. [31]

By contrast, Hume did indeed, as he admitted, 'shed a generous tear' for Charles I and Strafford.

As a monarch, too, in the exterior qualities he [Charles I] excelled; in the essential he was not defective. His address and manner, though perhaps inclining a little towards stateliness and formality, in the main corresponded to his high rank, and gave grace to that reserve and gravity which were natural to him ... But the high idea of his own authority, with which he had been imbued, made him incapable of submitting prudently to the spirit of liberty which began to prevail among his subjects. His politics were not supported with such vigour and foresight as might enable him to subdue their privileges and maintain his prerogative at the high pitch to which he had raised it... [32]

Although at first some were baffled by the inconsistencies of his moderate Toryism/sceptical Whiggism, it was as a Tory historian that Hume was taken up, and the revisions made to subsequent editions of his work provided increasing justification for so doing. But although Whig and radical opposition to Hume's *History* appeared in different forms, for a variety of reasons it was slow in undermining its influence. It was not until Macaulay took up his pen that the Whig interpretation was given its supreme statement and Hume began to be superseded.

In the meantime, however, one of the earliest and most extreme attacks on the new statement of Tory history came from Mrs Catherine Macaulay (1731-91) in her eight-volume *History of England from the Accession of James I to that of the Brunswick Line*, published between 1763 and 1783. Remarkable as the first serious female historian and as an avowed republican, Mrs Macaulay belongs to that line of 'Real Whigs' or neo-Harringtonians (as opposed to those Whigs in office) who transmitted the seventeenth-century republican ideology of such as Milton, Harrington, Neville and Nedham to the political world of the following century. [33] Well-written and carefully researched — Mrs Macaulay made use of recently published parliamentary debates and journals and of the Thomason collection of Civil War tracts acquired by the British Museum in 1762 — the early volumes of the *History* brought upon their author the general acclaim of Whig and radical circles and of the dissenting academies. Mrs Macaulay seemed at first to be well on the way to achieving her aim of refuting Hume's interpretation and of rivalling him in popularity. A statue, representing her as Dame Thucydides, was commissioned by one of her most ardent admirers, and still today adorns a public building in Warrington. For the twentieth century, however, a more appropriate memorial has been provided by Bridget and Christopher Hill's article which successfully attempts to rescue Mrs Macaulay from undeserved neglect.[34]

Neo-Harringtonian certainly in its emphasis on economic factors — 'industry and commerce had enabled them [the Commons] to make the full advantage of their new privilege by large purchases' — Mrs Macaulay stressed and justified the revolutionary character of seventeenth-century events.

> With regret do I accuse my country of inattention to the most exalted of their benefactors: whilst they enjoy privileges unpossessed by other nations they have lost a just sense of the merit of the men by whose virtues these privileges were attained; men that with the hazard and even the loss of their lives attacked the formidable pretensions of the Stuart family and set up the banners of liberty against a tyranny which had been established for a series of more than 150 years ... Neglect is not the only crime committed against these sacred characters. Party prejudice, and the more detestable principle of private interest, have painted the memoirs of past times in so false a light...[35]

The main outlines of Mrs Macaulay's interpretation are clear enough: the Stuarts were the aggressors, not to mention 'the criminal ambition of the Tudors', the ancient constitution the thing contested for, and the Parliamentarians its true champions.

> [James I] was himself the only dupe to an impertinent, useless hypocrisy. If the laws and constitution of England received no prejudice from his government, it was owing to his want of ability to effect a change suitable to the purpose of an arbitrary sway. Stained with these vices and sullied with these weaknesses, if he is ever exempt from our hatred, the exemption must arise from motives of contempt.

Pardoning Charles I, however, was even less excusable.

> [Charles I] had conceived an ineffable contempt for popular
> privileges with the most exalted notions of sublime authority in
> princes. Concessions he looked upon as derogations to the honour
> of a king, and opposition in subjects as such a flagrant breach of
> divine and moral laws that it called down from Heaven a sure and
> heavy vengeance on the aggressor. ... [Under his misrule] England
> carried the face of a conquered province. The liberties and properties
> of the subject lay prostrate at the mercy of a rash imperious monarch,
> a rapacious insolent minister, and a designing bigoted priest; the
> prisons were daily filling with patriots.[36]

Her denunciation of Strafford contrasts vividly with her account of the
praiseworthy John Hampden who 'combated this new state monster,
Ship money'.[37]

Although no democrat at any point — as the Hills show, her
confidence in the supine people was ultimate rather than immediate
— the radical republicanism in Mrs Macaulay's account became more
pronounced as her *History* proceeded. Those moderate Whigs who had
been impressed by the tone and contents of the first two volumes were
embarrassed or shocked to find Mrs Macaulay in the later instalments
revealing herself plainly as a 'Real Whig' and Wilkesite and defending
regicide at a time when the cry of 'Wilkes and Liberty' was resounding
in the London streets. She later *claimed* in the preface to Volume VI
(published in 1781) that she had 'shed many tears' over the fate
of Charles I, but if so she had obviously wiped them dry by the end of
Volume IV in time to justify the execution of the King. Charles I's
deplorable conduct, Mrs Macaulay argued, had removed from his
subjects the necessity of obeying him.

> His trust and right to government from that period are forfeited,
> the tie of allegiance is dissolved, and the law and constitution being
> rendered incapable of affording the subject protection, he is no
> longer bound by their forms and dictates and may justly by the
> right of self-preservation take every probable means to secure him-
> self from the lawless power and enterprises of the tyrant.[38]

Views such as these, boldly and unrepentantly put forward,
convinced Mrs Macaulay's readers beyond all doubt that hers was not
the safe, respectable Whig account of seventeenth-century history that
was needed to displace Hume. Catherine Macaulay's influence as a

political historian declined even in the course of the publication of her eight volumes. Her importance in the social history of English feminism rivals her significance as a historian. Her *History of England* became a minority taste, and in this restricted sense Mrs Macaulay's work continued to cater for the interests of a small, like-minded coterie of Commonwealthmen until it was itself superseded in the 1820s.

Chapter 4

The nineteenth century: from party polemics to academic history

Drawn to the subject by a conviction that prejudice had too deeply coloured the minds of those that had already dealt with it for their work to be in any respect final or satisfactory, and armed with a determination to be above all things open-minded and fair, he made up his mind to grapple with the whole material accessible ... It is not too much to say that Gardiner found the story of the first Stewarts and Cromwell legend and has left it history (E. York Powell, 'Samuel Rawson Gardiner', *English Historical Review*, XVII (1902), pp.276, 278.)

There was no clear-cut dividing line between the 'philosophical history' of the Age of Reason and that produced in the different climate of romanticism and nationalism in the early nineteenth century.[1] Hume's influence survived into the later period, despite the assaults of such as Mrs Macaulay, and his *History* was reprinted, re-edited, brought up to date, and even expurgated! (The title page of one such bowdlerized version, edited by a clergyman in 1816, proclaimed that Hume's work had been 'revised for family use with such omissions and alterations as may render it salutary to the young and unexceptional to the Christian.') But the radical opposition to the 'Tory' Hume was reinforced in the 1820s by the appearance of works by Mary Wollstonecraft's husband William Godwin (1756-1836) and J.T. Rutt (1760-1841).

Rutt, radical, Unitarian friend of Priestley and Gibbon Wakefield, and member of Cartwright's Society for Constitutional Information and later of the Society of the Friends of the People, was notable as an editor rather than as an author in his own right.[2] In 1828 he brought out an edition of the diary of Thomas Burton, a member of the Long Parliament, and used the opportunity to emphasize the importance of the Commonwealth period.

It was distinguished by the patriotic deeds of men, whom knowledge, energy and discretion had eminently qualified to dispute the claims of the crown to an unlimited and irresponsible authority. Such had been too long the extravagant pretensions of that royal race which an absurd notion of hereditary right ... had entailed on the acquiescing people of England.[3]

A more important and wide-ranging effort to redirect attention to the 1640s and 1650s was Godwin's *History of the Commonwealth of England* (1824-8). This was the first full-length study of England's experiment in republican government, the first systematic effort to fill (as Godwin termed it) 'this chasm in our annals'. Based on extensive research in the order books of the Council of State and in the Thomason tracts, Godwin's work aimed 'to remedy this defect, to restore the just tone of historical relation on the subject, to attend to the neglected, to remember the forgotten and to distribute an impartial award on all that was planned and achieved during this eventful period'.[4] His study was more temperate, less blatantly partisan than Mrs Macaulay's, but none the less Godwin held it to be an irrefutable truth that 'the opponents of Charles I fought for liberty and that they had no alternative'.[5] The early part of his work did full justice to 'the founders of the Commonwealth' — Coke, Selden, Hampden, and Pym — and he concluded here that 'the liberties of Englishmen are perhaps to no man so deeply indebted as to Sir Edward Coke'.[6]

Godwin's hostility to Charles I was undisguised, but he was political realist enough to appreciate that the King's execution was a grave tactical error.

It is not easy to imagine a greater criminal than the individual against whom sentence was awarded. Charles I, to a degree which can scarcely be exceeded, conspired against the liberty of his country ... [Yet his execution] instead of breaking down the wall which separated him from others gave to his person a sacredness which never before appertained to it ... I am afraid that the day that saw Charles perish on the scaffold rendered the restoration of his family certain.[7]

On Cromwell — always an embarrassment to republican historians — Godwin was much less severe than Mrs Macaulay, to whom the Protector had appeared 'the most corrupt and selfish being that ever disgraced an human form'. Godwin, however, although he could never really forgive Cromwell for what inevitably seemed like his betrayal of the Good Old Cause, nevertheless paid tribute to his many qualities. Cromwell was:

> ... a man of great virtues, sincere in his religion, fervent in his patriotism, and earnestly devoted to the best interests of mankind ... His reputation as a man born to rule over his fellow men increased every day, and the awe and reverence of the English name that he inspired into all other states can find no parallel in any preceding or subsequent period of our history....
>
> The character of Cromwell has been little understood. No wonder. The man who has many enemies will be sure to be greatly misrepresented. [But] he governed a people that was hostile to him. His reign, therefore, was a reign of experiments. He perpetually did the thing he desired not to do and was driven from one inconsistent and undesirable mode of proceeding to another...[8]

Interesting though Godwin was as a historian, he had too many shortcomings, the coverage of his work was too restricted, and he was insufficiently Whiggish in the orthodox sense to overshadow Hume's *History*. Hume's influence still continued and survived two further, more conventionally Whig, rejoinders from George Brodie and Henry Hallam, just as it had earlier survived the publication of T.H.B. Oldfield's *Representative History of Great Britain and Ireland* (1816) and Lord John Russell's *Essay on the History of the English Government and Constitution* (1821).

The Scottish lawyer Brodie brought out his *Constitutional History of the British Empire from the Accession of Charles I to the Restoration* in 1822. Despite its misleading title his work was a staunchly Whig account of English domestic history (with chapters on Scotland and Ireland) deliberately, and in the event unduly optimistically, intended to demolish Hume. The latter, Brodie argued in his preface,

> ... embarked in his undertaking with a predisposition unfavourable to a calm enquiry after truth, and being impatient of that unwearied research which, never satisfied while any source of information remains unexplored or probability not duly weighed, with unremitting industry sifts and collates authorities, he allowed his narrative to be directed by his predilections, and overlooked the materials

from which it ought to have been constructed. ... Mr Hume's view of the government and of public opinion — on which is founded his defence of the unfortunate Charles I and his minister Strafford — appears to me altogether erroneous...[9]

Brodie's view of the Stuarts, in contrast to Hume's, was extremely hostile. Under Elizabeth limited monarchy had existed and 'the grand constitutional principles were clearly defined as well as recognized'. Under the Stuarts, however, government proceeded in new and arbitrary directions. Brodie put forward an exceedingly low estimate of Laud and Strafford, but proclaimed that the name of John Hampden 'will be illustrious so long as patriotism and private virtue are venerated by men'. Under Charles I the grievances of his subjects were numerous and genuine, and the courage with which the King faced his execution, Brodie argued, should not make later generations forget his deep guilt and constant hypocrisy.[10]

Accustomed from his earliest years to intrigue and dissimulation he seems, like his father, to have regarded hypocrisy as a necessary part of 'king-craft'. He had reconciled his conscience to the most uncandid protestations, and had studied divinity in order to satisfy himself of the lawfulness of taking oaths to break them. Though he loved the Church of England only as a prop to his own power, he had latterly endeavoured to persuade himself that, by upholding it, he was rendering a service to religion; and he was now surrounded by a clergy who, regarding the ecclesiastical establishment with reverence, partaking in no small degree of the feeling of self-interest, were ready to assure him (and well did they practise the lesson they taught) that a pious fraud which promoted such an object was not only justifiable, but commendable in the sight of God ... His whole government and all his measures ... had been subversive of parliament, the privileges of the people, and in short of the law of the land, on which alone was founded his right to govern; and yet, like his two grand criminal ministers, Laud and Strafford — whose own correspondence, in the absence of all other proof, would indisputably establish their guilt — he averred on the scaffold that he had always been a friend to parliaments and the franchises of the people.[11]

The Whig standpoint was expressed just as clearly, though more moderately, in Henry Hallam's *Constitutional History of England* published in 1827. 'The Whigs', Hallam (1777-1859) roundly declared, 'appear to have taken a far more comprehensive view of the nature and ends of civil society; their principle is more virtuous, more flexible, to the variations of time and circumstance, more congenial to large and masculine intellects'.[12] So for this reason Hallam opposed the moves directed by the Stuarts towards absolutism in state and church. He was full of praise, therefore, for the Long Parliament which 'restored and consolidated the shattered fabric of our constitution'.

> But those common liberties of England which our forefathers had, with such commendable perseverance, extorted from the grasp of power, though by no means so merely theoretical and nugatory in effect as some would insinuate, were yet very precarious in the best periods, neither well defined, nor exempt from anomalous exceptions, or from occasional infringements. Some of them, such as the statute for annual sessions of parliament, had gone into disuse. Those that were most evident could not be enforced; and the new tribunals that, whether by law or usurpation, had reared their heads over the people, had made almost all public and personal rights dependent on their arbitrary will. It was necessary, therefore, to infuse new blood into the languid frame, and so to renovate our ancient constitution that the present era should seem almost a new birth of liberty. Such was the aim, especially, of those provisions which placed the return of parliaments at fixed intervals, beyond the power of the crown to elude.

But of all the reforms carried through by the Long Parliament in its early stages, the one which warmed Hallam's heart most was the abolition of the court of Star Chamber.

> Thus fell the great court of Star Chamber, and with it the whole irregular and arbitrary practice of government, that had for several centuries so thwarted the operation and obscured the light of our free constitution, that many have been prone to deny the existence of those liberties which they found so often infringed, and to mistake the violations of law for its standard.[13]

Hallam favoured all lovers of liberty, all those who believed in the ideal of 'the mixed government of England by King, Lords and Commons'.[14] His was party history of a more academic kind than had so far been current, but it was a shade too legalistic to become really influential, and for the most part he was too balanced rather than partisan to become the standard author in succession to Hume. He took Clarendon to task for the inconsistencies and half-truths of his *History* — 'a strange mixture of honesty and disingenuousness' he called it[15] — yet, when he felt it was appropriate, Hallam was just as capable of criticizing Parliamentarians and republicans. Hallam's early legal training, in fact, influenced his whole approach to history and was very evident, for example, when he discussed the political justice of the Civil War and the relative merits of the two opposing sides.[16] In the same way there were political limits beyond which Hallam himself was not prepared to go in the nineteenth century, and, though a Whig, he opposed the Reform Act of 1832.

So although Hallam had a respectful audience, although his *Constitutional History*, like his other major works, remained in print throughout the nineteenth century, his impact was not great enough to displace Hume from popular esteem. Even less calculated to achieve this object were the lightweight and anecdotal *Memoirs of the Court of Charles I* published in 1833 by Lucy Aikin (1781-1864). Only, in fact, with Lord Macaulay did a Whig historian appear on the scene who effectively combined popular appeal with party emphasis.

Politically identified with the Whigs by the 1820s and as a writer much influenced by Sir Walter Scott, Macaulay (1800-59) perfected a brilliant style. (It has been aptly described by a recent historian as 'a virtuoso's instrument played not to interpret the music but to glorify the performer!')[17] He aimed deliberately at a wide audience. 'I shall not be satisfied', he wrote to Napier, editor of the *Edinburgh Review*, 'unless I produce something which shall for a few days supersede the last fashionable novel on the tables of young ladies'.[18] He certainly set out to supersede Hume as the leading historian of England and debunked him unmercifully.

> Hume is an accomplished advocate. Without positively asserting much more than he can prove, he gives prominence to all the circumstances which support his case; he glides lightly over those which are unfavourable to it; his own witnesses are applauded and encouraged; the statements which seem to throw discredit on them are controverted; the contradictions into which they fall are explained away; a clear and connected abstract of their evidence is given. Everything that is offered on the other side is scrutinized with the utmost severity; every suspicious circumstance is a ground for comment and invective; what cannot be denied is extenuated, or

passed by without notice; concessions even are sometimes made: but this insidious candour only increases the effect of the vast mass of sophistry.[19]

Hume's 'sophistry' needed to be replaced by a more balanced account, which Macaulay first of all began to provide in his essays. An early statement of his views on the Stuarts was published in 1824 in *Knight's Quarterly Magazine*,[20] and in the following year with his essay on Milton, Macaulay triumphantly began a long and successful association with the Whig mouthpiece, *The Edinburgh Review*.

[Milton] lived at one of the most memorable eras in the history of mankind, at the very crisis of the great conflict between Oromasdes and Arimanes, liberty and despotism, reason and prejudice. That great battle was fought for no single generation, for no single land. The destinies of the human race were staked on the same cast with the freedom of the English people. Then were first proclaimed those mighty principles which have since worked their way into the depths of the American forests, which have roused Greece from the slavery and degradation of two thousand years, and which, from one end of Europe to the other, have kindled an unquenchable fire in the hearts of the oppressed, and loosed the knees of the oppressors with an unwonted fire...

[In England, the puritans] those who roused the people to resistance, who directed their measures through a long series of eventful years, who formed, out of the most unpromising materials, the finest army that Europe had ever seen, who trampled down King, Church, and Aristocracy, who, in the short intervals of domestic sedition and rebellion, made the name of England terrible to every nation on the face of the earth, were no vulgar fanatics ... We do not hestitate to pronounce them a brave, a wise, an honest and a useful body.[21]

His essays on Hallam, Sir James Mackintosh, and Lord Nugent's *Memorials of Hampden* presented the same Whig standpoint which Macaulay was to elaborate later at greater length in his *History of England* (1848-61).

And now began [in 1627] that hazardous game on which were staked the destinies of the English people. It was played on the side of the House of Commons with keenness, but with admirable dexterity, coolness and perseverance. Great statesmen who looked far behind them and far before them were at the head of that assembly. They were resolved to place the King in such a situation that he must either conduct the administration in conformity with the wishes of his Parliament, or make outrageous attacks on the most sacred principles of the constitution...

[Of Charles I's many faults] faithlessness was the chief cause of his disasters, and is the chief stain on his memory. He was, in truth, impelled by an incurable propensity to dark and crooked ways. It may seem strange that his conscience, which, on occasions of little moment, was sufficiently sensitive, should never have reproached him with this great vice. But there is reason to believe that he was perfidious, not only from constitution and from habit, but also on principle. [22]

Macaulay, active himself in Whig political circles, was pre-eminent among historians of his age, and he supplied an attractive and satisfying alternative to Hume in the changed political climate of 1832 and after. In a political speech in 1839 he declared:

I entered public life a Whig and a Whig I am determined to remain ... It seems to me that, when I look back on our history, I can discern a great party which has, through many generations, preserved its identity; a party often depressed, never extinguished; a party which, though often tainted with the faults of the age, has always been in advance of the age; a party which, though guilty of many errors and some crimes, has the glory of having established our civil and religious liberties on a firm foundation; and of that party I am proud to be a member ... It was a party which, in the reign of James I, organised the earliest parliamentary opposition, which steadily asserted the privileges of the people, and wrested prerogative after prerogative from the Crown. It was that party which forced Charles I to relinquish the ship money. It was that party which destroyed the Star Chamber and the High Commission Court. It was that party which, under Charles II, carried the Habeas Corpus Act, which effected the Revolution, which passed the Toleration Act, which broke the yoke of a foreign church in your country, and which saved Scotland from the fate of unhappy Ireland ... To the Whigs of the seventeenth century we owe it that we have a House of Commons. To the Whigs of the nineteenth century we owe it that the House of Commons has been purified... [23]

At first glance it may seem unfair to use a political speech as evidence of Macaulay's historical thinking. In fact, however, electioneering of this sort was freely imported into his essays and into the *History*. Macaulay's firm beliefs in the idea of progress, in parliamentary government, civil liberty, and toleration, directly conditioned his whole attitude to the past and the way in which he wrote about it. Although his work cannot be dismissed as an uncritical hymn to Victorianism, none the less Macaulay, supremely complacent and confident, contemplated the seventeenth-century past from the elevated standpoint of his own age. As he proclaimed at the beginning of the first chapter of his *History of England:*

> Unless I greatly deceive myself, the general effect of this chequered narrative will be to excite thankfulness in all religious minds, and hope in the breasts of all patriots. For the history of our country during the last hundred and sixty years is eminently the history of physical, of moral, and of intellectual improvement. Those who compare the age on which their lot has fallen with a golden age which exists only in their imagination may talk of degeneracy and decay; but no man who is correctly informed as to the past will be disposed to take a morose or desponding view of the present.[24]

The success of his *History* reflected the mood of relief and self-congratulation after England's avoidance of revolution in 1848.

Macaulay's partisan historical writing, written with unsurpassed vigour, flamboyance, and exaggeration, came at the end of an era in historiography; only twenty years after the appearance of the last volume of his *History* the work was being criticized as 'unhistorical'. [25] After Macaulay, English historical scholarship in general was never quite the same again. For from the middle of the nineteenth century the nature of historical research and writing, following the German model, was noticeably changing and was becoming more academic and scientific in character. (Macaulay himself, to all intents and purposes, ignored these developments in German historiography, and significantly when he reviewed von Ranke's *History of the Popes* he had virtually nothing to say about the writer's methodology.) The contrast between 'literary' and 'scientific' history, of course, was not absolute; 'scientific' history too, in the nature of things, still involved subjectivity, despite the contrary claims of its practitioners. But none the less there was a difference between the two varieties of history, albeit one of *degree* rather than of kind.

The more detached, more scientific approach to historical study in England was made possible first by the increased accessibility of primary source material, and second by developments in the training of historians stemming from the establishment of history as an academic discipline in its own right at the universities. The creation of separate Schools of History at Oxford in 1871, with William Stubbs as Regius Professor, and at Cambridge in 1873 helped to give the subject a firmer foothold, although it did not mean that the two universities from this date began to turn out a steady stream of professional historians. The colleges and most of the students saw history as part of a general education, well-suited for politicians, administrators and empire-builders. The 'history for its own sake' line taken by the Regius Professors was at first unsympathetically received.[26] Other changes were more immediately productive. The resources of the British Museum, for example, were made more readily available to historians through systematic cataloguing. A related move was begun in 1856 with the publication of the first calendars of state papers. The new Public Record Office was opened in 1862 and the Historical Manuscripts Commission was launched seven years later. The publication of source material by such bodies as the Camden Society (founded 1838) and the Chetham Society (founded 1843) was a step in the same general direction. The *English Historical Review,* the first journal of its kind in this country, began publication in 1886. The result of developments such as these was that painstaking research, based squarely on manuscript as well as on secondary material, was coming to be regarded as the essential element in the historian's business. J.B. Bury's 1902 inaugural lecture at Cambridge on 'The Science of History' accurately reflected this state of affairs.[27]

As far as the historiography of the English Revolution is concerned, the influence of these developments was obvious. A noticeable change occurred in the style of writing; one has only to contrast Macaulay's pages with the restrained and detailed scholarship of S.R. Gardiner (see pp.69-73). The emergence of more scientific history, in fact, produced a profound change in the nature of the debate on the English Revolution. The polemical element, the party political flavour receded, and since then the debate, for the most part, has been predominantly academic in tone.

Looking back, we can see that a move had been made in the direction of more critical, more scientific history by John Lingard (1771-1851). Lingard concerns us only briefly here since although he published a general *History of England from the First Invasion of the Romans to the Accession of William and Mary* (1819-30), his original researches were confined mainly to the sixteenth century rather than to the period of the English Revolution. Lingard, a Catholic priest, was the first English historian to look at Tudor policy from an international point of view, and by exploiting previously untapped European sources in the archives of Rome and Simancas he endeavoured to correct some of the most glaring distortions in the English Protestant/ nationalist view of the English past. But although his religious purpose at times obstructed his scholarly objectives, and although his later volumes on the Stuarts reveal mildly Whiggish opinions, none the less Lingard did consciously *try* to be objective about the past and to aim at scientific accuracy. He was no uncritical partisan either of Church or of party. Take, for instance, his reflections on the execution of Charles I.

> Such was the end of the unfortunate Charles Stuart, an awful lesson to the possessors of royalty, to watch the growth of public opinion, and to moderate their pretensions in conformity with the reasonable desires of their subjects ... But while we blame the illegal measures of Charles, we ought not to screen from censure the subsequent conduct of his principal opponents. From the moment that war seemed inevitable, they acted as if they thought themselves absolved from all obligations of honour and honesty. They never ceased to inflame the passions of the people by misrepresentation and calumny; they exercised a power far more arbitrary and formidable than had ever been claimed by the king...[28]

Lingard's views on historical method, which involved an explicit rejection of 'philosophical history', were put forward most clearly in the preface to the last revision of his *History* which he undertook in 1849.

> In disposing of the new matter derived from these several sources, I have strictly adhered to the same rules to which I subjected myself in the former editions; to admit no statement merely upon trust, to weigh with care the value of the authorities on which I rely, and to watch with jealousy the secret workings of my own personal feelings and prepossessions. Such vigilance is a matter of necessity to every writer of history, if he aspire to the praise of truthfulness and impartiality. He must withdraw himself aloof from the scenes which he describes and view with the coolness of an unconcerned spectator

the events which pass before his eyes, holding with a steady hand the balance between contending parties, and allotting to the more prominent characters that measure of praise or dispraise which he conscientiously believes to be their due. Otherwise, he will be continually tempted to make an unfair use of the privilege of the historian; he will sacrifice the interests of truth to the interests of party, national, or religious, or political. His narrative may still be brilliant, attractive, picturesque; but the pictures which he paints will derive their colouring from the jaundiced eye of the artist himself, and will therefore bear no very faithful resemblance to the realities of life and fact.[29]

For the final revision of his *History* Lingard made use of Carlyle's *Letters and Speeches of Oliver Cromwell* (1845), or at least of 'the letters and speeches themselves, not the running commentary with which the editor has accompanied them in language most glowing and oracular ... I feel no disposition to fall down before the idol, and worship him at the command of his panegyrist'.[30] In some ways Carlyle deserved Lingard's rebuke; Cromwell emerged from his pages as a Heaven-sent Hero of a kind, as the author saw it, that his own generation in the nineteenth century badly needed. But despite all appearances, it could be argued that Carlyle too, perverse and idiosyncratic though he was, like Lingard, in a sense took a step away from party history towards a more critical, scientific approach to the seventeenth-century past.

Judged by later standards, Thomas Carlyle (1795-1881) certainly would not rank as a scientific historian, and by the end of the century he was indeed much out of favour with the professionals. Seen in the context of his own times, however, Carlyle appears different from his predecessors in that, despite all his obtrusive subjectivity, his prejudices — vast though they were — were at least his own, and not those picked up in the Whig/Tory political arena. Carlyle preferred to use primary sources and described his researches on Cromwell as 'a mole's work, boring and digging blindly underground'.[31] But whereas later historians saw in research the main part of their scholarly activity, to Carlyle it was no more than a preliminary, sometimes disagreeable, to the main task of communicating ideas in society at large. He was always impatient to write down his conclusions even if he had still not genuinely reached them by his research. He wrote to a correspondent in 1845,

I would very gladly tell you all my methods if I had any, but really I have as it were none. I go into the business with all the intelligence, patience, silence and other gifts and virtues that I have; find that ten times or a hundred times as many could be profitably expended there, and still prove insufficient: and as for plan, I find that every new business requires as it were a new scheme of operations, which amid infinite bungling and plunging unfolds itself at intervals (very scantily, after all) as I get along. The great thing is not to stop and break down ... Avoid writing beyond the very minimum; mark in pencil the very smallest indication that will direct me to the thing again; and on the whole try to keep the whole matter simmering in the living mind and memory rather than laid up in paper bundles or otherwise laid up in the inert way. For this certainly turns out to be a truth: only what you at last have living in your own memory and heart is worth putting down to be printed; this alone has much chance to get into the living heart and memory of other men...[32]

Only to a limited extent, therefore, do Carlyle's *Cromwell* and his posthumously published *Historical Sketches of Notable Persons and Events in the Reigns of James I and Charles I* (1898) reveal their author as a critical, scientific historian in the later sense of the term. Far more positive and recognizable steps in this direction were taken by two distinguished European historians of seventeenth-century England, the one a Frenchman and the other a German. The first was François Guizot (1787-1874), liberal conservative politician and sometime professor of history who fell from power with the July monarchy in 1848. Guizot's historical writing can best be described, perhaps, as proto-scientific in character. As Professor Johnson has written in his study of the man and his background:

> It is easy to understand why Guizot appeared so outstanding. Nothing could appear more scientific than his detached and objective style. This is all the more striking when compared to that of his contemporaries...
>
> No one would deny that Guizot had prejudices. He appears to be less one-sided than many of his contemporary historians because these prejudices are concealed under an air of dispassionate reason, and are hidden by a screen of erudition. But he simply did not have antipathies on the same scale as Macaulay or Michelet.[33]

But it was not only Guizot's style which appeared scientific to his contemporaries both in France and England, but also his very conception of history. J.S. Mill, for example, in 1845 declared that Guizot's great merit was that he set out to *explain* the facts of history, whereas in England the mere unearthing and presentation of the facts themselves satisfied historians.[34]

Guizot wrote extensively on seventeenth-century England, and did so with the confidence of one who had himself experienced revolutions and their consequences. First, in 1826 came his *History of the English Revolution of 1640* which was followed by studies of Oliver Cromwell, Richard Cromwell, General Monck and others in the 1850s. Although J.W. Croker complained that Guizot tended to confuse the *Rebellion* with the *Revolution*,[35] his survey of seventeenth-century England was highly regarded both for its comprehensiveness and impartiality. Hallam, for instance, thought that if Guizot continued as he had begun, then 'he will be entitled to the preference above any one, perhaps, of our native writers, as a guide through the great period of the seventeenth century'.[36]

Guizot was in fact the first historian to use the term 'English Revolution', and in the preface to the first instalment of his *History* published in 1826, he drew an extended comparison between affairs in England and the French Revolution of 1789. He emphasized that both events, far from being unexpected, were the natural result of historical development.

> Produced by the same causes, the decay of the feudal aristocracy, the church, and royalty, they both laboured at the same work, the dominion of the public in public affairs; they struggled for liberty against absolute power, for equality against privilege, for progressive and general interests against stationary and individual interests. Their situations were different, their strength unequal; what one clearly conceived, the other saw but in imperfect outline; in the career which the one fulfilled, the other soon stopped short...
>
> In a word, the analogy of the two revolutions is such, that the first would never have been thoroughly understood had not the second taken place.[37]

Guizot elaborated his ideas on the seventeenth-century crisis in England in his pamphlet *Why was the English Revolution Successful?* (1850). Looking at the Revolution in its broadest social aspects, Guizot concluded in a way that was reminiscent of Harrington that:

> Political and religious parties were not alone in the field. Beneath their struggle lay a social question, the struggle of the various classes

for influence and power. Not that these classes were in England radically segregate and hostile one to another as they have been elsewhere....But in the last hundred years, great changes had taken place in the relative strength of the various classes in the bosom of society, without any analogous changes having been wrought in the government. Commercial activity and religious order had, in the middle classes, given a prodigious impulse to wealth and to thought ... Hence had arisen amongst them and the ranks beneath them a proud and powerful spirit of ambition, eager to seize the first occasion to burst forth. Civil war opened a wide field to their energy and to their hopes. It presented at its outset, no aspect of a social classification, exclusive and hostile: many country gentlemen, several even of the great lords, were at the head of the popular party. Soon the nobility on the one hand, and the middle class and the people on the other, ranged themselves in two masses, the one around the crown, the other around the parliament, and sure symptoms already revealed a great social movement in the heart of a great political struggle, and the effervescence of an ascendant democracy, clearing for itself a way through the ranks of a weakened and divided aristocracy.[38]

Written after his fall from office in 1848, Guizot's pamphlet reveals a writer who now had time, and added reason, to reflect on revolutions. His admiration for the English Revolution still remained. He stressed its constitutionalism, its appeal to Magna Carta, its resistance to tyranny. ('In the seventeenth century in England, royal power was the aggressor'.[39]) The political solution — wholly admirable in Guizot's view — which emerged from the seventeenth-century crisis was constitutional monarchy. 'But in the seventeenth century they had neither the enlightenment nor the political virtues which this government requires.'[40] Regrettably, the Revolution which began so promisingly got out of hand. The execution of Charles I was a 'high crime', religious extremism degenerated into an arrogant fanaticism, and a thoroughly un-English republic was created. 'Revolutionists, even the ablest of them, are short-sighted. Intoxicated by the passion, or dominated by the necessity of the moment, they do not forsee that what today constitutes their triumph will be tomorrow their condemnation.'[41] As Guizot saw it, therefore, the English Revolution, immensely important though it was, was in some ways important for indirect reasons; it was a lesson, painfully learnt.

After the great revolutionary crisis of 1640-1660, the English people had the good fortune and the merit of appreciating experience, and of never giving themselves up to extreme parties. Amidst the most ardent political struggles and violence, in which they sometimes impelled their chiefs, they always on great and decisive occasions reverted to that sound good sense which consists in recognising the essential benefits it is desired to retain and attaching itself without wavering to them; enduring the inconveniences attendant on them and renouncing the desires which might compromise them. It is from the time of Charles II that this good sense which is the political intelligence of free nations has presided over the destinies of England ... Whether we look at the destiny of nations, or at that of great men — whether a monarchy or a republic is in question — an aristocratic or a democratic society, the same truth is revealed by facts; definitive success is only obtained by the same principles and in the same way. The revolutionary spirit is as fatal to the greatness it raises up as to that which it overturns. The policy which preserves states is also that which terminates and founds revolutions.[42]

Clearly, it was Guizot the failed, ousted, helpless politician as much as Guizot the historian who reached this verdict.

Not a politician himself, the second of these distinguished European historians of seventeenth-century England was more detached from his subject. Leopold von Ranke (1795-1886), the great German historian and the real founder of the new school of history in the nineteenth century, wrote his six-volume *History of England chiefly in the Seventeenth Century* in the 1860s, and it soon appeared in an English translation in 1875. Ranke emphasized the advantages of an outsider's view of this important and controversial period of English history.

It is surely good that in epochs of such great importance for the history of all nations, we should possess foreign and independent representations to compare with those of home growth; in the latter are expressed sympathies and antipathies as inherited by tradition and affected by the antagonism of literary differences of opinion. ... A historical work may aim either at putting forward a new view of what is already known or at communicating additional information as to the facts. I have endeavoured to combine both these aims.[43]

Not surprisingly in view of its author, Ranke's work was particularly
valuable for its treatment of England's relations with the continent.
And it was entirely characteristic of his careful and exacting scholarship
to attach extensive documentary and historiographical appendices to
his history.

But although he wrote as an outsider whose 'only concern is to
become acquainted with the great motive powers and their results',
this did not mean that Ranke's volumes consisted only of a colourless
and neutral collection of facts. English history in general and the
seventeenth-century crisis in particular were presented from a European
point of view. The seventeenth century emerged from Ranke's pages as
a heroic period for England, and the Revolution of 1688 as an event
which served the interests of a Europe menaced by the ambitions of
Louis XIV. The Civil War, he argued,

> ... is an event which concerns all, this shaking of the foundations of
> the old British state. Whether they would stand the shock or, if not,
> what shape public affairs would in that case assume was a question
> which must concern the continent also. The civilised world is still
> busy day by day with more or less conspicuous complications of the
> spiritual and political struggles arising from similar opposing
> principles. [44]

Particularly interested in the diplomatic and religious aspects of the
seventeenth century, for a German Ranke treated the religious
controversies of the period with unaccustomed seriousness, and
underlined the differences between the English Revolution and the
French Revolution of 1789, of which he thoroughly disapproved.
Unimpressed by Cromwell and republicanism, Ranke's charitable
treatment of the Stuarts was based, in part at least, on their
contribution to the unification of Great Britain which indirectly served
the cause of a beleaguered Europe.

> James I had probably during his lifetime too high an idea of the
> strength of his opponents; Charles I certainly had too slight a one ...
> He knew neither the depth of the lawful desires of Parliament nor
> the purport of the opposition already begun: he cherished splendid
> hopes when nearest to his ruin. For he trusted chiefly to the intrinsic
> power of the rights and ideas for which he fought ... So far there was
> certainly something of a martyr in him, if the man can be so called
> who values his own life less than the cause for which he is fighting,
> and in perishing himself, saves it for the future. [45]

English historians, too, were active in the work of research and reinterpretation. J.R. Green (1837-83) was the oddity among them. His popular *Short History of the English People* appeared in 1874 and was novel in both its treatment and sympathies. In Green's work the 'people' held the centre of the stage, and the book as a whole was suffused with his Liberal convictions. Green believed, as his editor later wrote, that 'political history could only be made intelligible and just by basing it on social history in its largest sense'. As a schoolboy studying Charles I, 'it had suddenly burst upon him that Charles was wrong'. Green's *Short History* embodied the same sentiments. 'Modern England, the England among whose thoughts and sentiments we actually live, began however dimly with the triumph of Naseby'.[46]

Ultimately, however, it was S.R. Gardiner (1829-1902), who produced the classic, large-scale, new-style work on the period 1603 to 1656. For Gardiner, recognition was an uphill task, and he held no university appointment until late middle age. Lord Acton wrote an unenthusiastic review of the first instalment of his history in 1863. But tributes to him abounded by the end of the century. 'No man did more by his personal efforts to forward the progress of historical studies in England', wrote Sir Charles Firth after Gardiner's death.[47] 'With the possible exception of Stubbs's *Constitutional History,* his [Gardiner's] volumes form the most solid and enduring achievement of British historiography in the latter half of the nineteenth century.' So wrote G.P. Gooch a few years later.[48] And from America, too, came glowing praise in the *Yale Scientific Monthly.* Gardiner, it was said,

> ... firmly grasped the profound distinction which lies at the root of all science, between the judgement of fact and the judgement of value, and knew that the validity of the first can only be secured if it is provisionally treated as an end in itself, in perfect abstraction from any possible application of it.[49]

It was his methodology, certainly, which was Gardiner's distinctive contribution to historical studies. Rejecting the impressionism of earlier historians, such as Carlyle, and the oratorical style and judge-like pose of Macaulay, Gardiner embarked on his multi-volume history with the determination to be satisfied with nothing less than the truth, and to break with the whole notion of Whig and Tory history.

When I first undertook to investigate the history of this momentous period, I felt a certain hesitation. Libraries positively bristled with the names of great writers who had given their thoughts to the world on the subject of these years. But I was not long in discovering that there was still room for further investigation. We have historians in plenty, but they have been Whig historians or Tory historians. The one class has thought it unnecessary to take trouble to understand how matters looked in the eyes of the King and his friends; the other class has thought it unnecessary to take trouble to understand how matters looked in the eyes of the leaders of the House of Commons. I am not so vain as to suppose that I have always succeeded in doing justice to both parties, but I have, at least, done my best not to misrepresent either....

Certainly the politics of the seventeenth century when studied for the mere sake of understanding them, assume a very different appearance from that which they had in the eyes of men who, like Macaulay and Forster, regarded them through the medium of their own political struggles. Eliot and Strafford were neither Whigs nor Tories, Liberals nor Conservatives. As Professor Seeley was, I believe, the first to teach directly, though the lesson is indirectly involved in every line written by Ranke, the father of modern historical research, the way in which Macaulay and Forster regarded the development of the past — that is to say, the constant avowed or unavowed comparison of it with the present — is altogether destructive of real historical knowledge. [50]

Although a fine lecturer and a writer of school textbooks, Gardiner was primarily a historians' historian, and in contrast with Macaulay and Green his first ventures into publishing were miserably unsuccessful. But he persevered in the task and with the method with which he had begun. The hallmark of Gardiner's historical method was a strict adherence to chronology, taking into account only those sources relating to each moment in time which he examined in progression. The method had its drawbacks, of course. Above all, it was not conducive to consistency, although in this, too, Gardiner believed that he was faithfully representing the times. But the main value of chronology, as he saw it, was that it was an antidote to bias.

Hitherto no book has come into existence which has even professed to trace the gradual change which came over English feeling year by year ... Much confusion has been caused by the habit ... of classifying events rather according to their nature than according to their chronological order, so that the true sequence of history is lost. It is needless to add that where, as too often happens, no attempt whatever is made to understand the strong points in the case of the King or the weak points in the case of his opponents, the result is a mere caricature.[51]

Gardiner based his research securely on the primary sources and was helped in this by the work of the Historical Manuscripts Commission and by the calendaring of state papers. 'Evidence worth having must be almost entirely the evidence of contemporaries who are in a position to know something about that which they assert.'[52] Gardiner, however, was no narrow specialist, but was careful to place the Civil War and the reigns of the early Stuarts in a long perspective. Also, as a considerable linguist well versed in continental sources, Gardiner gave, so far as English historians were concerned, unprecedented attention to European affairs in this period.

No one can really study any particular period of history unless he knows a great deal about what preceded it and what came after it. He cannot seriously study a generation of men as if it could be isolated and examined like a piece of inorganic matter. He has to bear in mind that it is a portion of a living whole.[53]

Gardiner's interpretation of seventeenth-century events, unlike that associated with Macaulay's hammering technique, was relatively unobtrusive; 'The Puritan Revolution' is a convenient but inadequate summary of his model. He avoided making summaries of general trends and did not interrupt his chronological narrative to provide full-length character portraits. But Gardiner, like all historians, could not leave himself out of account. There was naturally a subjective as well as an objective element in his method and interpretation, and this was systematically exposed by the American historian R.G. Usher. 'In reality', Usher concluded, 'Gardiner has done exactly what he blamed Macaulay for doing: he has decided a great issue in history, which was by no means clear to the men of the time, by applying to it his later knowledge.'[54] Usher, too, criticized Gardiner for the inconsistencies into which his historical method led him; his many volumes demonstrated his intellectual growth as a historian but did not provide the reader with a considered and structured account of a controversial period of English history.

Others pushed criticism to unreasonable lengths (see p.74). But Gardiner's method had simply exposed the central frailty of the assumptions on which scientific history was based. With or without a strictly chronological method, complete objectivity was an impossible goal for the historian to attain. Gardiner's Liberal Nonconformist background could hardly fail to make an impact on his historical writing. That he was a member of the Irvingite sect, a great admirer of Gladstone, and himself a descendant of Oliver Cromwell, all helped to shape his historical perception. What emerged, then, from Gardiner's account of seventeenth-century England was a record of a struggle for political and religious liberty. 'The interest of [English] history in the seventeenth century lies in the efforts made to secure a double object — the control of the nation over its own destinies, and the liberty of the public expression of thought, without which parliamentary government is only a refined form of tyranny.'[55] His national pride comes through.

> England was then, as she has always been, decidedly in advance, so far as political institutions are concerned, of the other nations of Europe. She had to work out the problem of government unaided by experience, and was entering like Columbus upon a new world, where there was nothing to guide her but her own high spirit and the wisdom and virtue of her sons.[56]

It was the English nation itself which was the repository of liberty.

> The English people had never entirely relinquished their control over their own destinies, nor had ever so put themselves like sheep into the hands of any king as to suffer themselves to be tended or shorn at his arbitrary will. Not in statute or precedent, not even in the Great Charter itself, but in the imperishable vitality of the nation, lay the fundamental laws of England.[57]

There was a certain inevitability about the Civil War, and puritanism's role was absolutely central.

> Above all, it was Puritanism which gave to those whose energies were most self-centred the power which always follows upon sub-mission to law. Puritanism not only formed the strength of the opposition to Charles, but the strength of England itself. Parliamentary liberties, and even parliamentary control, were worth contending for.[58]

With all these resonances of the Whig interpretation, it is easy to see how the label 'Puritan Revolution', despite the oversimplification it brought with it, came to be attached to Gardiner's great, but quintessentially Victorian, work.

Chapter 5

The twentieth century: the nineteenth century inheritance and its development

[Gardiner's works] cover the period from 1603 to 1656 with unexampled thoroughness. Even after the lapse of fifty years it is difficult to add substantially to or to make more than minor corrections of this narrative ... (Godfrey Davies, *The Early Stuarts 1603-1660* (Oxford, 1937, 2nd ed. 1959), p.418.)

The criticism of Gardiner's historical method made by R.G. Usher in 1915 was carried to much greater lengths by an anonymous correspondent in the *Times Literary Supplement* in 1919. This writer, whose tone became increasingly irascible week by week as the correspondence developed, denounced Gardiner as 'a subtle and dangerous partisan. The truth is that nothing he says can be trusted. Every reference note should be checked.'[1] Leading academic historians like A.P. Newton, A.F. Pollard and C.H. Firth rallied to the defence of Gardiner's reputation. Without the latter's pioneering efforts, they argued, the state of knowledge of seventeenth-century history would have been immeasurably poorer. 'It is an ungrateful act', one of them said, 'to kick down the ladder whereby you have climbed.'[2] Appropriately, it was Sir Charles Firth (1857-1936) who took the lead in vindicating Gardiner against this violent attack, and on this occasion, as on others, he proved himself a true disciple. In the obituaries he wrote for the *Quarterly Review* and for the *Proceedings* of the newly formed British Academy, he helped to ensure that Gardiner received the honour that was due to him as one of the leading English historians.

For years before Gardiner's death Firth had been his friend and amanuensis. As Gardiner wrote in the preface to the revised edition of his *History of the Great Civil War:*

I wish it were possible for me to give adequate expression to my sense of the obligation under which I am to Mr Firth. He has generously allowed me to draw on his vast stores of knowledge concerning the men and things of this period and has always been ready to discuss with me any point of importance as it arose, often very considerably modifying the opinion at which I had originally arrived.[3]

Firth was the obvious choice to continue Gardiner's history from the point where he had broken off in 1656, and he did so specifically at Gardiner's request. The result was *The Last Years of the Protectorate 1656-58* published in 1909. This in turn was eventually carried forward in *The Restoration of Charles II* published as recently as 1955 by Firth's own friend and former student Godfrey Davies.[4] By this process of apostolic succession, therefore, the Gardiner tradition was ensured of a long and vigorous life. In an obituary notice the *American Historical Review* accurately claimed that Davies 'did much to maintain the central tradition regarding [seventeenth-century English history] against eccentric revisions from writers of the left and of the right'.[5]

It was not that Firth's view of history and of the seventeenth century was simply an exact replica of Gardiner's. Firth did not share Gardiner's own religious convictions and, appropriate to one drawn from a well-known family of Sheffield metalmasters, he gave more emphasis to social and economic aspects than his predecessor had done. Firth, too, far excelled Gardiner in his broad and intimate knowledge of English literature — significantly he played a prominent part in the foundation of the English School at Oxford — and his style was undoubtedly superior.[6] Firth was inferior to Gardiner, however, as a linguist, and his historical knowledge was in some ways less wide-ranging. 'I am conscious that I do not possess either the comprehensive knowledge or the perfect equipment which he [Gardiner] brought to his task.' So Firth wrote in the preface to *The Last Years of the Protectorate*. But Firth thought that Gardiner's early writings at times adhered too rigidly and mechanically to a chronological sequence. Far from exactly modelling himself on Gardiner, therefore, in this respect, Firth wrote his history of the years 1656-8 in the conviction that 'it seemed to me as important to show the temper of the time as to narrate the events'.[7] Firth's capacity for generalization was even more clearly revealed in his short study of *The Parallel between the English and American Civil Wars* (1910). And Firth was not averse to publishing historical works of an unashamedly topical nature. His study of *The House of Lords during the Civil War* (1910) appeared at the height of Lloyd George's struggle with the upper house, and it expressed the hope that the evidence concerning seventeenth-century parliaments would serve 'for the instruction of their descendants'.

But such differences apart, Firth acknowledged Gardiner as his mentor and continued, extended and, in his *Oliver Cromwell and the Rule of the Puritans in England* (1900), popularized Gardiner's model of the seventeenth-century crisis.[8] In Firth's view of the Civil War, puritanism was still at the heart of things, as he made abundantly clear in his critical comments on Clarendon's neglect of the religious factor (see p.32). Firth's scientific method, too, had some of Gardiner's weaknesses, as W.S. McKechnie pointed out in a perceptive review of his book on the House of Lords.

> His interests reveal themselves as centering round principles and tendencies rather than families or individuals. Carefully suppressing, so far as that is possible, all personal prejudices or predilections of his own, he strives to allow the bare facts to speak for themselves subject to such colour as they may receive from the estimates of contemporaries.

The result of this method, McKechnie argued, was to some extent deceptive; conclusions seemed to emerge of their own accord whereas in fact, of course, it was the author who prised them out.[9]

Trained at Oxford, where he was much influenced by Stubbs as Regius Professor, and remaining there for most of his academic career, Firth's earliest work was of an editorial kind. He brought out, for example, critical editions of the *Memoirs of Colonel Hutchinson* in 1885 and of *The Life of the Duke of Newcastle* in the following year. Firth's chief contribution as an editor, however, was in publishing *The Clarke Papers* in four Camden Society volumes between 1891 and 1901. (William Clarke was an influential member of the republican secretariat, and his papers are a tremendously important source for the military campaigns of the period, the relations between parliament and the army, and for the events leading up to the Restoration in 1660.) Besides this important editorial work Firth was later an extremely active member of the Royal Commission on Public Records and contributed no fewer than 275 articles to the *Dictionary of National Biography*.

Firth had a keen interest in historiography, as the chapters on

Raleigh, Milton, Clarendon and Burnet in his *Essays Historical and Literary* made clear. In 1904 he contributed three detailed articles to the *English Historical Review* which established the way in which the final version of Clarendon's *History of the Rebellion* had been constructed from originally separate works. (See p.25.) Also in 1904 he supplied an important critical introduction to an edition of Carlyle's *Letters and Speeches of Oliver Cromwell*, while in 1913 he published a useful general survey of 'The development of the study of seventeenth-century history'.[10] Firth's major work in the field of historiography was his *Commentary on Macaulay's History of England*, which Godfrey Davies edited for publication in 1938. The book consisted of a series of Firth's lectures, the purpose of which had been,

> ... not merely to criticize the statements made by Macaulay and the point of view adopted by him, but also to show the extent to which his conclusions had been invalidated or confirmed by later writers who had devoted their attention to particular parts of his subject, or by the new documentary materials published during the last sixty years...[11]

By systematically examining such aspects as the genesis of Macaulay's *History*, his historical method, his use of authorities, and his treatment of particular subjects and characters, Firth tried to place Macaulay in perspective.

Apart from his editorial work, his general surveys of the Civil War and Interregnum and his writings on historiography, Firth had a special interest in military history. His well-known study of *Cromwell's Army* made its appearance in 1902, and at the time of his death he was still working on his *Regimental History of Cromwell's Army*. Firth approached military history in the broadest possible way. 'A civil war is not only the conflict of opposing principles', he wrote in the preface to *Cromwell's Army*, 'but the shock of material forces.' [12] Firth's chief concern was to explain parliament's military superiority, and he became deeply involved, therefore, with questions of military organization, with discipline, pay, religion, and politics.

Firth became Regius Professor of History at Oxford in 1904 and did much to improve research facilities and the professional training of historians at the university. His intentions were announced in his inaugural lecture, *A Plea for the Historical Teaching of History* (1904), which caused such a stir that the college tutors petitioned against it. Firth's difficulties stemmed from the anomalous position of history at

Oxford. Although established as a course of study at the university, few of its students in fact went on to become historians themselves. These defects Firth set out to remedy by providing instruction in the handling of sources, and by encouraging postgraduate research.[13]

Godfrey Davies (1892-1957) was one of Firth's students, and with his book on the Restoration, he reached the point which Gardiner himself had originally aimed at when he launched his massive narrative history. Davies began his teaching career at Oxford, his own *alma mater*, but moved to America in 1925 to take up appointments first at the University of Chicago, and then, from 1930, more congenially, at the Huntington Library, San Marino, California. Besides his book on *The Restoration of Charles II*, Davies collaborated on Firth's *Regimental History of Cromwell's Army* (1940). In 1937, the year of Firth's death, he published *The Early Stuarts 1603-1660* in the Oxford History of England series, a work which in many ways was a summary of Firth's and Gardiner's volumes. Davies's book was a densely packed factual narrative, and the clearest statement of his overall view of the period is found not in the text itself but in the introduction. 'The keynote of the seventeenth century', he wrote, 'was revolt against authority. Modern times as distinct from the Middle Ages had begun under the Tudors and were now developing rapidly.' However, Davies went on to say that:

> In some ways the 'Great Rebellion' is a better label than 'Puritan Revolution' for the movement that led to the execution of Charles I and the establishment of the protectorate. It is true that most puritans sided against the king, that the parliamentary commissions ran in the name of the king and parliament and thus afforded their holders a somewhat transparent screen against being called rebels, and that a war concerned mainly at the start with political sovereignty rather changed its character and became a crusade for religious freedom. Nevertheless the struggle, though at no time a class war, was to a large extent a revolution by the middle classes against personal government. They had been growing steadily in power under the Tudors when they had been allowed to participate in government at the will of the sovereign. Now they were no longer content merely to register approval of royal edicts...[14]

Davies collaborated with William Haller in editing *The Leveller Tracts 1647-53* (1944), and his *Essays on Later Stuart History* were published posthumously in 1958.

Other writers, too, acknowledged an indebtedness to Firth and Gardiner and followed their lead. One such historian was F.C. Montague (1858-1935) whose textbook on the period 1603-60 in a multi-volume *Political History of England* was first published in 1907.[15] Another was Sir J.A.R. Marriott (1859-1945), who in 1930 brought out a book called *The Crisis of English Liberty*. Marriott, whose own main research interests were not in this field, in his preface acknowledged a special debt to Gardiner and Firth. But Gardiner especially would have been horrified at the use to which his research was being put. Gardiner firmly believed that the mingling of past and present was anti-historical; Marriott's approach to the seventeenth century was unashamedly present-minded.

History, it has always seemed to me, is something more than a mere record of the past; it must necessarily represent the past as seen through the medium of the present. Consequently, each generation must look at the past from a fresh angle. True of all periods, this is pre-eminently true of the history of the seventeenth century and of those who look back upon it from the twentieth. For this reason. The seventeenth century was confronted by problems which we thought it had permanently solved. Unexpectedly, they have in these latter days re-emerged; they are still, it seems, living issues; they still stir the blood of those who mingle in public affairs ...

I regretfully recognize that this avowal will cost me the good opinions of some 'orthodox' historians, and that I shall be accused of the deadly sin of 'reading history backwards'. But all history, save contemporary history, must, in a sense, be read backwards.[16]

As Marriott saw it — and as well as being a historian he had first-hand political experience as a conservative M.P. — twentieth-century England faced much the same kind of crisis of liberty as seventeenth-century England had done.

This much is clear that under conditions greatly altered and in forms not always recognizable, devices adopted by the Stuart kings in their contest with parliament and in their relations with the judges are today making an unwelcome re-appearance...

Recent tendencies have thus invested the history of the seventeenth century with new and arresting significance. It may not then be amiss to con once more the lessons which that period is pre-eminently calculated to teach.[17]

Twentieth-century Englishmen found themselves swamped by an ever-growing volume of legislation and confronted by a 'new despotism' in which the position of the central government and its experts was becoming daily more unassailable.

Yet another writer whose writings in a way helped to perpetuate Gardiner's influence in the twentieth century was G.M. Trevelyan (1876-1962). But Trevelyan, like Marriott and unlike Firth and Davies, could hardly be classified as Gardiner's disciple in the conventional sense; in his style of writing and view of the social function of history he owed far more to his great-uncle Macaulay. 'I have not been an original but a traditional kind of historian', Trevelyan wrote in his autobiography.

> The best that can be said of me is that I tried to keep up to date a family tradition as to the relation of history to literature, in a period when the current was running strongly in the other direction towards history exclusively 'scientific', a period therefore when my old-fashioned ideas and practice have had, perhaps, a certain value as counterpoise.[18]

In his famous textbook *England under the Stuarts* (1904) Trevelyan tried to bring together Gardiner's research and Macaulay's style. The American historian W.C. Abbott, in one of the few serious academic reviews which the book received, saw its value as a work of popularization even though it made 'no great original contribution to knowledge'. 'That it bears any such relation to the seventeenth century as the work of Professor Gardiner bears to the period 1603-1660 or that of Bishop Stubbs to the constitutional development of England before 1485 no one could seriously maintain.'[19]

Despite his rejoinder to Professor J.B. Bury's 1902 Cambridge inaugural lecture on 'The Science of History', Trevelyan did not oppose 'scientific' history in any wholesale and indiscriminate way. As a student at Cambridge he developed a deep respect and admiration for Lord Acton. In the bibliography of *England under the Stuarts* he described Ranke's work on England as 'one of the great histories of our country, too much neglected'. In the same book, Trevelyan spoke of Gardiner as '*the* authority on the period for both general readers and students', Firth's *Cromwell* was listed as 'the highest authority on the subject', while his *Cromwell's Army* was praised as 'the best book and the most learned authority on the military side of the war'.[20] It was not scientific history as such which Trevelyan attacked, but the excesses committed in its name, its harmful effects on style and therefore on history's role as a social educator, and by no means least, its German origins. As he wrote in the second edition (1919) of his essays:

> If the first and most important essay [The Muse of History] was received better than I hoped at the time of its publication [1913], it will scarcely be regarded with more disfavour now, seeing what a dance German 'scientific' history has led the nation that looked to it for political prophecy and guidance. The wheel has indeed come full circle. Treitschke worship and Kultur are at a discount, and Englishmen need no longer apologise for the free traditions of their own history and of their own great national historians.[21]

Historians like Carlyle, Macaulay, and indeed Sir Walter Scott, formed an important part of this national heritage, and it was wrong to ignore or reject them. Scott, he claimed in his inaugural lecture at Cambridge in 1927, 'did more for history, I venture to think, than any professed historian in modern times'. In the same lecture he praised Carlyle.

> The past was full of passion and passion is therefore one element in historic truth. Sympathy is a necessary part of understanding. Carlyle helped as much as Gardiner to elucidate the forgotten truth about the English Puritan era and the character and career of Cromwell about whom generations of dispassionate historians, Whig as well as Tory, had unerringly missed the point.[22]

Trevelyan's work, therefore, attempted to combine what was best in the two schools of history, although in the last analysis, like Macaulay, it was his literary style which was its hallmark. *England under the Stuarts* was a textbook, but as J.H. Plumb has remarked, 'surely no textbook has ever before or since been written with such gusto'.[23] Continuing in the 'family tradition', Trevelyan revived not only the art of narrative, but also in a frank and explicit way the Whig interpretation of the seventeenth century. 'The historian's bias', Trevelyan wrote, 'may sometimes help him to sympathize with the actual passions of people in the past whose actions it is his business to describe. Clio should not always be cold, aloof, impartial.'[24] In the pages of *England under the Stuarts,* therefore, the idea of a Puritan Revolution, a struggle for liberty, was presented forcefully and vividly.

> England has contributed many things, good and bad, to the history of the world. But of all her achievements there is one, the most

insular in origin, and yet the most universal in effect. While
Germany boasts her Reformation and France her Revolution,
England can point to her dealings with the House of Stuart ... At
a time when the continent was falling a prey to despots, the English
under the Stuarts had achieved their emancipation from monarchical tyranny by the act of the national will; in an age of bigotry,
their own divisions had forced them into religious toleration
against their real wish; while personal liberty and some measure of
free speech and writing had been brought about by the balance of
two great parties. Never perhaps in any century have such rapid
advances been made towards freedom. [25]

The 'Glorious' Revolution of 1688/9, of course, occupied an
honoured place in Trevelyan's vision of seventeenth-century England
— as in Macaulay's — and he devoted a separate study to it in
1938. [26] But the Civil War period, too, had a share in this 'glorious'
achievement and belonged to the same basic struggle for constitutional liberty. In Trevelyan's view the Civil War was fought over ideas
and principles.

> For it was not, like the French Revolution, a war of classes ... It was a
> war not of classes or of districts, but of ideas. Here there was a
> nobler speculative enthusiasm among the chiefs and their
> followers, but less readiness to fight among the masses of the
> population, than in other contests that have torn great nations.
> The French Revolution was a war of two societies; the American
> Civil War was a war of two regions; but the Great Rebellion was a
> war of two parties. [26]

This concern for liberty was one of the central motifs of Trevelyan's
voluminous output. It conditioned his historical approach, and even
helped to determine the subjects he chose to deal with. It was not
fortuitous that Trevelyan wrote on Wyclif, on Italian unification, and
on seventeenth-century England. Such was Trevelyan's identification
with the Whig tradition, in fact, that when Herbert Butterfield's book
The Whig Interpretation of History appeared in 1931, it was widely
taken as a thinly veiled attack on Trevelyan himself.

Trevelyan's liberal, patriotic interpretation of seventeenth-century
England was restated, more briefly, in his *History of England* (1926),
and in his *English Social History* (1944). In the first of these two
general works he declared:

The English Civil War was not the collapse of an out-worn society in a chaos of class hatred and greed, but a contest for political and religious ideals that divided every rank in a land socially sound and economically prosperous.

The causes of the war were not economic and were only indirectly social. Nevertheless the old aristocratic connection was apt to favour the King while the world that had arisen since the Reformation was apt to favour Parliament...

Trevelyan too, made his contribution to perpetuating the hoary myth that 'all the Roman Catholics were for the King and more particularly for the Queen who was the real head of their party'.[27]

Trevelyan's *English Social History*, so patriotic that it can almost be regarded as an integral part of the war effort, repeated the same basic interpretation of the Civil War that he had first outlined forty years earlier.

The Cromwellian revolution was not social and economic in its causes and motives; it was the result of political and religious thought and aspiration among men who had no desire to recast society or redistribute wealth. No doubt the choice of sides that men made in politics and religion was to some extent and in some cases determined by predispositions due to social and economic circumstance; but of this the men themselves were only half conscious ... Every class in town and country was itself divided ... [The Civil War was] more ubiquitous in its scope and area than the Wars of the Roses, but fought from less selfish and material motives.[28]

Few, perhaps, would have disagreed with this verdict if it had been written by S.R. Gardiner in the nineteenth century at a time, for instance, when the discipline of economic history was still in an infant state. But by 1944, recollections of Victorian self-confidence and prosperity were fast receding. Vastly different conditions now prevailed. Marxism was providing an intellectual and political alternative to liberalism. The traumatic effects of the Second World War were being experienced. Thus Trevelyan's unashamedly 'old-fashioned' view of seventeenth-century English history appeared at a time when the Gardiner/Firth historical orthodoxy — and all the assumptions on which it was based — was being called into question. Some historians at least were now arguing that the crucial element in the seventeenth-century crisis was precisely those 'material motives' and their social milieu which Trevelyan had disregarded. The most prominent (though not the most radical) of these historians was R.H. Tawney.

Chapter 6

The twentieth century: society and revolution

The test of an historian is not so much the final validity of his theories as the originality of his approach, his talent in devising new and more fruitful ways of looking at the problems of the past ... Because he first posed the questions in the answers to which lie the key to historical understanding of the period, 1540-1640 will remain 'Tawney's century' for an indefinite period to come. (Lawrence Stone, 'R.H. Tawney', *Past and Present*, 21 (1962), p.77.)

The most serious objection to Christopher Hill's historical method is not the influence of Marx; indeed, if this is what Marxism does to historians, one might wish that it could infect a few more. It is much more his tidy-mindedness and his firm conviction that rules are rules and exceptions are exceptions, that there must be correlations between patterns of fundamentally abstract ideas and pragmatic political and ecclesiastical movements, which give us pause to think. (G.E. Aylmer, *English Historical Review*, LXXXI (1966), p.789.)

R.H. Tawney (1880-1962), although he disagreed with Trevelyan's political presuppositions and found his conclusions unsatisfying, would at least have concurred with the Cambridge Regius Professor's hostile views on the cold detachment of scientific academic study. 'There is no such thing as a science of economics, nor ever will be,' Tawney wrote in 1913. 'it is just cant, and Marshall's talk as to the need for social problems to be studied "by the same order of mind which tests the stability of a battleship in bad weather" is twaddle.'[1] Tawney studied history in order to understand present problems, a fact which he freely admitted in his inaugural lecture in 1932 at the L.S.E.

I found the world surprising; I find it so still. I turned to history to interpret it, and have not been disappointed by my guide though often by myself ... [The historian's] object is to understand the world around him, a world whose cultural constituents and dynamic movements have taken their stamp and direction from conditions which the experience of no single life is adequate to interpret ... If he visits the cellars, it is not for love of the dust, but to estimate the stability of the edifice, and because, to grasp the meaning of the cracks he must know the quality of its foundations...[2]

Tawney's political writings — he became, of course, one of the great intellectual fathers of the Labour movement — and his work on history shared common origins, and both were suffused with his deep-rooted Christian Socialism. Tawney's pre-First World War common-place book shows him wrestling with historical and modern problems simultaneously. Later, *The Acquisitive Society* (1922) and *Equality* (1931) told as much about his approach to the past as about his view of the twentieth-century crisis. For Tawney, history was not a source of 'dead' information; it was first a means to understanding, and then a guide to action.

Tawney was drawn to the economic and social history of pre-Revolutionary England partly as a result of his dissatisfaction with a purely political approach. ('It says so much and explains so little.'[3]) His experience of W.E.A. teaching also contributed. 'The friendly smitings of weavers, potters, miners, and engineers, have taught me much about problems of political and economic science which cannot easily be learned from books.' So Tawney wrote in the preface to *The Agrarian Problem in the Sixteenth Century* (1912).[4] Above all, however, Tawney developed a particular interest in the sixteenth and seventeenth centuries because he saw this as a crucial period in the emergence of capitalism and of the changing relationship between economic power and political power.

The Agrarian Problem in the Sixteenth Century was Tawney's first book, and his preoccupation with the historical origins and conse-quences of capitalism was as clearly expressed there as it was in all his later writings on the early modern period. Small-scale peasant farming was overcome, he argued, by the aggressive forces of a growing rural capitalism, which gained strength from the redistribution of monastic lands in the sixteenth century and achieved victory in the Civil War and the settlements of 1660 and 1689.

With the destruction in 1641 of the Court of Star Chamber and the Councils of Wales and of the North, an end was put to the last administrative organs which could bridle the great landed proprietors ... Henceforward there was to be no obstacle to enclosure, to evictions, to rack-renting, other than the shadowy protection of the Common Law; and for men who were very poor or easily intimidated, or in the enjoyment of rights for which no clear legal title could be shown, the Common Law with its expense, its packed juries, its strict rules of procedure, had little help. Thus the good side of the Absolute Monarchy was swept away with the bad ... For to the upper classes in the eighteenth century the possession of landed property by a poor man seemed in itself a surprising impertinence which it was the duty of Parliament to correct, and Parliament responded to the call of its relatives outside the House with the pious zeal of family affection.[5]

Having opened up a new economic perspective on the English Revolution, Tawney moved on in his next and most famous major work to explore a socio-intellectual dimension of the seventeenth-century crisis. This was *Religion and the Rise of Capitalism* (1926), a work which brought together Tawney's own religious concerns and his interest in the origins of capitalism. 'I wonder if Puritanism produced any specific attitude towards economic matters?', Tawney had asked himself in his commonplace book in September 1912.[6] His own book, written in the light of Weber's *The Protestant Ethic and the Spirit of Capitalism* (1904), was an attempt to answer the question, and a whole generation of historians was influenced by its conclusions. Professor W.H.B. Court, a student at Cambridge when Tawney's classic was first published, recalled that this,

> ... was one of the books which everyone read. It responded brilliantly in typically Tawney fashion to the mood of a time of sharp disillusion and changing social values. He linked the study of history with sociology on the one side and with social philosophy on the other and asked where changes of social values in the past had come from.[7]

Tawney's modification of the Weber thesis lay in his stress on the initial conservatism of the reformed religion; it was only in the long run, he argued, as the result of a dual relationship between puritanism and society, that the godly discipline became compatible with the religion of trade.

Puritanism was the schoolmaster of the English middle classes. It heightened their virtues, sanctified, without eradicating, their convenient vices, and gave them an inexpugnable assurance that, behind virtues and vices alike, stood the majestic and inexorable laws of an omnipotent Providence, without whose foreknowledge not a hammer could beat upon the forge, not a figure could be added to the ledger. But it is a strange school which does not teach more than one lesson, and the social reactions of Puritanism, trenchant, permanent and profound, are not to be summarized in the simple formula that it fostered individualism ... There was in Puritanism an element which was conservative and traditionalist, and an element which was revolutionary ... That it swept away the restrictions imposed by the existing machinery is true; neither ecclesiastical courts, nor High Commission, nor Star Chamber, could function after 1640. But if it broke the discipline of the Church of Laud and the State of Strafford, it did so but as a step towards erecting a more rigorous discipline of its own. It would have been scandalized by economic individualism, as much as by religious tolerance, and the broad outlines of its scheme of organization favoured unrestricted liberty in matters of business as little as in the things of the spirit...[8]

Tawney's book made a seminal contribution to a historical debate which has ever since continued to attract the attention of historians, sociologists, theologians and economists.[9]

The large-scale work on sixteenth- and seventeenth-century England which for many years Tawney was known to be writing, unfortunately never saw the light of day. The project had been outlined in rough as early as 1914. The scheme was to treat:

The rise of capitalism, beginning with the end of the sixteenth century, describing the economic policy of the Tudors and first two Stuarts, the economic causes for the opposition of the middle classes to the monarchy, the growth of the sects, the economic ideas of the Levellers, Diggers, ending with the economic results of the Revolution of 1688.[10]

'But shall I ever have time'? Tawney ended. In fact, Tawney only found time to publish, in 1941, his two articles on 'The Rise of the Gentry 1558-1640' and 'Harrington's Interpretation of His Age' and to bring out, in 1958, his monograph on *Business and Politics under James I*.[11] Even so, it was a remarkable achievement and provided glimpses, at least, of the grand survey that might have been. The Ford Lectures he gave at Oxford in 1936 were never prepared for publication.

Business and Politics under James I: Lionel Cranfield as Merchant and Minister was a case study of those general themes in seventeenth-century history with which Tawney had been concerned throughout his academic career. Through the biography of this one influential individual Tawney explored once more that 'seductive border region where politics grease the wheels of business and polite society smiles hopefully on both'.[12] The book's historiographical significance was partly that it revealed a new facet of Tawney's attitude to capitalism. As T.S. Ashton pointed out, 'Tawney, who in his earlier works, had tended to treat merchants and financiers with distrust here comes near to presenting a capitalist turned administrator as a hero'.[13] The change surprised even Tawney himself. He wrote to William Beveridge, his brother-in-law, in 1961, explaining that he began the book,

> ... with a prejudice against [Cranfield] as a capitalist on the make. I ended with a respect for the man who, without being over-scrupulous in business, was in courage and public spirit head and shoulders above the awful gang of courtly sharks and toadies with whom, as a minister of the crown, he was condemned to mix, and sacrificed his career for the service of the state.[14]

From a wider point of view, the historiographical significance of the book was that it brought historians away from the parliamentary opposition back to the weaknesses of the central government.

> The monarchy, in short, does not fight a losing battle against a remorseless tide of rising prices. Before it can be submerged by the advancing flood it is well on the way to drown itself ... Tendencies already visible before the death of James make a too exclusive emphasis on the follies and misfortunes of his son difficult to accept. Among these tendencies not the least important ... was the decline in the prestige of the monarchy...[15]

It was in his two famous articles on Harrington and on the rise of the gentry, published in 1941, that Tawney reached out most explicitly for a theory of the Civil War, and in so doing started a long controversy which became one of the *causes célèbres* of modern historiography. Tawney's essay on Harrington enlarged on the economic explanation of the seventeenth-century crisis put forward in *Oceana*, that it was the imbalance between economic realities and political structure which produced the Civil War. Tawney stressed the relative decline of the aristocracy ('In a period of sensational monetary depreciation, the economy of many noble landowners was an obsolete anachronism' [16]) and the rise of a new class of hard-headed, business-like gentry, alert to the opportunities provided by an expanding market. Using the detailed statistical evidence provided, for example, in Savine's *English Monasteries on the Eve of the Dissolution* and in *The Domesday of Crown Lands* by S.J. Madge, Tawney charted the process whereby land was redistributed away from the one group towards the other.[17]

The theme was elaborated, with all Tawney's customary eloquence, in his article on 'The Rise of the Gentry'.

> To say that many noble families — though not they alone — encountered in the two generations before the Civil War, a financial crisis is probably not an overstatement. The fate of the conservative aristocrat was, in fact, an unhappy one. Reduced to living 'like a rich beggar, in perpetual want', he sees his influence, popularity and property all melt together ... [But] the conditions which depressed some incomes inflated others; and, while one group of landowners bumped heavily along the bottom, another, which was quicker to catch the tide when it turned, was floated to fortune. The process of readjustment was complex; but two broad movements can be observed, affecting respectively the technique of land management and the ownership of landed property.[18]

Tawney buttressed the rhetoric of his thesis with statistics, demonstrating firstly a fall in the number of manors held by the aristocracy and, secondly, the growing importance of medium-sized landowners.

Tawney's thesis of the rise of the gentry was supported by a young Oxford historian, Lawrence Stone, when he rashly published an article on 'The anatomy of the Elizabethan aristocracy'.[19] Backed by some impressive (though in fact almost baseless) statistics, Stone underlined Tawney's point about the decline of the aristocracy and argued that this was largely the result of their over-expenditure.

The 'storm over the gentry' broke in 1951 with the first of two contributions from H.R. Trevor-Roper (1914-   ), already well-known for his biography of *Laud*.[20] The article was directed against Stone, and in one of the most savage and devastating attacks ever to appear in the pages of a learned journal, Trevor-Roper ruthlessly undermined the foundations (statistical or otherwise) of his fragile thesis. 'An erring colleague is not an Amalekite to be smitten hip and thigh,' snapped Tawney, angered by the tone of the debate.[21] Stone came back with 'The Elizabethan aristocracy: a re-statement'[22], but this was as much an apology as a rejoinder, and it took some years and much laborious research before this deflated author had sufficiently regained his confidence to launch his magisterial work of mature scholarship, *The Crisis of the Aristocracy*. But soon it was not just the disciple but the master himself who was under attack from Trevor-Roper. The tone was more respectful now. *The Gentry 1540-1640* opened with a compliment.

> Perhaps no man has stimulated the study of English history in the sixteenth century more effectively than Prof. Tawney: the century from 1540 to 1640, the century which separates the Dissolution of the Monasteries from the Great Rebellion, may almost be defined, thanks to his radical reinterpretation of it, as 'Tawney's century'. All historians who have since studied that period are inevitably, even if unconsciously, affected by his reinterpretation: they can no more think of it now in pre-Tawney terms than sociologists can think of society in pre-Marxist terms.[23]

But the compliment given, Trevor-Roper, one of the most brilliant historical essayists of the twentieth century, none the less elegantly but vigorously launched his attack. Trevor-Roper attempted to counter and discredit Tawney's notion of the rise of the gentry with a rival and persuasive alternative thesis of the decline of the 'mere gentry', middling men whose precarious wealth was drawn from land alone at a time when inflation was playing havoc with landed incomes. These 'mere gentry' were the basis of the country party which, in opposing the stranglehold of the court, ultimately overthrew Charles I, and later were the chief advocates of decentralization under the republic. Those who rose in this period were rather, on the one hand, those gentry who had access to other, more lucrative sources of income (office-holding, trade and the law), and on the other hand the yeomen, who combined direct intensive farming with austere living.[24] An article by J.P. Cooper ('The counting of manors', *Ec.H.R.*, 2nd series, VIII, 1956) lent support to Trevor-Roper's alternative explanation of social change and revolution by completely discrediting the statistical basis of the case which Tawney and Stone had put forward.

It was not long, however, before the tables were turned, and the Trevor-Roper thesis itself came under heavy attack from Christopher Hill and the American, Perez Zagorin.[25] Both these writers emphasized the extreme frailty of some of the supposedly logical connections in Trevor-Roper's argument and its entirely non-statistical approach; his long essay was mainly an exercise in rhetoric. In particular, Trevor-Roper was criticized (quite rightly) for the ease with which 'mere gentry', 'small gentry', and 'declining gentry' came together in his argument, the three terms being used virtually synonymously. Hill was no more satisfied with Trevor-Roper's identification of the Independents with the 'mere gentry'.[26] Trevor-Roper was (with equal justice) called to account for asserting that in a period when food prices were still rising, agriculture was not a route to wealth. Conversely, Trevor-Roper's critics argued, his thesis exaggerated the ease with which court fortunes could be built up. The links which Trevor-Roper postulated between economic decay and religious nonconformity were similarly unconvincing to his critics; *either* kind of religious extreme (puritanism or Catholic recusancy) would do equally well, apparently, as a refuge from decline. The American historian J.H. Hexter (1910-   ) joined the chorus of critics almost simultaneously, but broadened his front to attack Tawney as well. His stylish essay 'Storm over the Gentry' was first published in *Encounter* in 1958, but appeared in an extended and more scholarly form three years later as part of his *Reappraisals in History*. Both Tawney and Trevor-Roper, for different reasons, were accused of subscribing to a narrow economic determinism. Hexter's contribution, like others from the same author, tended to point in a negative rather than in a constructive direction, but the demolition work cheerfully completed, Hexter offered a modified version of Lawrence Stone's earlier thesis stressing, however, a *military* rather than an economic decline of the aristocracy in the century before 1640.

Tawney himself took no further part in the debate on the gentry after his postscript of 1954. His age, of course, disinclined him from so doing, but there were other reasons. Given the limited sources available to the disputants, Tawney frankly saw no additional value in the controversy, or in engaging further in a debate, the tone of which he found increasingly distasteful.[27] Tawney began the debate but did not expect or desire that his interpretation would become a stifling orthodoxy. Although he firmly believed that historians should generalize and draw out the main outlines, Tawney recognized that the only way forward in this subject, as in others, lay in further research; a new synthesis of the evidence would then become possible.

One obvious direction in which further research on the gentry was possible was at the local and regional level. (These studies are examined in the next chapter.) Another was explored with commendable thoroughness in *The Crisis of the Aristocracy 1558-1640* (1965). Lawrence Stone (1919-   ), its author, graduated from Oxford and taught there until 1963 when he joined the brain drain to America and became Dodge Professor of History at Princeton. Although a noted historian of art and architecture — his father was an artist — Stone's main field of interest has been that of social structure and social change in early modern England. His books on *Social Change and Revolution in England 1540-1640* (1965), *The Causes of the English Revolution 1529-1642* (1972), his article on 'Social mobility in England 1500-1700' and, most recently, his work on English education all bear witness to his work in this area.[28] Despite his unfortunate 1948 article on the Elizabethan peerage it is this subject which Stone has made his own. A massive piece of scholarship, the result of fourteen years' research, *The Crisis of the Aristocracy* is Stone's *magnum opus*.[29]

Tawney was given pride of place in the acknowledgements to this 841-page epic.

> My greatest intellectual obligation is to the late Professor R.H. Tawney. He was always ready with information, advice, and encouragement and I owe him more than perhaps he realized, for it was his writings which first stimulated my interest in Tudor history. Above all he taught me to shun the temptation to which economic and social historians are so exposed, of taking the mind out of history. I am particularly anxious to acknowledge my dependence on his inspiration and example, since I have ultimately come to differ substantially from many of his conclusions.[30]

A vast and impressive undertaking, Stone's *Crisis of the Aristocracy* had twin objectives.

> This book sets out to do two things: firstly to describe the total environment of an *élite*, material and economic, ideological and cultural, educational and moral; and secondly to demonstrate, to explain and to chart the course of a crisis in the affairs of this *élite* that was to have a profound effect upon the evolution of English political institutions. It is therefore at once a static description and a dynamic analysis; it is a study in social, economic and intellectual history, which is consciously designed to serve as the prolegomenon to, and an explanation of, political history.[31]

The 'crisis' thesis which Stone advanced combined some of his earlier ideas from the days of the gentry controversy with those of J.H. Hexter. The result was an interpretation which stressed the aristocracy's loss not just of military power but of lands and prestige. In Elizabeth's reign the real income of the peers declined sharply so that in the seventeenth century, above all, they were in a disadvantageous position as compared with the greater gentry. It was the decline in the authority and power of the aristocracy, argued Stone, which ultimately made possible the collapse of Charles I's government in 1640, since its effect was to leave the monarchy in a dangerously exposed and isolated position.

It was a provocative thesis which in the nature of things was unlikely to produce general assent, even though all reviewers paid tribute to the vast research effort involved. Alan Everitt, for instance, criticized what he found to be Stone's tendency to tie himself up in a statistical straitjacket. As a local historian he was critical, too, of Stone's insensitivity to the richness of provincial life, and expressed doubts as to whether the 'crisis' was as catastrophic as Stone argued or indeed whether it was quite so central to the outbreak of the Great Rebellion. [32] Quantification, of course, was an essential part of Stone's method, and was what chiefly distinguished it from the inspired or unfortunate sampling of the gentry controversy. What Stone offered in his book was not a few well-chosen examples to illustrate his points, but a survey of *all* the titular aristocracy with estimates of the mean net income of the peerage in 1559, 1602 and 1641.

> I think one has an obligation today to try to quantify. It is true that in the pre-statistical age of the sixteenth and seventeenth centuries, accurate figures are very hard to come by: error is enormous, and one is dealing very probably with highly hypothetical figures if one is dealing globally. My only defence of my figures is that they are better than nothing.[33]

But as one reviewer of *The Crisis of the Aristocracy* pointed out 'Professor Stone's confidence in his statistics appears to increase in direct relation to their distance from his original qualifying remarks'.[34] D.C. Coleman was even more sceptical about the value of many of Stone's calculations.[35] Stone, however, has stuck unrepentantly to his historical method and there is a pronounced statistical emphasis in his more recent book, *Family and Fortune: Studies in Aristocratic Finance in the Sixteenth and Seventeenth Centuries.*

Stone's final conclusions on the aristocracy were not closely in line with Tawney's views on the subject. Indeed the hallmark of Tawney's influence on other historians was not the creation of an orthodoxy to which growing numbers subscribed; Tawney, unlike Sir Lewis Namier, did not found a historical 'school'. His main legacy was not his methods or even his conclusions as such, but his stress on a questioning approach to the past and on a humane concept of economic history.[36] Tawney encouraged historians to go out in new directions and, responding to his invitation and stimulus, they have enlarged, extended, and in some cases corrected his own work on English society before the Revolution. The roll-call of seventeenth-century historians acknowledging an intellectual debt to R.H. Tawney is impressive and extends over a long period. A.P. Wadsworth (a student from Tawney's W.E.A. days) and Julia de Lacy Mann produced their classic study of *The Cotton Trade and Industrial Lancashire* under Tawney's guidance. W.G. Hoskins dedicated his book on *The Midland Peasant* to him. Tawney supplied an introduction for D. Brunton and D.H. Pennington's *Members of the Long Parliament* (1954). Alan Everitt in his study of Kentish society in the Civil War period and Peter Bowden in his book on the wool trade both acknowledged Tawney in their respective prefaces. The American historian J.U. Nef and the Australian George Yule both owed something to Tawney's influence.

As a tribute to Tawney on his eightieth birthday a Festschrift of essays was prepared with F.J. Fisher as editor.[37] Fisher (1908-   ) himself, Tawney's friend, amanuensis and colleague, supplied an appropriate introduction on 'Tawney's century'. The other contributors included Joan Thirsk, Ralph Davis, D.C. Coleman and Robert Ashton, all former research students of Tawney's at the L.S.E., as well as Christopher Hill and Lawrence Stone. Fisher had helped Tawney with the Gentry article and with the Cranfield book and his own work, chiefly on the growth of London, has been very much in the Tawney tradition.[38] D.C. Coleman (1920-   ), now Professor of Economic History at Cambridge, contributed an essay on government borrowing under the later Stuarts, a foretaste of his book on the same subject and one which owed something to Tawney's study of Lionel Cranfield.[39] Robert Ashton (1924-   ), now Professor of Economic History at the University of East Anglia and whose book *The Crown and the Money Market 1603-40* had appeared in the previous year, wrote on 'Charles I and the City' for the Festschrift.

Joan Thirsk (1922-   ), now Reader in Economic History in the University of Oxford, wrote on 'Industries in the countryside' for the Tawney volume and here, as in a later essay for another Festschrift and in her 1975 Ford Lectures, proved that she was equally at home with the history of industry as with that of agriculture.[40] Dr Thirsk had done the research for her doctorate under Tawney's direction between 1947 and 1950 and the fruits of that research were distilled in two articles on 'The sales of Royalist lands during the Interregnum' and on 'The Restoration Land Settlement'.[41] Her continuing interest in sixteenth- and seventeenth-century agriculture and rural society was expressed firstly in *Fenland Farming in the Sixteenth Century* (1953) for which Tawney wrote a preface, then (in 1957) in her book *English Peasant Farming*, and (in 1959) in *Tudor Enclosures,* a subject with which Tawney had earlier grappled. She has since edited *The Agrarian History of England and Wales. IV. 1500-1640*, a mammoth project over which Tawney himself once presided. One of the most important works of the decade, it was the result of an impressive collective research effort and, amongst other things, presented a stimulating hypothesis about the kind of rural settings conducive to dissent. Here, as elsewhere, Dr Thirsk made plain that she shared Tawney's zest for taking on big subjects and his capacity for generalization. The same eagerness to ask new questions has come out in her more recent articles on 'Younger sons in the seventeenth century' and on 'Seventeenth-century agriculture and social change'.[42] And the collection of *Seventeenth-Century Economic Documents* which she edited in 1972, looks like doing for the Stuart period what Tawney and Power's *Tudor Economic Documents* (1924) has done for the previous century.

Christopher Hill's contribution to the Tawney volume was on 'Protestantism and the rise of capitalism', and its opening paragraph paid tribute to Tawney's classic on that subject. Hill, more so than Tawney, stressed the central Protestant doctrine of justification by faith and its accompanying idea that 'what a man did was less important than the spirit in which he did it'. Hill concluded that,

> Since opposition to the Roman Church in sixteenth- and seventeenth-century Europe drew its main strength from the big cities, protestantism could be developed in ways which favoured the rise of capitalism. But there is nothing in protestantism which leads automatically to capitalism: its importance was rather that it undermined obstacles which the more rigid institutions and ceremonies of catholicism imposed.[43]

Hill had never been a student of Tawney's, his political opinions were more left-wing than those of the L.S.E. professor, and it was not Tawney but T.S. Eliot who first attracted him to the study of seventeenth-century ideas and society. None the less Hill deeply admired Tawney as a historian and as a man. 'One thing that made Tawney great in my eyes', Hill has said, 'was his politics. He was a deeply committed Christian Socialist. [For him] heavenly intervention went hand in hand with human action.' But it is impossible to conceive of Tawney, Hill has argued, without Karl Marx, 'Marx because the main feature of Tawney's work is a never failing concern for the underdog in history'.[44] Hill was the young Marxist historian from Oxford, 'a fine scholar of Tudor and Stuart England', whom Tawney once defended in the 1950s from attack by an anti-communist colleague. On another occasion, Tawney said, 'I don't mind Hill being a Marxist, but I do wish he wouldn't sing the doxology at the end of every piece he writes'. 'That got right under my skin', Hill has written in some reminiscences of Tawney, 'because it showed me that to him I looked exactly what I was reacting against. I have tried ever since to keep the doxological element in my writing under control.' In the same piece, Hill has made clear that his main criticism of Terrill's biography of Tawney was that it missed the *essence* of its subject.

Above all Mr Terrill seems to me to miss one crucial aspect of Tawney — his irreverence, his undergraduate desire to shock and provoke, sometimes irresponsibly when he thought his victim was being irresponsibly smug. Mr Terrill has flead Tawney's rump and pared his claws, made him far too reasonable, sensible, moderate. He might have done better to talk to more of Tawney's pupils (especially his W.E.A. pupils) and to fewer of his colleagues. I suspect that Tawney showed most of his creative self to those whom he thought he could help.[45]

Tawney, however, 'a Victorian in all but essentials', was in no sense a Marxist. Was the Civil War a 'bourgeois revolution', Tawney was once asked? 'Of course it was a bourgeois revolution. The trouble is the bourgeoisie were on both sides.'[46] Tawney took Marx and Marxism seriously but did not subscribe to its ideology. Terrill writes in his biography of Tawney:

He studied the French Revolution the better to understand the heritage which confronted the young Marx, he wrestled keenly with what Marx had to say about religion. But Tawney felt no compulsion to make Marxism the orienting point of his view of history or of his socialism. Nor did political pressure or intellectual fashion draw him into either blind adherence or obsessive hostility to Marxism.[47]

Until the 1920s and 1930s, in any case, British socialism was not divided into separate Marxist and social democratic fronts. It was not until the break with the Labour Party in the 1920s that communism began to run a separate course in Britain and not until the crisis years of the 1930s, when the Left Book Club was campaigning for an alliance with the Soviet Union, that it began to acquire an intellectual wing. Although a ceaseless critic of social injustice, Tawney never felt a cultural alienation from his own society, nor did he feel that Stalinism was a workable or appropriate solution to Britain's social and political problems.[48] Events, however, overtook Tawney. The current of enthusiasm for Marxism in the 1930s left him to some extent out on a limb both politically and historiographically. He remained there for different reasons in the 1950s in the hysterical anti-Marxism of the Cold War.

Christopher Hill (1912-   ), at Balliol College, Oxford, for the whole of his academic career, apart from a brief interval at Cardiff in 1936-8, has been one of the most prolific of all historians of the English Revolution; 'the master historian of his chosen field — Hill's half century', is how the American historian, R.B. Schlatter, has described him.[49] Hill's dominant position in the field of Revolutionary studies today rests both on the quality and quantity of his output, and it was not easily or rapidly achieved. It would be unrealistic to treat his books and articles produced over the last forty years as a single unified whole. There are common characteristics, certainly, but a historian's work and method mature over time as his knowledge deepens. Marxism has been the most obvious of these common characteristics, but this, too, has changed greatly both in emphasis and intensity. There is a strong case, then, for treating Hill's earlier work separately rather than as part of a monolithic whole as John Sanderson has done in a recent article.[50] And it is not only the earlier work itself which needs to be considered but also the context — the world of the left-wing intellectuals of the 1930s — in which it appeared.

Hill's earliest published work on the English Revolution came in the form of two articles in the respectable journals of the historical profession. The first was 'Soviet interpretations of the English Interregnum', in which Hill summarized the views of the Russian historians Savine, Pashukanis, Angarov and Arkhangelsky on the significance of the seventeenth-century crisis in England.[51] An entirely utilitarian piece of writing, never since reprinted, its evangelistic purpose was simply to introduce English historians, still largely committed to the Gardiner/Firth model of the 'Puritan Revolution', to the envigorating challenges of Marxist reinterpretation.[52] He summarized Soviet views on the central class conflict in seventeenth-century England between a landed aristocracy and a landed church (sheltering behind the landed power of the crown) on the one hand and the bourgeoisie and progressive country gentry on the other. Soviet historians, Hill pointed out, saw the split between Presbyterians and Independents as a struggle between commercial and industrial capital and emphasized the way in which the Civil War unleashed a whole range of democratic theories. The other article, published in 1940 in the *English Historical Review*, dealt with 'The agrarian legislation of the Revolution', and was largely a summary of the two-volume research work on this subject by Arkhangelsky. 'In trying to summarize Professor Arkhangelsky's conclusions', Hill wrote, 'I have added quotations from some sources not available to him, and have expanded certain points; but I have followed his ideas in the main.'[53]

The significance, then, of these early articles by Christopher Hill was that they publicized Marxist ideas on the seventeenth century at a time when very little of that kind was available in English. The German Marxist historian Eduard Bernstein's *Cromwell and Communism* (sub-titled *Socialism and Democracy in the Great English Revolution*) had come out in an English translation in 1930. Harold Laski's semi-Marxist 'essay in interpretation' on *The Rise of European Liberalism* appeared in 1936. Holorenshaw's *The Levellers and the English Revolution* was published in 1939 by the Left Book Club, while in the previous year the same organization brought out A.L. Morton's *A People's History of England*.[54] In this work, Morton (1903–   ), communist teacher, bookseller and journalist, offered the first full-length Marxist history of England. 'Its 150 pages on the sixteenth and seventeenth centuries', Hill wrote in 1950, 'offered the first large-scale re-interpretation of the period from the Marxist point of view and much the best popular introduction to the subject.'

In spite of all that has been said to the contrary,' Morton proclaimed, 'it cannot be too strongly insisted that the Civil War
was a class struggle, *was* revolutionary and *was* progressive. A
Royalist victory would have meant a dead hand imposed upon
the development of the country, feudal forms devoid of real content
ossified into a monarchical tyranny, the persistence of a less
advanced form of social and political organisation.[55]

In 1940 David Petegorsky's semi-Marxist account of *Left-Wing
Democracy in the English Civil War. A Study of the Social Philosophy
of Gerrard Winstanley* was published by the Left Book Club.[56]
Maurice Dobb's *Studies in the Development of Capitalism* came out
in 1946 and was joyously hailed by fellow Marxists as 'the most
important single work on British history so far produced by an English
marxist'. 'This erudite work', Christopher Hill declared, 'puts the
English Revolution into perspective as part of the rise of capitalism on
a European scale.' R.H. Hilton, writing in the *Labour Monthly*,
readily agreed.

> Maurice Dobb has demonstrated in a most striking way the
> superiority of the marxist approach to historical problems over
> the bourgeois eclecticism which nowadays passes as a substitute for
> proper analysis ... There are treasures of analysis in this remarkable
> book. If the case for a historical and marxist outlook as the 'essential
> foundation for any realistic system of economics' (the original aim
> of these studies) is proved up the hilt, the work has also proved that
> a marxist approach is the only possible one for the solution of
> historical problems. It is to be hoped that both historians and
> economists learn the appropriate lesson.[57]

The war years apart, the 1940s were an important period in the
development of the Marxist historiography of the Revolution, and in
it, Christopher Hill, back at Balliol after 1945, played a prominent
part. In 1940 Hill edited *The English Revolution 1640*, a Marxist
textbook designed to celebrate the 300th anniversary of 'perhaps the
most important event that has yet occurred in English history'. The
book contained three essays, one by Hill and the others by Edgell
Rickword and Margaret James, a former student of Tawney whose
book *Social Problems and Policy during the Puritan Revolution* had
appeared in 1930; all 'sought to link up the past with the present,
theory with practice, the particular with the general'.[58]

The bold opening paragraph of Hill's own essay followed on naturally from these precepts.

The English Revolution of 1640-60 was a great social movement like the French Revolution of 1789. An old order that was essentially feudal was destroyed by violence, a new and capitalist social order created in its place. The Civil War was a class war, in which the despotism of Charles I was defended by the reactionary forces of the established Church and feudal landlords. Parliament beat the King because it could appeal to the enthusiastic support of the trading and industrial classes in town and countryside, to the yeomen and progressive gentry, and to wider masses of the population whenever they were able by free discussion to understand what the struggle was really about.

Discussing the capitalist penetration of agriculture and industry in this period, Hill lost no opportunity to make analogies with the modern world.

The seventeenth-century English revolution changed the organisation of society so as to make possible the full development of all the resources of that society. A transition to socialism will be necessary to win the same result in England today.

'We have still much to learn from the seventeenth century,' was Hill's last sentence in this essay.[59]

Christopher Hill wrote a number of articles in these years for such journals as *The Modern Quarterly, The Communist Review,* and for the American Marxist periodical *Science and Society.* One of these *Science and Society* articles, on 'Land in the English Revolution' (XIII, 1948-9), enlarged on what Hill had previously written on this subject in 1940. The other two articles in this *Science and Society* group were explicitly historiographical, and attempted to offer a challenging alternative to the 'blind-alley specialization' of 'present day bourgeois scholarship'.[60] The first of these was 'The English Civil War interpreted by Marx and Engels' (XII, 1948) and there Hill,

… tried to illustrate their ideas about the English Revolution, not to synthesize them. They never wrote a consecutive history of the period, and the niggling may be able to find verbal inconsistencies. But their view of the revolution as a whole is consistent and illuminating. I have occasionally suggested how modern research has confirmed their analysis. But my concern was less to show that Marx and Engels spotted a lot of winners than to demonstrate the value for historians today of their interpretation. Because their philosophical insight was deeper than that of Macaulay, Guizot or Gardiner, Marx and Engels were able to grasp the dualism of the English seventeenth-century revolution: to see that it was at once bourgeois and progressive; that in putting forward the claims of their class the parliamentary leaders of 1640 were also in a real sense speaking for the mass of the population; and yet that because of the inherent contradictions of their position in society they were forced ultimately to turn against the democracy in whose name they had defeated the old order, and to make that compromise with their defeated adversaries which has coloured English history ever since.[61]

The last of these articles for *Science and Society* in this period was again historiographical and similarly evangelistic in purpose. 'Historians and the rise of British capitalism' (XIV, 1950) dealt with the need to replace Gardiner's politico-religious model of the 'Puritan Revolution' which reflected — so Hill felt — all the smug complacency of Victorian liberalism and capitalism, with one which encompassed economic development and social conflict. 'No serious academic historian today could defend the thesis of a "Puritan Revolution" in the form in which Gardiner put it forward. Yet no alternative synthesis has been advanced by bourgeois academic historians to take its place.' 'As capitalism enters its final crisis all the bourgeois assumptions come under criticism.'[62] To Hill, writing in 1950, there was only one alternative model which could possibly replace Gardiner's. 'It is difficult to see what satisfactory synthesis *could* be advanced other than the Marxist view that the English Revolution was a bourgeois revolution. This interpretation alone can explain all the new facts, fit them into a coherent story which makes sense.'

> Marxism restores unity to history because it restores real, live, working and suffering men and women to the centre of the story and does not deal merely with their abstract ideas and rationalizations ... Finally the Marxist approach, and it alone, can restore to the English people part of their heritage of which they have been robbed...[63]

Hill's *The Good Old Cause. The English Revolution of 1640-1660* (1949), edited with Edmund Dell, had an identical purpose. Its object was 'to establish by contemporary evidence the general Marxist thesis of the nature and consequences of the English Revolution: to show that the men who actually took part in the Revolution were much less confused about it than bourgeois historians have been during the past century'.[64] The introduction described how 'one class was driven from power by another' and how 'advances towards democracy were the product not of a beneficent spirit of compromise, but of class struggle'.[65] Sections of documents on, for example, social classes before 1640, the sects and democracy, the Levellers, the Diggers, provided abundant illustration.

In the 1950s Hill continued to publish in *Science and Society* — an article on 'The English Revolution and the brotherhood of man' appeared in 1954 — but by this time he had helped to create an English counterpart to the American journal, *Past and Present*. Originally sub-titled 'a journal of scientific history', *Past and Present* was launched in 1952, and no journal has since done more for seventeenth-century studies. R.H. Hilton and Maurice Dobb joined Hill on the editorial board and John Morris and Eric Hobsbawm were the first editors. Christopher Hill's article on 'Puritans and the poor' appeared in the second issue of the journal in November 1952.

The Marxist-oriented *Past and Present* struggled for existence in its early years, and it would have been difficult then to predict its present position in the historical 'establishment'. For English Marxists, too, as well as for Marxist journals, the 1950s proved a critical period. Discontent with Stalinism and with the Communist Party leadership in Britain was being expressed by the Party's intellectual wing. E.P. Thompson and John Saville moved into open attack in 1956, Thompson denouncing the Party's 'uncritical and inaccurate propaganda about the Soviet Union extending over a period of twenty years'. Both Thompson and Saville were suspended from Party membership as a result. The rising in Hungary, and official Communist Party reactions to it, brought the crisis to a head. The Party leadership was challenged from the branches and a massive loss of membership followed, including many of the Party's intellectuals such as Christopher Hill.[66]

Intellectually as well as politically, the crisis of the mid-1950s must have been a traumatic and chastening experience. Certainly, the aggressive propagandist element and the doxology which Tawney had complained about have since receded in Hill's writing. *Economic Problems of the Church From Archbishop Whitgift to the Long*

Parliament (1956), Hill's first major research work, published at the age of forty-four, signalled a new period in his writing and a much more flexible and sophisticated use of the Marxist model. As one (decidedly anti-Marxist) reviewer of the book trenchantly put it.

> Mr Hill is a Marxist who has come out of his trance. He does not say so himself, either because he is still a little dazed or because a candid confession would be too painful. But anyone who remembers *The English Revolution* or its companion volume [*The Good Old Cause*] can see that the spell is broken.[67]

D.H. Pennington, a former student of Hill's, reviewing the book in *History*, took a similar line, contrasting the two Christopher Hills, the one a Marxist progagandist and the other a critical scholar. Pennington pointed to the 'undogmatic realism' of Hill's new book, its self-mockery about 'that ubiquitous class the rising bourgeoisie', and its invitation to 'ignore his occasional genuflexions [to Party dogma] and listen to the sound sense he talks'.[68]

Since 1956 and *Economic Problems of the Church*, Christopher Hill's output of books and articles has been immense. Invariably full of insights, informative, and frequently controversial, Hill's work rests on a secure mastery of the printed word in the seventeenth century. Two volumes of his essays have been published — *Puritanism and Revolution* (1958) and *Change and Continuity in Seventeenth-Century England* (1975) — and they by no means exhaust the full store from which they were selected. Two widely used textbooks came from his pen in 1961 and 1967, *The Century of Revolution 1603-1714* and *Reformation to Industrial Revolution. A Social and Economic History of Britain 1530-1780*. The rest of his books are research works. *Society and Puritanism in Pre-Revolutionary England* (1964) was a companion volume to *Economic Problems of the Church. The Intellectual Origins of the English Revolution* (1965), his Ford Lectures at Oxford, has been Hill's most provocative book, variously regarded as one of the most stimulating studies of the seventeenth-century crisis or, by a particularly cantankerous American historian, as a 'blunt instrument' from which ensued a 'historiographic disaster'.[69] Compared with this thunderbolt, Hill's *God's Englishman. Oliver Cromwell and the English Revolution* (1970) and *Antichrist in Seventeenth-Century England* (1971) were positively low-key. Hill's *The World Turned Upside Down. Radical Ideas during the English Revolution* (1972) was more stirring and is arguably his finest book.

His study of Milton is in the making, and the lively debate which followed from its trailer ('Milton the Radical') in the *Times Literary Supplement* in November 1974 suggests that its publication will inaugurate a further controversy.[70]

No attempt will be made here to discuss Hill's books individually; to do so would burst the bounds of what is already an over-long chapter. It would be more profitable, in any case, to look at the main features of Hill's interpretation of the English Revolution, at the controversies in which his work has figured, and at the criticism which has been made of his historical method.

One of Hill's most consistent preoccupations has been with the need to find a satisfactory synthesis to replace Gardiner's model of the 'Puritan Revolution'.[71] His first instinct in his early writings, as we have seen, was simply to dismiss the notion out of hand. But such brusque treatment, as Hill himself came to recognize, did Gardiner less than justice. 'We all stand on his shoulders,' he wrote in *God's Englishman*. In *The Century of Revolution*, writing of the historian's tendency to emphasize social and political causes of the Civil War at the expense of its religious dimension, Hill argued that 'the very idea of a Puritan Revolution is more complex than we used to think'. Nevertheless, 'the Puritan Revolution was an unfortunate concept. It suffered both from exaggeration by Gardiner's epigones and from an equally exaggerated reaction away from it by some twentieth-century historians.' 'In some recent explanations of the English Revolution', Hill wrote in *Economic Problems of the Church*, 'the material conflicts seem to me to have been presented too simply, in terms of outs versus ins, country versus court gentry, the bourgeoisie versus a "social justice" state ... Puritanism would not have been the historical force it was if it had been a mere economic reflex.' 'Puritan Revolution' in a real sense, Hill has argued in his latest book, put historians on the wrong tack.

> For this implied, or could appear to imply, a revolution made by Puritans in order to establish a Puritan society. It assumes an element of conscious will among an identifiable group of those who made the revolution. Most historians reject the Puritan Revolution these days, and interpret the events of 1640-60 in more sociological terms. There is no need why such interpretations need make any assumptions about purpose. The object indeed of a sociological interpretation should be to account for events which cannot be explained in terms of human intentions.[72]

Before either using or discarding the term 'Puritan Revolution', Hill has insisted, historians obviously need to be clear about what they understand by 'puritanism' and 'revolution'. And in his book of essays published under that title in 1958, Hill argued that from this point of view English historians had laboured under a double disadvantage.

> First, few of us have any experience of revolutions. The British tradition since the seventeenth century has been almost entirely gradualist: revolutions are things we learn about from books. Secondly, most of us think that we do know all about Puritanism. But too often we are thinking — whether with conscious hostility or unconscious sympathy — not of Puritanism at all but of later non-conformity ... So we have to make a deliberate intellectual effort to open our minds to revolutionaries, and to clear them of erroneous prepossessions about Puritans. When we are dealing with men who were simultaneously Puritans and revolutionaries the task is doubly exacting. [73]

The whole corpus of Hill's mature work can be summed up as an attempt to come to terms with the complexities of puritanism and revolution, and with the role of ideas and ideology. One could cite the fact, for instance, that Hill has devoted two whole books (*Economic Problems of the Church* and *Society and Puritanism*) to 'some of the non-theological reasons which might lead men to oppose the Laudian régime in the English church' and indeed to the 'non-theological reasons for supporting the Puritans, or for being a Puritan'. [74]

Although Hill's definitions of revolution occasionally have had a circular tendency and although the distinction between cause and consequence has not always been clearly made, his interpretation has been that the changes associated with the events of the mid-century were so momentous that 'revolution' is the only term that can describe them. 'The 1640s and 50s marked the end of medieval and Tudor England' in government, agriculture, commerce, colonial and foreign policy, industry, finance, religion and ideas. [75]

In a broadcast talk Hill said:

> I certainly think it was a revolution, and I don't think much of some recent attempts to argue the contrary — on the grounds, for instance, that nobody planned it, or that nobody in the Long Parliament (when it met in 1640) intended to have a civil war. All

this is perfectly true, but things do happen without being planned by people ... I would see the English Revolution of the seventeenth century as clearing the path for the sort of economic development which made the Industrial Revolution happen in England first.

Judged by its *consequences*, the English Revolution was a bourgeois revolution in the Marxist sense.

I would think of what happened in the seventeenth century as being, in the marxist sense, a bourgeois revolution. I don't think that two classes lined up to fight, any more than they have done in any revolution. There were members of all classes on both sides. But what I think I understand by a bourgeois revolution is not a revolution in which the bourgeoisie did the fighting — they never do that in any revolution — but a revolution whose outcome is the clearing of the decks for capitalism.[76]

'The word ''Puritan'' ', Hill has argued, 'is an admirable refuge from clarity of thought.'[77] It was used by contemporaries in a variety of ways, and no simple religious or politico-religious definition is adequate to describe its whole range of meanings. Originally it was 'a reproachful name', and its political and religious ramifications also had a pronounced social dimension. Puritanism, Hill contended in *Society and Puritanism in Pre-Revolutionary England* and elsewhere, appealed particularly to the 'industrious sort of people', 'those smaller employers and self-employed men, whether in town or country, for whom frugality and hard work might make all the difference between prosperity and failure to survive in the world of growing competition'.[78] 'There were social reasons for the puritan ministers' special emphasis on the duty of working hard, for extolling the dignity of labour.' Puritanism, then, was primarily the ideology of the large group of economically independent yeomen, artisans and small and middling merchants. Sabbatarianism was, as much as anything, a means of conducting industrial life on a more rational and methodical basis. 'Without the backing of large numbers of humbler men, Puritanism could never have challenged the crown and the bishops: the civil war could never have been fought and won.'[79] Hill's interpretation of puritanism — and, of course, he covers far more ground than this brief summary can suggest — is interesting and important, but lingering doubts remain firstly as to whether Hill has entirely succeeded in defining accurately the socio-economic context in which puritan ideas were received, and secondly shown how the puritan gentry can be accommodated in his model.

'Puritanism was perhaps the most important complex of ideas that prepared men's minds for revolution, but it was not the only one.' In his *Intellectual Origins of the English Revolution*, Hill looked at some of the others, 'particularly at those which appealed to "the middling sort", to merchants, artisans, and yeomen', and in so doing produced his most controversial work.[80] 'Within less than a decade successful war was levied against the King; bishops and the House of Lords were abolished; and Charles I was executed in the name of his people. How did men get the nerve to do such unheard of things? ... If there was no Rousseau, perhaps there were Montesquieus, Voltaires and Diderots of the English Revolution?.'[81] Hill argued that there were such counterparts, and he devoted his book to looking at the ferment of ideas associated with Bacon, Raleigh, Coke and the London scientists.

> Bacon, Raleigh, Coke, together with the many lesser figures whom we have studied in this book, helped to undermine men's traditional belief in the eternity of the old order in Church and state, and this was an immense task, without the successful accomplishment of which there could have been no political revolution ... Scientific utilitarianism and radical Protestantism grew up side by side in the urban centres, with support from some gentlemen but deeply rooted in the middle and lower middle class...
>
> The Civil War was fought largely by Puritans, with useful support from the scientists, against (among other things) the "inquisitorious and tyrannical duncery" of the bishops and consequent intellectual frustration. This struggle had its counterpart inside Oxford and Cambridge: only the Puritans and scientists could never have won there without support from outside.[82]

Hill's preface to *Intellectual Origins of the English Revolution* expressed the view that 'my object was not to write a definitive work, but with luck to start a discussion'. He certainly succeeded. A lively debate ensued on the jousting ground of *Past and Present* and elsewhere, which criticized Hill's view of scientific advance in England for being too insular in conception, treating England in isolation from Europe. The debate also called in question Hill's use of evidence and the connections he postulated between puritanism and science.[83]

Hill's special province has always been that of relating ideas to society. 'Historians are interested in ideas', he has asserted, 'not only because they influence societies, but because they reveal the societies which give rise to them. Hence the philosophical truth of the ideas is irrelevant to the historian's purpose...'[84] Explicitly confronting the vexed question of the relationship between the climate of ideas, ideology and the Revolution in his *Intellectual Origins*, Hill wrote:

> Ideas were all-important for the individuals whom they impelled into action; but the historian must attach equal importance to the circumstances that gave these ideas their chance. Revolutions are not made without ideas, but they are not made by intellectuals. Steam is essential to driving a railway engine; but neither a locomotive nor a permanent way can be built out of steam. In this book I shall be dealing with the steam.[85]

Intellectual breakthroughs, old ideas with new content, 'class' differentials in interpreting those ideas, time-lags in securing their acceptance, have all received Hill's attention. Nor has he been content to restrict himself simply to those ideas which happened to win. His *Antichrist in Seventeenth-Century England* (1971) is a case in point. Similarly in his *The World Turned Upside Down*, Hill focused on the fascinating undergrowth of ideas which was revealed in the freer climate of the 1640s, and the unsuccessful 'revolt within the Revolution' which went with it. This was the work not of a lunatic fringe but of earnest, soul-searching men, and the historian, he pleaded, ought to take them seriously.[86]

Hill himself has been one of the first to admit that 'a sociological approach to intellectual history carries its own risks'. Ideas have a history of their own and are not simply a reflection of economic conditions or needs. But equally, pedigrees of ideas can be plotted with a totally spurious precision. 'It is always easy to construct chains of causes once you know what you have to explain.' There is the danger, too, of being over- (and falsely) selective in treating the evidence. In the preface to *Intellectual Origins* Hill wrote:

> The origin of this book in lectures should be borne in mind by the reader. I was advancing a thesis, not attempting to sketch the intellectual history of England in the fifty years before 1640. I therefore picked out evidence which seemed to me to support my case. So, though I hope I have suppressed no facts which make against me, I have often ... omitted facts which seemed to me 'neutral'.

In *Puritanism and Revolution* there is a related statement.

> I am selecting unfairly, for in each case Perkins qualifies heavily by
> insisting that riches are good *as they are used*, that men must desire
> them to glorify God, not for themselves. And he denounces
> engrossers, forestallers, usurers in the traditional manner. But I
> suspect that many good bourgeois in the congregations of Perkins
> and his followers would follow the same principles of selection as I
> have done: the new concessions would be noted, the traditional
> qualifications would be forgotten, as with Calvin's shift of emphasis
> in dealing with usury.[87]

Hill's critics, however, have argued that although he recognized
these traps, this has not prevented him from falling into them. 'The
trouble is,' wrote Trevor-Roper, 'when we skim through sources
looking only for such evidence as supports our case, we tend only to
notice such convenient evidence: and thus in spite of our efforts to be
impartial, scholarship is transformed into advocacy.' The case against
Hill has been put even more forcefully by the accomplished American
demolition expert J.H. Hexter, who accused him of systematic 'source-
mining' to accumulate material on specific points, and then of
compulsive 'lumping' of evidence together into a pre-conceived
pattern.

> Each historian lives under an especially heavy obligation to police
> himself. Far from just looking for evidence that may support his
> thesis, he needs to look for vulnerabilities in that thesis and to
> contrive means of testing them. Then, depending on what he finds,
> he can support the thesis, strengthen its weak points, or modify it to
> eliminate the weaknesses it it. He should in effect always be
> engaged in an inner dialectic, compensating for history's limitations
> with respect to codified, externalized conditions of proof by being a
> hard master to his own mind. For a historian of great erudition and
> vivid imagination to fail to do this is for him to fail his colleagues,
> to place on them a burden that should have been his. Christopher
> Hill so fails his colleagues. It is too bad.[88]

It seems that venom may have taken over from reason in the way
that it did over half a century ago in the debate on the historical
method of S.R. Gardiner (see p.74). Hill's method involves 'source-
mining', certainly — doesn't that of any historian? — and, to use
Hexter's unhappy term, it also involves 'lumping', if by that is meant

interpreting and synthesizing; most historians, in fact, want to make some sense out of history. Hill's method and approach to history, however, like anyone else's, have their limitations. There is much repetition in his work. He has relied almost exclusively on printed sources, even though ideas and attitudes are expressed in manuscripts as well as in books and often with greater immediacy, openness, and local understanding. One reviewer has written:

> He does not display the intimate knowledge of provincial England of, say, W.G. Hoskins or Alan Everitt. So, despite Dr Hill's very real sympathy for the poor and underprivileged they tend to appear in his books as intellectual abstractions, vehicles for ideas within an impersonal historical process rather than as human beings rooted in precise but varied physical and socio-economic environments.[89]

He has been more interested in change than in continuity.

But Hexter was surely unreasonable to attack Hill's method *as such*, and in a spirited and convincing reply, Hill defended not just himself, but also a view of the purpose of historical study to which most historians would probably subscribe.

> The professor's division of historians into lumpers and splitters (his elegant phrases) revives an old distinction, familiar to those who used to set general papers a generation ago, between those who try to make sense of history and those who see nothing in it but the play of the contingent and the unforeseen, who think everything is so complicated that no general statements can safely be made, who are so busy making qualifications that they forget that anything actually happened. "Splitters" may make minor additions or alterations to traditionally received opinions, but they prefer to leave undisturbed those conventional prejudices in their readers' minds on which they rely....
>
> Historians whose sole concern is with tortoise watching have an enjoyable hobby which satisfies the academic's sense that he is different from the vulgar. But it is not self-evidently superior.[90]

No one could accuse Christopher Hill of tortoise watching! Few historians have done as much to enlarge our understanding of the social history of the English Revolution and of the changes in ideas that went with it. And indeed few English historians have contributed more to the development of social history as a discipline. His influence, even outside the seventeenth-century field, has been enormous. (E.P. Thompson's work on the eighteenth and nineteenth centuries provides eloquent testimony to this effect.) Not surprisingly, then, the names of many of Christopher Hill's former students will figure prominently in the remaining chapters.

Chapter 7

The twentieth century: local and regional studies

Local and regional studies of seventeenth-century England have
become one of the most thriving branches of the recent historiography
of the English Revolution, and most of this chapter will be concerned
with analysing first the reasons for this development and second the
main trends in this kind of research. Such studies, however, have a
long and fascinating ancestry and we should begin by briefly recalling
it.

Civil War local histories, in fact, date back to the seventeenth
century. The puritan divine John Corbet, for instance, produced *An
Historical Relation of the Military Government of Gloucester ...* in
1645, and in it stressed the peculiar value of the close-up portrait of a
particular area.

Authors more universal could never gain to be styled the writers of
unquestionable verities, for they see at a greater distance, and by a
more obscure and dusky light. Certainly a nearer approach, and
some kind of interest is required of him that desires to show not
only some track and footsteps but the express image of things.

Corbet was an acute observer of the local scene and his comments on
the social composition of the Parliamentary side in the Civil War put
future historians in his debt.[1] Royalist local history of the same
period is represented by such works as *The Most True and Exact*

Relation of that as Honourable as Unfortunate Expedition of Kent, Essex and Colchester (1650) by Matthew Carter.

But it was in the nineteenth century, with a receptive audience of gentry, clergymen and others from the swelling ranks of the professions, that the local history of the English Revolution took on a new lease of life. Robert Halley's valuable study of *Lancashire: its Puritanism and Nonconformity* (1869) dealt at some length with the Civil War in that county. J.R. Phillips's *Memoirs of the Civil War in Wales and the Marches 1642-46* appeared in 1874. Alfred Kingston's two books on *Hertfordshire during the Great Civil War* and *East Anglia and the Civil War* came out in 1894 and 1897 respectively. These works, some of them very good indeed, took their place among a growing collection of county histories of the Civil War period. But the main achievement of Victorian local historians in this field, it could be argued, lay in making available a vast number of seventeenth-century texts. In Lancashire, for example, the Chetham Society brought out as one of its earliest volumes a collection of *Tracts Relating to Military Proceedings in Lancashire During the Great Civil War ...* (1844). This was shortly followed by an edition of the lives of two puritan clergymen of this period, *The Life of Adam Martindale* (1845) and *The Autobiography of Henry Newcome* (1852), an edition of a seventeenth-century *Discourse of the War in Lancashire* (1864) and, later, *Tracts Relating to the Civil War in Cheshire* (1909). The Lancashire and Cheshire Record Society produced an edition of *The Commonwealth Church Surveys of Lancashire and Cheshire 1649-1655* as its first volume in 1879. The same society's *Memorials of the Civil Wars in Cheshire* appeared ten years later. The publishing activities of these two societies were representative of others of the period. The Surtees Society, the Yorkshire Archaeological Society, the Somerset Record Society, to name but three, all contributed in a similar way by printing valuable source materials relating to the local history of the English Revolution.

In the early years of the twentieth century, with Gardiner and Firth's outline of national events to guide them, local historians offered a new crop of county studies. J.W. Willis-Bund's *The Civil War in Worcestershire 1642-1646 and the Scottish Invasion of 1651* (1905) made use of Gardiner's volumes on the Commonwealth and of Firth's *Cromwell's Army*. No fewer than three other new, and very good, county studies appeared in 1910. Ernest Broxap's *The Great Civil War in Lancashire 1642-51* and A.R. Bayley's *The Great Civil*

War in Dorset 1642-1660 were both written at Firth's suggestion.[2] Firth also gave an encouraging hand to Sir Charles Thomas-Stanford, whose *Sussex in the Great Civil War and the Interregnum 1642-1660* appeared in the same year. W.J. Farrow's book on *The Great Civil War in Shropshire 1642-49* (1926), like Broxap's study of Lancashire, originated as a University of Manchester M.A. thesis. Unlike Broxap and the other local historians of his vintage, however, Farrow did not restrict himself only to an account of the war itself, but said something about the growth of parties and of neutralism, and devoted a whole chapter to 'some social aspects of the struggle'.

Farrow's book heralded a changing trend in the writing of county histories of the Civil War period which was expressed more fully in two works published in 1933 and 1937 respectively. The first was *Cornwall in the Great Civil War and Interregnum 1642-1660* by the Oxford historian Mary Coate (1886-1972), and her book placed the Civil War firmly in the context of the intense localism and isolation of Cornish society.

> The history of Cornwall is that of a county with a strong personality, priding itself on its peculiarities and alive with a local patriotism rooted in racial differences and fed by geographical isolation ... Again and again this local patriotism ... knit together in a common unity men of differing political and religious opinions.
>
> Similarly in the economic life of the people, the custom of the manor, the petty life of the borough, and the traditional relation of landlord to tenant survived the changes and chances of Civil War, for they were the very fibre of which society was constituted, and beside them the political conflict appeared transient and superficial.[3]

The second of these two books to break new ground in the 1930s in offering a social, rather than a political and military, history of the Civil War in a particular county was *Nottinghamshire in the Civil War* by A.C. Wood (1896-1968).

> The war in Nottinghamshire was predominantly local in character and it can be isolated for separate treatment without distortion or omission of the facts. I have endeavoured throughout to keep the parish pump linked up to the main stream, but my primary object has been to narrate the fortunes of this county during the twenty most febrile and dramatic years of its history.[4]

The social and economic characteristics of Nottinghamshire were clearly delineated at the outset, a separate chapter was devoted to Royalist and Roundhead organization, and, like Mary Coate, Wood covered the religious history of the county in his period in a final chapter.[5]

Although county studies of a fairly traditional kind have continued to be written, other local and regional historians of the Civil War have moved out in a number of new directions.[6] This has been made possible by the opening of county record offices since 1945 and, going with this, the increased availability of private collections of family papers. Almost invariably, as well as being natives of the counties whose history they have explored, the local historians in question have been professionals; local history has become firmly established at the universities, though Leicester still has the only separate department devoted to its study.

The 'gentry controversy' provided the stimulus to the opening up of one new direction in local and regional studies, since as its original participants, especially Tawney, came to realize, it was futile to continue the debate at the level of generalization. More research, more case studies of particular counties and particular families were preferable to further wild hypotheses. The American historian Alan Simpson (1912-　) made the point very clearly in one such case study of the gentry's fortunes which appeared in 1961. In *The Wealth of the Gentry 1540-1660. East Anglian Studies* Simpson argued that the 'gentry controversy', stimulating though it had been while it lasted, was no more than a 'cleansing operation' in which 'anyone with a good general knowledge of the century, and a clear head can have his say'.

> [But] the simple fact remains that the economic history which the whole controversy presupposes has still to be determined. It is an argument about incomes and expenditures, and the number of economic biographies which exist can be counted on two hands, with a few fingers to spare. It is an argument about land management, and there are even fewer studies of that, which clearly demonstrate its methods and its profits. It is an argument about movement upwards and downwards among the ruling classes, and there is not a county in England for which the attempt has been made to compare the leading families of 1640 with those of 1540 and to explain the differences.[7]

Honestly describing his own work as 'more limited than the range of the controversy which stimulated it', Simpson processed some difficult evidence from a part of the country (East Anglia) which had been surprisingly absent from the generalized treatments of Tawney, Stone and Trevor-Roper. Without offering any dogmatic conclusions, Simpson none the less, in a way which lent support to Tawney's thesis, was able to identify:

> ... the patterns which the demographic factor could produce — the possibilities of subdivision where there were too many children, of consolidation when some lines failed, and of extinction if there was no male heir. We learn something of the expenses as well as the profits of office; if the founder of the family owed everything to a career at court, the children of the second marriage knew all about its hazards. Finally, we discover the capacity of landed estates to weather the inflation.[8]

Overall, it was Simpson's impression that:

> Apart from a few Bacons that rose, a few Heydons that crashed, and rather more who disappeared through lack of male heirs, it is an interesting possibility, after all the talk of rise and fall, that the rest may just have endured. If so, it would be something of an anti-climax; but to one student, at least, the agrarian history of this century has turned out to be far more prosaic than he ever expected.[9]

A cautious and judicious case-study approach to the gentry of another county had characterized one of the first studies of this kind produced under the stimulus of the Tawney/Trevor-Roper debate. Mary Finch's careful and well-documented monograph of *The Wealth of Five Northamptonshire Families 1540-1640* (Northants Record Society, XIX, 1956) acknowledged Tawney and Stone in its preface. Dr Finch, (1923-   ) like Simpson later, argued that steady if unspecttacular profits could be gained from landowning in this period, provided that the gentry selected, consolidated and improved their estates carefully and firmly grasped the realities of credit and investment.[10] But complicating any theory of the rise and decline of sections of the gentry was an erratic, unquantifiable aspect. 'Personality of the individual landowner', she concluded, 'is always the decisive factor.'

This conclusion was echoed in another case study of the gentry.

Although general economic factors could be important, the financial success or failure of a landed family depended in the last resort on individual character. Whatever the prevailing conditions an estate could be seriously, even disastrously, impaired if the owner was an incompetent or negligent landlord, a lunatic or a spendthrift.[11]

This was J.T. Cliffe's observation in his weighty volume on *The Yorkshire Gentry from the Reformation to the Civil War* which looked at the economic fortunes, religious affiliations and political attitudes of the social élite in that county. Dr Cliffe (1931-   ) drew a distinction between the economic opportunities open to the minor gentry and to those further up the scale in the social hierarchy.

Although the theory that the 'mere landowner' rarely prospered cannot be sustained as a general proposition, it undoubtedly has some validity when applied to the small landed families with no other form of income. For them there was little prospect of economic advancement.[12]

Bad management, extravagance, lavish hospitality, litigation, demographic crises, could all help to put gentry families in a difficult position.

H.A. Lloyd's study of *The Gentry of South-West Wales 1540-1640* (1968) grew out of an Oxford D.Phil. thesis supervised by Professor Trevor-Roper. Lloyd's work was less quantitative in approach than some of the other studies of this genre; 'statistical contrivances', he wrote, 'do not offset fundamental deficiencies of evidence'.

The only general observation to be admitted is that the characteristics of the gentry as here portrayed are not consistent either with the aspirations or with the impact attributed to rising or declining 'generalized gentry' in England as a whole. This is a comment not upon the likely characteristics of gentry elsewhere, studied in accordance with the terms of this analysis, but upon the doubtful admissibility, for purposes other than that of academic stimulus, of broad hypotheses taking insufficient account of the variations within that agglomeration of localities which in this period made up the kingdom of England.

For South-west Wales, Lloyd (1937-   ) concluded that the gentry suffered from an economic and political lassitude.

That community [of Wales] was conditioned by a heritage of disharmony and conflicting forces. Its leaders were able neither sufficiently to abandon old ways for new opportunities, nor effectively to seek development and adjustment of native forms to meet new circumstances. With the old order crumbling and the new world unexplored, south-west Wales lingered in limbo.[13]

For regional studies of this kind, the 'gentry controversy' provided a stimulus rather than a constraining framework. Work on the economic fortunes of the gentry easily, and naturally, led on to reassessments of their role in county society and politics. Following the lead taken by W.B. Willcox in *Gloucestershire: A Study in local government 1590-1640* (1940), in 1961 T.G. Barnes produced his study of *Somerset 1625-1640. A County's government during the 'Personal Rule'*. Earlier, in 1957, D.H. Pennington and Ivan Roots had published *The Committee at Stafford 1643-1645. The Order Book of the Staffordshire County Committee*. Another county committee was one of the subjects documented in Alan Everitt's *Suffolk and the Great Rebellion 1640-1660*.[14]

Primarily a collection of source material, Everitt's book on Suffolk hardly gave its author scope to produce a rounded interpretation of provincial society in the 1640s and 1650s. Such an opportunity, however, was offered and was firmly grasped in his study of *The Community of Kent and the Great Rebellion 1640-1660*, a landmark in this branch of the recent historiography of the Revolution.[15] The book's title accurately indicated where its main emphasis lay; the county community came first in Everitt's interpretation.[16] Himself a native of Kent, Everitt (1926-), now Hatton Professor of English Local History at the University of Leicester, offered a refreshingly different and stimulating approach to the regional history of the English Revolution.

> In many respects, despite its ancient centralized government, the England of 1640 resembled a union of partially independent county-states of communities, each with its own distinct ethos and loyalty ... One important aspect of the history of the Great Rebellion is certainly the gradual merging or submerging of these communities, under the stress of revolution, in the national community of the New Model Army and the Protectorate.[17]

Unlike older local historians who had set out simply to illustrate the familiar pattern of national events, Everitt emphasized the need to penetrate the internal intricacies of the local world itself. In the crisis years of the Civil War the community divided, though at first the two 'parties' in Kent were minorities of extremists with the majority preferring to remain neutral for as long as possible; 'the most striking political feature of Kent during 1640-1660 was precisely its insularity'. [18] Local resistance, however, to the centralizing efforts of Parliament during the Interregnum was as strong as any opposition which had confronted Charles I, and sprang from the same origins. In this way the county community reunited, and the 'natural rulers', the old gentry families, by 1660 were back in the saddle. 'The local power of the gentry had not been diminished but rather increased by the Great Rebellion' even though 'the community of 1660 was not identical in character with that of 1640'.[19]

The 'community' of Kent, as Everitt defined it was essentially that of the *gentry*, almost three-quarters of whom (an unusually high proportion) were indigenous to the county. Intermarriage reinforced the insularity and separateness of the Kentish gentry.

> A casual eye cast over English society in 1640 naturally tends to alight on celebrated names of national importance like Sackville and Sidney. But far more numerous, and in county affairs more important, were those like the Oxindens and Derings, families of ancient standing, local outlook and moderate fortune. Quite two thirds of the Kentish community was composed of such families, who as far as we can tell usually owed in their rise little or nothing to trade or office, and whose connexions were confined to the circle of neighbours and cousins whom they met in their manorhouses day by day.

Such men formed the backbone of the county community, and from them arose the distinctive ideals and the ethos of provincial society.[20] Everitt has returned to these themes repeatedly in his later work. For instance, in 1969 he brought out two complementary essays on *Change in the Provinces: the seventeenth century* and *The Local Community and the Great Rebellion.*[21] Despite its title, the first of these essays devoted rather more attention to the conservatism and continuity of provincial life than it did to changing patterns of social relations associated with the arrival of the 'new gentry', the growth of the wayfaring community, the professions and the pseudo-gentry.[22] None the less, Everitt argued that the growth in provincial self-awareness was one of the most important developments of the seventeenth century.

It emerged with the growing power of the county commonwealths of England. It emerged with the rise of the county capitals, focusing as they did so many aspects of the shire communities around them. It developed, too, with the rise of the professional classes, called into being to serve the new needs of both town and countryside. It arose with the expansion of trade and wealth generally, for this expansion greatly increased the wealth of provincial townsmen and yeomen. Indeed, it was one of the ironies of provincial life that even the revolutionary developments of the time, such as the rise of the new gentry and the emergence of the wayfaring community, in the end came to be accepted and neutralized within it and to buttress its independence. The new developments were grafted into the old tree, so to speak, rejuvenating and invigorating its productive powers without fundamentally altering its identity. In a real sense the events of 1660 were a compromise between the power of this provincial world and the power of the nation-state. Or rather they were an agreement to differ, an *entente*, a recognition that each world needed the other in order to survive.[23]

It was the continuities of everyday social and economic life rather than the dramatic, but short-lived, impact of the Civil War that Everitt dwelt on in the second of these essays, on *The Local Community and the Great Rebellion*.

A superficial reading of contemporary tracts sometimes gives the impression that it was a total war. But tracts, by their nature, do not usually record the *ordinary* facts of daily life, but its disruptions. It is the background of common existence that we need to visualise.

Following the suggestion made more tentatively by Mary Coate thirty years earlier, Everitt pleaded at the end of his essay that, above all, the English Revolution ought to be placed firmly in a wider local perspective. It should be seen,

... as one of a succession of problems to which society at the time was peculiarly vulnerable. The recurrent problems of harvest failure, and the malnutrition and disease that often followed in its wake, were, for most English people, more serious and more persistent than the tragic but temporary upheaval of the Civil War ... The stubbornness and the resilience of country people, over the generations, in the face of this alternating harshness and generosity of nature were equally remarkable. Their experiences certainly go some way to explain that latent intransigence of the provincial world which, in the last resort, was one of the principal factors in the failure of both Charles I and Cromwell. For if you have been engaged for centuries in hand-to-hand warfare with the forces of nature, you naturally develop a certain dumb obstinacy towards the world at large — and not least towards the strange doings of princes and protectors. [24]

Professor Everitt's 'gentry community' perspective on the English Revolution has been an important influence on subsequent county studies of this period. It was discernible, for instance, in Anthony Fletcher's massive and erudite work *A County Community in Peace and War: Sussex 1600-1660.* [25] Perhaps mistakenly, since at times it made the book diffuse, the chronological coverage of Fletcher's study was longer than Everitt's, although his definition of the 'county community' was the same. The gentry held the centre of the stage throughout; their wealth, social standing, political experience, administrative service, religious allegiance, kinship and friendship networks all received due attention. Little was offered on the aristocracy, who by the 1620s had lost control in the county, and even less, except through the eyes of their betters, on the great mass of the rural and urban population. Popular agitation, such as the Sussex episodes in the Clubmen movement in 1645 got only perfunctory treatment. The tensions between gentry and an urban oligarchy — as at Chichester — had more interest for a historian such as Mr Fletcher (1941-   ).

Everitt's work also clearly influenced David Underdown's *Somerset in the Civil War and Interregnum*, although in line with this historian's previous work the main emphasis here was political; [26] his local study drew both strengths and weaknesses from being written in tandem with his work on parliamentary politics, *Pride's Purge* (see pp. 137-8). But Professor Underdown's dual interest in politics at the centre and in the counties enabled him to explore the relationship between the two, the way, for instance, in which M.P.s' attitudes were based on local conditions.

A similar concern with the constant interaction between regional and national politics underlay Clive Holmes's study of *The Eastern Association in the English Civil War.* [27] Everitt had broached this subject earlier in his book on Suffolk, and there had offered a regional explanation of the Association. Circumstances in East Anglia, he argued, were especially conducive; there was 'a considerable body of Suffolk people who were capable of thinking in terms not only of their native village and county, but of East Anglia as a whole'.[28] Holmes (1943-   ) however, showed convincingly that the rise and fall of the Eastern Association in the 1640s could not be explained primarily in local and regional terms. 'The Association was formed in spite of, rather than because of, the socio-economic substructure of the region.' Nor could the Association be explained as another dimension of the puritanism of the eastern counties, a factor emphasized since Gardiner's day; 'the supposed religious homogeneity of the region', he contended, 'has been over-emphasized'. In a political sense, too, it was necessity rather than choice which brought the eastern counties together. 'The initial pressure for the formation of the Eastern Association came from those counties which were least enthusiastic in their support for the Parliamentary cause.'[29] Local and regional forces, then, were not in themselves strong enough either to justify the Association in the first instance or to hold it together subsequently. The impressive and practically unique success of the Eastern Association was made possible by the 'complex and tension-ridden dialogue' between local and national politics, and in the last analysis it was the politicians at Westminster who first created and then dismantled this instrument of aggression.

While Holmes challenged Everitt's emphasis on purely local explanations, J.S. Morrill (1946-   ) in his *Cheshire 1630-1660. County government and society during the 'English Revolution'* took a critical look at Everitt's definitions of 'county community' and 'crisis'.[30] 'My aim', the author wrote, 'has been to convey an impression of a whole community [not just the gentry] under stress'. [31] The kind of crisis facing society in the 1640s, Morrill argued, went much deeper than Everitt had allowed. (The latter's preference for the term 'Great Rebellion' was significant.) A new self-consciousness was developing at *village* level, and the stirrings of this grassroots social revolution induced a fear in the county élite which was translated into political action.

Everitt's stress on county communities of gentry has been countered also by the development of specifically *urban* case studies of the English Revolution. For example, A.M. Johnson explored 'Politics in Chester during the Civil Wars and the Interregnum 1640-1662', while a full-length study of *Newcastle-upon-Tyne and the Puritan Revolution* by Roger Howell (1936-   ) appeared in 1967.[32]

Howell's book, however, reinforced Everitt's stress on the importance of local determinants of Civil War politics. The main significance of the English Revolution for Newcastle was that it provided new opportunities to attempt to prise open the grip of the ruling oligarchy on the corporation and the coal trade.

Newcastle's coal trade gave it a special relationship with London (its main customer), and the capital itself has received due attention from Valerie Pearl (1926-   ), a former student of Hill and Trevor-Roper at Oxford and now Reader in the History of London at University College, London. The publication of her book on *London and the Outbreak of the Puritan Revolution. City government and national politics 1625-43* in 1961 had been eagerly awaited by seventeenth-century historians and its appearance amply justified the high expectations.[33] Dr Pearl's book on the structure of government and course of politics in the capital took a long and highly critical look at the notion, repeated so frequently by historians that it had become an accepted cliché, that London supported Parliament even before the outbreak of the Civil War. Her conclusion, in fact, was very different and was that 'the eventual alignment of London with Parliament was the result of *force majeure*, that is to say, of the seizing of power in the City by the parliamentary puritans'.[34] It was in 1642 that this group captured control of the city government and of the trained bands, and by enlarging the role of the Common Council heralded the formal reduction, in 1649, of the powers of the Lord Mayor and aldermanic bench. The revolutionary character of these changes, however, Dr Pearl argued, should not be exaggerated. As in the case of Newcastle, once new men took power, they did not set out to destroy the oligarchical structure which they had entered; their own position, after all, *vis-à-vis* those below them was a highly privileged one. But the new men were socially different from their predecessors, amongst whose ranks had been numbered monopolists, customs farmers, and high-ranking members of the chartered trading companies. The most significant group of these new men who came to power in London after 1642 were middle-rank merchants.

Both Dr Howell and Dr Pearl gave some attention to religion in their urban studies of Newcastle and London; other historians have concentrated specifically on the local and regional history of this important subject. R.A. Marchant looked at *The Puritans and the Church Courts in the Diocese of York 1560-1642.*[35] R.C. Richardson's *Puritanism in North-West England. A regional study of the diocese of Chester to 1642*, though it did not deal with the Civil War period itself, covered part of the background to it by analysing the structure and organization of the puritanism of that area and the forces at work within it.[36] The Catholic community of the English counties (and of London) has been examined in the works of John Bossy, Keith Lindley, M.J. Havran, and Hugh Aveling.[37]

New research continues (and a vast amount remains to be done) at local and regional level, and few would doubt the importance of this branch of the recent historiography of the English Revolution. No single county or town in the seventeenth century, of course, was *typical* of the whole country, and local historians would no longer define their function as that of simply *illustrating* the national picture. The relationship between local and national events in the seventeenth century was much more complicated than that. But undoubtedly one of the ways forward in English Revolutionary studies will be in exploring that relationship still further, and in confronting and trying to explain the bewildering variety of local structures, experience and attitudes that has begun to be opened up before us.

Chapter 8

The twentieth century: political history: continuity and experiment

However ancient and well-established the writing of political history may be, it is at present under something of a cloud. At least some professional historians incline to treat it as a rather old-fashioned and manifestly inadequate — even an uninteresting form. Some think it too 'easy'. (G.R. Elton, *Political History. Principles and Practice* (London, Allen Lane, 1970), p.57.)

Much of the emphasis in recent writing on the English Revolution, as the previous chapters have demonstrated, has been on its social and economic aspects. Reacting against relics of Victorian liberalism and the prominence given to political events and political explanations by Gardiner and Firth and their 'school', historians moved out into those areas of the period which were still most open and in whch the need for research seemed most urgent. It was widely felt that the political history of the Revolution had already been established, had already been mapped out in laborious detail, and for a time therefore, this branch of the historiography of the subject seemed threatened with eclipse. Labelled as Whig history, it became unfashionable. Although political histories of the Revolutionary period continued to be written, they were done under Gardiner's shadow. It was only comparatively recently, in fact, that a renewed concern began to be expressed with the politics of these years, assimilating the work of the social, economic and regional historians, and with new questions being asked and with new analytical techniques being applied. The recent historiography of the English Revolution, then, has by no means been exclusively social and economic, and there are few historians today who would argue that the events of the mid-seventeenth century can be explained exclusively in those terms. For the political history of this period the result has been that what once seemed so certain and clear-cut has now begun to look quite different when viewed from another angle. Although it will deal partly with the continuity of writing in the Gardiner tradition, this chapter will be concerned mainly with new developments, reinterpretations, and new avenues of research in this field. It follows on, therefore, in a logical sequence from the two previous chapters. Many of the historians discussed here belong specifically to a context which is post-Namier, post-Tawney, post-Hill, and post-Everitt.

Amongst the traditionalists, C.V. Wedgwood (1910-   ) has justly acquired the reputation of being the most accomplished of the nineteenth-century narrative historians' successors. Although she has written extensively on European history, she has become best known for her work on seventeenth-century England.[1] C.V. Wedgwood's greatest skill has been in telling a story, in making clear how and in what order political events occurred. Apparently, after graduating at Oxford, she had been about to embark on research under Tawney. 'Had I gone on with it', she later stated, 'I would have become a *why* historian, but I didn't. I discovered that in *why* history research is more important than writing, and I wanted to do both....'[2] In the event it was not Tawney but Trevelyan whose influence she came under, and in this way she emerged as a *how* historian. Both the achievements and limitations of this kind of historical approach were displayed in her volumes on *The King's Peace 1637-1641, The King's War 1641-1647*, and on *The Trial of Charles I*.[3] 'She is a shortbread historian,' it has been asserted. 'She tells stories simply and entertainingly in the manner of Somerset Maugham.'[4] Reviewing *The King's War*, Christopher Hill, too, was obliged to admit that,

> Miss Wedgwood's book as a whole is a narrative, not an explanation. It tells us all about the war except what they fought each other for ... Many of her pages are full of one rather breathless incident after another ... Two hundred facts do not make an interpretation ... Too often Miss Wedgwood leaves us bewildered in a flux of events ... [Her] refusal to analyse makes it impossible to see below the surface of mere events.[5]

C.V. Wedgwood has freely admitted as much herself. She has never made false claims for her kind of history and has obviously been content to follow in the footsteps of illustrious predecessors like Macaulay and Trevelyan. She has more than once defended Macaulay's reputation.

'400 editions', thundered Carlyle incensed at the levity [of the style of Macaulay's *History*], 'could not lend it any permanent value'. He failed to see that 400 editions in themselves may well constitute a permanent value; his attack was based on the groundless faith that there is an absolute standard outside the praise and agreement of the public. For the historian there is not. Macaulay may have been inaccurate and biased: but he preached a good cause eloquently.[6]

Wedgwood's *The King's Peace 1637-1641* was dedicated to Trevelyan, her mentor, and was written in a manner which the master himself would have been proud of. In the introduction she justified her decision to produce what was first and foremost 'a straightforward and chronological narrative'. Her aim in writing the book, she declared, had been above all to restore 'the immediacy of experience', 'the admitted motives and the illusions of the men of the seventeenth century'. Historians themselves had intruded too frequently in their efforts to reconstruct the seventeenth-century past.

> The application of modern methods of research, together with modern knowledge and prejudice, can make the past merely the subject of our own analytical ingenuity or our own illusions. With scholarly precision we can build up theories as to why and how things happened which are convincing to us, which may even be true, but which those who lived through the epoch would neither recognize nor accept.

'It is equally legitimate', Wedgwood insisted, 'to accept the motives and explanations which satisfied contemporaries.' 'The behaviour of men as individuals', she went on, 'is more interesting to me than their behaviour as groups or classes.' Her book, therefore, was 'not an economic analysis, not a social study; it is an attempt to understand how these men felt and why, in their own estimation, they acted as they did'.[7]

Miss Wedgwood's preference for studying 'the behaviour of men as individuals' could obviously be gratified most completely in biography. Her study of *Strafford* (1935) was, in fact, her first book, and it was revised and reissued in the light of subsequent research in 1961 as *Thomas Wentworth. First Earl of Strafford 1593-1641: A Revaluation*.[8] Charles I's other chief minister, Archbishop Laud, found his biographer in H.R. Trevor-Roper. First published in 1940, Trevor-Roper's book was reissued twenty-two years later with some prefatory apologies for the youthful overconfidence and insensitivity of the original.[9] Biography was, in fact, one field in which continuous interest in the politics of the English Revolution was noticeably maintained, and Wedgwood's and Trevor-Roper's volumes took their place in a growing gallery of portraits. The list of biographies, of course, has continued to expand, and there have been recent studies, for example, of Lord Cottington, Charles I's Chancellor of the Exchequer, and of Sir Richard Weston, the King's Lord Treasurer.[10] But there have been considerably fewer biographies of royalist figures than of leaders on the Parliamentarian/puritan side. Maurice Ashley, for instance, tried valiantly to define *The Greatness of Oliver Cromwell* (1957), and more recently, in an unconventional biography, Christopher Hill took on *God's Englishman. Oliver Cromwell and the English Revolution* (1970).[11] Pauline Gregg's *Free-born John. A Biography of Lilburne* came out in 1961, while *Marginal Prynne. 1600-1669* by W.M. Lamont followed two years later. Violet A. Rowe brought out in 1970 a biography of *Sir Henry Vane the Younger. A study in political and administrative history.* Ruth Spalding's *The Improbable Puritan. A life of Bulstrode Whitelocke 1605-1675* appeared in 1975.[12]

C.V. Wedgwood's traditional approach to seventeenth-century history and biography has been more than adequately countered by the development of fresh methods and ways of thinking, expressed both in general surveys and in specialized monographs. First of all, the political thought of this period has been reinvestigated and reinterpreted. The first volume of J.W. Allen's *English Political Thought 1603-1660* (1938) reached 1640 but unfortunately the project was never completed. But the American historian Margaret Judson's stimulating study of *The Crisis of the Constitution. An essay in constitutional and political thought* (1949) both reworked some of the same material and advanced chronologically. In a short but astonishingly wide-ranging *History of Political Thought in the English Revolution* (1954), another American historian, Perez Zagorin (1920-), pushed the survey even further, dealing with the theorists of the Commonwealth and Protectorate and also with Filmer's contribution to the political ideas of Royalism.[13] J.W. Gough explored the importance of *Fundamental Law in English Constitutional History* (1955), while J.G.A. Pocock's indispensable study of *The Ancient Constitution and the Feudal Law. A study of English historical thought in the seventeenth century* appeared in 1957.

C.B. Macpherson's controversial book on *The Political Theory of Possessive Individualism* was published in 1962, and offered some provocatively original reassessments of the Levellers, Harrington, Locke, and Hobbes.[14] Hobbes was also the subject of a sequence of articles by Quentin Skinner.[15] The Canadian political scientist J.A.W. Gunn investigated the notion of 'public interest' in seventeenth-century thought, while Anne Pallister and Sir Herbert Butterfield re-examined the use made of Magna Carta in seventeenth-century politics and historiography.[16]

On the political history as opposed to the political thought of this period much new work has been done on allegiance, party groupings, institutions, and personnel. American historians have taken a prominent part in such studies, and in 1969 one of their number, Perez Zagorin, Professor at the University of Rochester, New York, offered a new synthesis of the evidence. Zagorin had earlier intervened in the gentry controversy, and his new book *The Court and the Country. The beginning of the English Revolution*, amongst other things, was designed as a rejoinder to the Marxists.[17] The Civil War, he insisted, was not a class war. Marxist historians had committed a grave error in accepting contemporary Royalist propaganda about the social inferiority of their opponents at face value.

> The social system in which the revolution occurred was not based on economic classes. It was based, rather, on status, and the terms in which we must perforce delineate it — peers, gentry, yeomen, citizens, etc. — are fundamentally not economic classifications at all.

Nor, Zagorin argued, did men in the seventeenth century have a political conception of revolution.

> It is the total absence of this highly charged idea of revolution born in France and elevated to a theoretical principle by Marx that we have to notice as we look back across the abyss of time to the 1640s. 'Revolution' had then another, mainly non-political meaning.

The English Revolution was, in fact, the result of a division *within* the political élite itself, a division which contemporaries recognized as a cleavage between 'Court' and 'Country'.

> Around this widening split, all the various conflicts in the kingdom gradually became polarized. The antagonism was thus not a lateral one between the orders of society; it was vertical, by degrees

dividing the peerage, the gentry and the merchant oligarchies of the towns. At last it drew in also the unprivileged and normally inarticulate mass of men.[18]

'The Country was the first opposition movement in English history whose character transcended that of a feudal following or a faction.' But it was a conservative opposition and, although there were political and religious differences, socially speaking, according to Zagorin, it was drawn from the same ranks as the Court group it opposed.

The outstanding characteristic of the Country from a social-structural standpoint was its uniformity with the governing class. To imagine the Country as 'progressive' in the sense of incarnating, even unwittingly, a new ordering of society, is completely erroneous. Equally so is the supposition that its relation to the Court was the antipathy of 'Outs' to 'Ins' — the social resentment of men denied admission to influence and favour. What made the Country so formidable was that its adherents were pillars of society.[19]

Later events, of course, Zagorin recognized, changed the course and character of the Revolution. There was a substantial realignment of political forces in the years 1640-2, in which a new Royalism was discovered, and Charles I built up, almost out of nothing, a party and an army with which to fight the Civil War. The labels 'Parliamentarian' and 'Royalist' replaced those of 'Country' and 'Court', the religious issue in the struggle became more central, and political arguments which a conservative opposition had first used against the King came in time to be directed against Parliament itself by groups like the Levellers.[20]

As a general survey of political developments, Zagorin's book had much to recommend it, but more than one reviewer underlined the weak points in his argument. The labels 'Court' and 'Country', to which Zagorin attached such great significance, were not in fact the political novelty of the 1620s which he claimed, nor were these the only party tags then current. Similarly, Zagorin's attack on simplistic social explanations of the seventeenth-century crisis, although in some respects salutary, none the less ended in an unwillingness to see *any* social patterns in the evidence concerning puritanism and the political struggle.[21] His denial that there was any recognizably modern concept of revolution in the seventeenth century undervalued the role of popular movements and of millenarianism. (Results as well as conscious motives, in any case, should surely be taken into account in any assessment or definition of revolution.) Zagorin's claim that the peers and the gentry never lost the initiative in their own well-managed revolt has not convinced other historians such as Brian Manning who have emphasized the decisiveness of the popular contribution (see pp.143-5).

Work on the alignment of forces during the Civil War period itself has been carried forward by other historians. P.H. Hardacre, for example, presented a general outline sketch of *The Royalists during the Puritan Revolution* (1956). Based only on printed sources rather than on the unpublished private papers of Royalist gentry families necessary for a social analysis of his subject, Hardacre's book was able to raise more questions than it could answer about their social structure and internal divisions. Part of the same subject was dealt with at much greater length by David Underdown (1925-) in his *Royalist Conspiracy in England, 1649-1660* (1960). An expanded version of his Oxford thesis written under Christopher Hill and Trevor-Roper, Underdown's book was principally a narrative history of the continuous efforts of Royalists on behalf of the future Charles II. But the subject of his study was such that it naturally involved a discussion of the structure of the Royalist 'party' and its component factions, which led on to an assessment of the Royalist problem to all successive régimes in the Interregnum. 'As long as the Cavaliers remained unconverted, a freely elected parliament was impossible unless the republicans were willing to sign their own death warrants.' Underdown had a chapter on Penruddock's Rising in 1655, the one occasion when the Royalists attempted a rebellion entirely by themselves without allies, and he also weighed the importance of Royalist conspiracy in making possible the Restoration of 1660. Underdown, however, offered a careful analysis of the organizational and financial weaknesses of the Royalist party and of the tensions caused by the mingling in the resistance movement of the newer recruits of the 1650s with those who had fought and lost in the Civil War.[22]

Other recent work on the formation of the Royalist party has included that by Brian Manning (see p.144) which has stressed that, above all, the Royalists were a party of order brought into being as a counter to popular discontent and intimidation. Recent research, in fact, has suggested that parties — both Royalist and Parliamentarian — grew quite as much as a result of the attitudes and actions of their opponents as of those of their supporters. Puritan opposition to popery pushed neutral Catholics into the Royalist ranks.[23] In the same way the alliance between puritanism and Parliamentarianism became a fact partly as a consequence of Royalist propaganda to that effect. 'The connection between puritanism and revolution', one historian has written recently, 'was largely of Charles I's making.' Arguably, even in religious terms, puritanism was a reaction to the Arminian revolution and only belatedly became radicalized itself.[24] Clearly the connections between religion and politics were infinitely more complex than nineteenth-century historians believed, and one important strand in the recent historiography of the English Revolution has been the attempt to understand and define those connections more exactly.[25]

Political groupings within Parliament rather than those outside it have tended to attract more attention from historians and have certainly been at the centre of more controversy. The American historian J.H. Hexter explored the emergence and management of a middle group in the House of Commons in the early 1640s in his brilliant study of *The Reign of King Pym* (1941).[26] Pym emerged from Hexter's pages as a political artist of consummate skill. He was no idealist. Above all 'he was a political tactician, a political engineer'. Of the three men in the middle group — Essex and Hampden were the other two — holding the balance between the extremes of the war party and the peace party, it was Pym whose role was in a real sense most crucial, particularly after the outbreak of war when Parliament had no effective organization, no military or administrative machine of its own. [Pym] had the dull but useful knack of squeezing the maximum political energy out of the most unpromising raw materials, and of applying that energy at the time and in the place where it would be most effective; somehow or other he kept things going.'[27]

Always at home in historical controversy — 'If you can't stand the heat stay out of the kitchen' has been his motto — Hexter in 1938 with his article on 'The Problem of the Presbyterian Independents' fired the first shots in what has since proved a lively debate.[28] Hexter's argument against the notion that Presbyterians and Independents were distinct and mutually exclusive groups was challenged by Tawney's former pupil George Yule (1919-) in his book on the religious, political and social identity of *The Independents in the English Civil War* (1958).[29] The debate widened with further contributions from Brunton and Pennington (see pp.135-7), David Underdown, Valerie Pearl and Lotte Glow.[30]

An article in *Past and Present* in 1969 by an American historian, Stephen Foster, sent the sparks flying yet again by boldly suggesting that 'the whole controversy, fallacies, misinterpretations and all, rests at its base on a statistical illusion' and that for years historians, who ought to have known better, had been enthusiastically chasing the ghosts of the 'Presbyterian Independents up and down the pages of a variety of journals and monographs'. The old contestants, and one new one, were quick to reply, and the issues of political and religious terminology were given a further airing. [31]

The investigation of seventeenth-century parliaments and their composition has proved inherently controversial, and not only because of the need to attach some sort of labels to the elusive groups or parties involved. The controversy has also concerned historians' methodologies, and in particular the validity of applying the technique of static analysis to an institution that was itself changing and increasingly engaged in self-discovery, and all this, moreover, in a contentious period in which principles were at stake and were eventually fought over.

American historians, again, have been prominent in this field and the chief of them, undoubtedly, was Professor Wallace Notestein (1878-1969), whose teaching career was spent in the universities of Kansas, Minnesota, Cornell and Yale. Part of Notestein's contribution to the re-examination of parliamentary history in the seventeenth century was in editing source material. In 1921 he brought out an edition of the *Commons Debates for 1629* and the seven volumes of *Commons Debates 1621* followed in 1935. [32] In addition, in 1923, Notestein began the publication of *The Journal of Sir Simonds D'Ewes*. [33] Notestein, however, is best remembered for his famous essay on Jacobean parliaments, 'The Winning of the Initiative by the House of Commons'. His narrative history of *The House of Commons 1604-1610* was posthumously published in 1971. [34]

Some of Notestein's former students joined him in the work that he had begun. D.H. Willson's *The Privy Councillors in the House of Commons 1604-1629* came out in 1940. Robert Zaller acknowledged Notestein's guidance (and that of J.H. Hexter) in his study of *The Parliament of 1621. A Study in Constitutional Conflict* (1971). Earlier, in 1958, T.L. Moir's book on *The Addled Parliament of 1614* had appeared, while in 1971 a further contribution to the parliamentary history of the reign of James I arrived in the form of R.E. Ruigh's reassessment of *The Parliament of 1624. Politics and Foreign Policy*.

Other parliamentary studies of this period have included the ambitious but ultimately rather unsuccessful effort by W.M. Mitchell to trace *The Rise of the Revolutionary Party in the English House of Commons 1603-29* (1957). Much more convincing was Colin Tite's learned volume on *Impeachment and Parliamentary Judicature in Early Stuart England* (1974), a case study of the advance in parliamentary authority during the early seventeenth century.[35]

Notestein's studies of parliament rested, partly at least, on a biographical analysis of its members, and the American historian was in fact associated with the official History of Parliament Trust in England.[36] The aim of this body, founded in 1928, was to compile a biographical register of all M.P.s who had sat in parliament between 1264 and 1901. Its leading light was Sir Lewis Namier, Professor of History at Manchester University from 1931 and author of *The Structure of Politics at the Accession of George III* (1929). But the 'Namierization' of parliamentary history by means of collective biography extended outside the eighteenth century, Namier's own research field, and was applied, for example, to the Long Parliament.

Members of the Long Parliament by Douglas Brunton (1917-52) and Donald Pennington (1919-   ) came out in 1954. The research for it was begun at Namier's suggestion in 1947 when both authors were junior members of his History Department at Manchester, and, although Namierite methods were not uncritically adopted in a wholesale fashion, none the less the book was clearly written under his influence.[37] *Members of the Long Parliament* dealt with the composition and organization of that body in the period 1640-53, with chapters on the original members, the recruiters who came in after 1645, and on the Rump. Case studies of the members from the eastern counties and from the south-west were included as well as a separate chapter on the merchant body in the House. Statistical tables of the numbers of Parliamentarian and Royalist members, their experience in earlier parliaments, and their family links with other M.P.s were appended, as were lists of county and borough members with their political affiliations. Although in essence, like Namier's work, an analysis of collective biography, *Members of the Long Parliament* did not, in fact, include individual biographies of each M.P. These were deliberately omitted in view of the impending publication of another work on the same subject, *The Long Parliament 1640-1641. A biographical study of its members* by the American historian Mary F. Keeler. In the event this, too, came out in 1954, the same year as Brunton and Pennington's own volume. Mrs Keeler contented herself with a study of the original M.P.s in the firm belief that:

> To attempt a composite portrait of the membership for the whole period of the Parliament ... would be useless. A series of group portraits would be better. The picture of the Commons of 1640 and 1641 would not be the same as the picture drawn for 1646 or 1649 or 1653. Changes in personnel developed a body quite different from the one which made its bold attack on the structure of absolutism in the early period.[38]

Accordingly, although the lengthy introduction dealt with such matters as elections and returns, attendance, management, factions, M.P.s' religious and political allegiances, their previous political experience, age, wealth, social, occupational and educational backgrounds, the body of the book consisted of a detailed biographical dictionary of the 547 members in question.

Because of its wider scope and no doubt also because of its potential anti-Marxist ammunition, Brunton and Pennington's work attracted particular attention and criticism. Brian Manning accused the two authors of asking the wrong questions and looking in the wrong places for answers, of failing to examine the relations between the M.P.s and their constituents, and above all of omitting the House of Lords (the stronghold of Royalism) from their study.[39] Christopher Hill was similarly unconvinced by Brunton and Pennington's findings and by their method. Namier himself had been accused of taking the mind out of history by concentrating exclusively on the structure and organization of politics at the expense of its ideas and practice.[40] If this was true of Namier's own work on the eighteenth century, ostensibly a period of stability, it was obviously even more true of the work of his two disciples on parliament in a period when civil war was fought over serious matters of principle. Hill, like Manning, felt the *Members of the Long Parliament* obscured the differences between Royalists and Parliamentarians.[41]

Criticism of this kind, however, ran the risk of distorting what Brunton and Pennington *themselves*, as opposed to their defenders and opponents, actually said. The claims which the authors made for their work were in fact extremely modest, and it was certainly not launched as a kind of anti-communist manifesto. They claimed for their work 'only a limited and largely negative value', and admitted that their evidence did not 'go far enough to enable us to make any confident generalizations on the relation of the Civil War to the great economic changes of the age'. 'There is no such thing as a typical county. Each county and each borough has its own history' and until very much more research had been done on politics, society and economic change in the seventeenth century 'it is very well to be guarded in explanations of the causes and consequences of the Revolution'.[42]

It was not part of Brunton and Pennington's brief to explain why and how the Long Parliament acted in the way that it did, how its multiple groupings actually operated and how allegiances shifted. But the attention of historians has been redirected to such problems (unresolved in many ways despite all Gardiner's heroic efforts to establish the true chronological sequence of events) in three works published since 1971. The first of these, J.R. MacCormack's *Revolutionary Politics in the Long Parliament* (1973), although not without some redeeming features, tended to lose itself amidst its unproven hypotheses and inconsistencies, and has been completely overshadowed by the two other studies in this trilogy.[43]

David Underdown's magisterial re-examination of *Pride's Purge. Politics in the English Revolution* came out in 1971, and, as its title made clear, provided not just an elucidation of one major event in 1648 but threw light on a whole area of the English Revolution. Following the lead taken by Hexter and others, Underdown's analysis of the complexity of political groupings in this period demonstrated beyond all doubt that old notions of two-party conflict were false and misleading.

> Parties, it is clear, were at best vague, ephemeral and transitory, loose associations of individuals or groups who might temporarily co-operate on some of the major issues of the day, but might equally well be divided quite differently on others.

National politics, in any case, had a local dimension.

> Pride's Purge was not the straightforward outcome of the familiar party division of Presbyterians and Independents. Nor can the revolution be understood exclusively, or even mainly, in terms of parliamentary politics. To grasp its meaning it is necessary to explore the relationship between politics at the national and the grass-roots levels, between the revolution at Westminster and the

revolution in the counties and boroughs, and between the State and the local communities.

Pride's Purge, like other major events of the Interregnum, had wider social implications and highlighted different conceptions of political rights; Oliver Cromwell was 'impaled between the dictates of Providence and gentry constitutionalism'.

> Pride's Purge was both a symptom and a cause of the failure of the Puritan Revolution. The circumstances which produced it, and the way in which it was conducted, demonstrate the revolutionaries' fatal divisions, their inability to agree on a common programme. The real pressure for revolution came from the Army, the Levellers, and the sects, but the leaders who made policy both then and in the weeks that followed, shared only a few of the desires of their supporters. [44]

The Rump Parliament 1648-1653 by Blair Worden (1945-) ably complemented Underdown's earlier work and triumphantly demonstrated the value of re-exploring the politics of the English Revolution.

> The study of politics, which are both a reflection and a determinant of men's thoughts, beliefs, economic activities and social attitudes, can tell us as much about a past age as can research into its other aspects ... The problem of the political historian is not that he is working in a vacuum, but, on the contrary, that in seeking to understand political events he is seeking to understand the society which gave rise to them.

Dr Worden's main concern was with the politics of parliament — its factions and internal mechanics — rather than with the Rump's efforts at government, although he did examine the problem of why the Rump, supposedly a revolutionary body, achieved so little in the way of reform. The reason, according to Worden, was that the Rump was in fact far less revolutionary than historians, including Underdown, had supposed. Its members were largely moderates who had stayed on after the Purge simply to prevent direct military rule. The reforming impulse came from the army not from Parliament. But the Rump's 'failure' to carry through a programme of social reform ought to be placed in a longer perspective. Worden reminded his readers that:

> Seventeenth-century parliaments were never the most eager of reforming institutions. The great reformers of the earlier seventeenth

century, Cranfield, Bacon, Strafford, were all broken by parliaments. Cromwell, as Lord Protector, came — like Strafford before him — to rely on administrative rather than legislative reform, and achieved it only when parliament was in abeyance ... Seventeenth-century politicians, unlike their twentieth-century counterparts, did not normally look to state legislation as the obvious instrument of social amelioration ... Most M.P.s, whether Cavaliers or Round-heads, were apolitical in outlook, regarding political differences as of secondary importance to the preservation of the ordered world they knew, and sharing conventional and non-partisan assumptions about the ends of government.[45]

The books by Underdown and Worden were symptomatic of a general upsurge of interest in the Interregnum. For example, Ivan Roots (1921-), Professor of History at Exeter, devoted a substantial part of his useful survey of *The Great Rebellion 1642-1660* (1966) to the 1650s, in the belief that 'this decade is too readily brushed aside as a mere tottering obstacle to the inevitable Restoration of 1660'. He has since written separate studies of the early legislation of the Protectorate and of Cromwell's Major Generals.[46] Austin Woolrych (1918-), Professor of History at Lancaster, has also made an important contribution to the reinvestigation of this period in essays and articles and in his edition of volume VII of the *Complete Prose Works of John Milton* (1977).[47] The American historian Lois G. Schwoerer had a chapter on the public debate on the New Model Army in her book *'No Standing Armies!' The anti-army ideology in seventeenth-century England* (1974). Recent studies have appeared on *Cromwellian Ireland* by T.C. Barnard and on *Cromwell and the New Model Foreign Policy* by C.P. Korr. Joan Thirsk has redirected attention towards the political, economic, religious and cultural significance of the 1660 settlement in her book *The Restoration* (1976). G.E. Aylmer brought together a col-lection of essays by eminent contributors dealing with various aspects of *The Interregnum. The Quest for Settlement 1646-1660* (1972).[48]

Gerald Aylmer (1928-), a former student of Hill at Oxford and since 1962 Professor of History at the University of York, has become best known for his monumental studies of seventeenth-century administration. *The King's Servants: The Civil Service of Charles I 1625-1642* came out in 1961, and was a pioneering and experimental study of the institutions and personnel of the central government. It was, of course, a heavily detailed work aimed primarily at the specialist.

But, as Aylmer pleaded in his introduction 'details need not be dull; they can often be more interesting than generalities, besides being less misleading'.[49] Professor Aylmer's subject was not just the actual machinery of administration but those who worked the system, and he painstakingly analysed their recruitment, terms of service, social background and their political and religious allegiances.

The King's Servants, impressive though it was in its own right, was designed as a prologue to, or framework of reference for, a study of the administration of the Republic. *The State's Servants. The Civil Service of the English Republic 1649-1660* appeared in 1973 and used the same analytical techniques employed in its predecessor. Its quantitative method, however, was more sophisticated and its conclusions were even more cautious and guarded. Aylmer's second book, none the less, was more wide-ranging than *The King's Servants* and raised a number of general questions about the development of bureaucracy and its place in society. 'Institutional pressures and practices can operate causally upon the economy of a country as well as on people's ideas about government and about society.' So Aylmer contended on his first page, and his book, among other things, was an illustration of that claim. The author looked at the economic cost of government to seventeenth-century society as well as examining the financial benefits of office-holding for the administrators themselves. Aylmer's approach and method, although it was not an exact replica of either of them, clearly owed much to the combined influence of Sir Lewis Namier and R.H. Tawney. 'This is a study of the interaction between administration and politics, and of the relationship between bureaucracy and social structure,' Aylmer wrote in his introduction. [50] The book began with a largely chronological account of the institutions of republican government which looked at the successive régimes in relation to each other, to the army, and to the general quest in these years for political settlement. It moved on to deal with the terms of administrative service, and, most interesting of all, with the social biography of the republican bureaucrats themselves. It was this section, full of statistical tables, which revealed Namier's influence most clearly. Having identified a total of 1200 civil servants in the period 1649-60, Aylmer first took from them a random objective sample of 200, and then 'to concentrate attention away from those at the very top and the bottom' a subjective selection of 100 middle-rank administrators was made. Analysis of these two groups suggested that office-holding in the Interregnum was acting as 'an agent of distributive justice'. The social complexion of the administration was changing under the republic and, as in the counties, men of lower rank were becoming increasingly conspicuous in the machine of government. The notion of 'revolutionary bureaucrats' was not a contradiction in terms. A new kind of public service — with salaries going up and illicit fringe benefits being reduced — was taking shape in those years, and only the Restoration in 1660 halted its development.

One of the important component groups in the republic's administration identified in Aylmer's social analysis was that of the lawyers. Other historians, too, have been concerned with this group and several political studies of the legal profession and of the question of law reform in the seventeenth century have appeared in recent years. W.R. Prest, a former student of Christopher Hill, examined *The Inns of Court under Elizabeth I and the Early Stuarts 1590-1640* (1972). J.D. Eusden attempted an exploration of the connections between *Puritans, Lawyers and Politics in Early Seventeenth-Century England* (1956). W.J. Jones's learned volume on *Politics and the Bench. The Judges and the origins of the English Civil War* came out in 1971. The American historian Brian P. Levack published *The Civil Lawyers in England, 1603-41. A political study* (1973). The complex issue of the demand for law reform in the English Revolution attracted two studies by S.E. Prall and Donald Veall.[51]

Administrative history is not exclusively history 'from above' and its writing does not necessarily embody a 'right-wing' bias. (Aylmer's *State's Servants*, full of biographical information, included a brief self-portrait of its author as 'middle-aged, middle-class, middle of the road'.)[52] But certainly another unmistakable strand in recent writing on the political history of the English Revolution has been the development — partly under Marxist stimulus — of the new perspective of history 'from below'. Christopher Hill's *The World Turned Upside Down* (see p.109) was a superb example of the genre, and in its exploration of radical ideas during the English Revolution dealt with groups such as the Levellers and Diggers, Ranters, and Quakers, and with the enhanced role of women encouraged by extreme forms of puritanism. Others have shared Dr Hill's interest in these fields. Roger Thompson, for example, attempted a comparative study of *Women in Stuart England and America* (1974), while Keith Thomas examined 'Women and the Civil War Sects' and Patricia Higgins women petitioners to Parliament.[53] A.L. Morton shed light on *The World of the Ranters* (1970), while Hugh Barbour published a study of *The Quakers in Puritan England* (1964). W.A. Cole wrote a stimulating article on 'The Quakers and the English Revolution'.[54] A considerable body of literature has accumulated dealing with the Levellers and Diggers. New editions of their debates and tracts have appeared, and their political, religious and economic significance has been reassessed.[55] Popular pressures, popular involvement in seventeenth-century politics have also been dealt with in two recent and important studies by Derek Hirst and Brian Manning, the first a work of pathfinding research and the other a stimulating reinterpretation.

The Representative of the People? Voters and Voting in England under the Early Stuarts by Derek Hirst (1948-) dealt with a theme which his own mentor, J.H. Plumb, had first begun to open up.[56] Based on a formidably large research effort in the archives using parliamentary journals, private correspondence, corporation records and surviving voting lists, Dr Hirst argued that popular participation in politics was much greater than historians had allowed.

> Both in the numbers of people voting, in the relative freedom with which they voted and the kind of issues they voted on, and the responsiveness of members of the House to outside pressures, there was some justification for Parliament's claims to be representative. Before the reaction consequent on the mid-century troubles set in, and when under the early Stuarts the political consensus and the workings of patronage broke down, genuine consultations took place with large numbers of ordinary people.[57]

Politics under the early Stuarts, Dr Hirst found, were not simply élite politics. Both the number of elections and the number of election contests were increasing in this period. Constituency pressures were exerted on M.P.s after their election. There were more voters than previously. In the countryside the simple process of inflation brought more men into the fold of the forty shilling freeholders at a time when in any case the electoral definition of 'freehold' was becoming more flexible. A number of borough franchises were formally widened by the House of Commons, often for tactical reasons, in the 1620s. Enlarged electorates, it was widely felt, were less amenable to royal, and later Royalist, pressures and intimidation. Moreover, in Dr Hirst's words, 'a state of franchisal innocence' existed in the early seventeenth century which meant that the commons could take advantage of

uncertainties about franchise qualifications and election management
and exercise the vote whether or not they were so entitled. (Polling was
unpopular with candidates and electors alike because of the time it
took.) Both in town and countryside, then, voters were no longer a
small, respectable minority; York's freemen franchise, for example,
meant in practice that 75 per cent of the adult male population had
the vote. By 1640, in Hirst's estimate, over the country as a whole, the
electorate must have consisted of 27-40 per cent of adult males.[58]

An enlarged electorate, of course, brought more people into direct
contact with the political process and, certainly by 1640, with national
issues, and it meant increasingly that votes had to be won and could
not be automatically relied upon.

> The common people were certainly actively involved in national
> political affairs by this time [1640] ... The political passions and
> interests of the populace could be a powerful factor ... The most
> common issues (such as opposition to royal taxation) were the ones
> most likely to gain the widest support ... The Crown's financial
> problems not only ensured that Parliament survived as an institu-
> tion, but also that significant developments took place in the
> relationship between the country and its representatives.

Partly due to the pressure of the commons themselves, and partly due
to gentry willingness to use that pressure against the King, the popular
presence was one of the most crucial elements in the political situation
of 1640-1.[59]

Although quite accidentally, in a real sense Brian Manning's *The
English People and the English Revolution 1640-1649* (1976) followed
on from where Hirst's book left off. His starting point was the
elections of 1640 in which the political consequences of an enlarged
electorate were unmistakably revealed.

> This enlarged electorate was less easy for the gentry to control and
> more capable of asserting its own opinions ... Political and religious
> questions became issues in the contests partly because of the inter-
> vention of the lower classes.

Dr Manning (1927-), a radical himself, a former student of
Christopher Hill and since 1959 in the History Department at
Manchester University, concentrated on 'the middle sort of people'
and set out 'to discover the role of popular grievances, popular
movements and popular aspirations in the revolutionary struggles of

the decade 1640 to 1649'. Initially popular discontent focused on the trial of Strafford, and the death of the King's hated minister was a popular triumph. The aftermath, Dr Manning continued, was a growing split in parliament between those who reacted against the popular presence and those who responded and accommodated themselves to it. On the one hand the Royalist party 'arose from dislike of popular tumults: it was less the party of episcopalians or Straffordians than the party of order'. On the other hand, the Parliamentarian party in 1641 was a popular party whose members saw that popular support was essential if moderate reform was to be grasped from an obdurate King. The popular party, however, 'would ally with the people with the aim of drawing the teeth of popular movements, so as to ensure the safety of the ruling class'.[60]

Popular attitudes and intervention, Dr Manning argued, were one of the principal determinants of the English Revolution. It was the intervention of 'the mass of the ordinary people of London', a political move although it was fuelled by economic distress, which saved Parliament in the dark December days of 1641. 'The City was now the Parliament's — or rather the Parliament was now the City's.' 'The Royalists were right in thinking that their most formidable opponent was the ordinary citizen of London.' The grievances of urban craftsmen against restrictive practices and monopolies forcefully penetrated the Parliament's cause.

> Whatever reservations wealthy M.P.s may have had, and did have, about such movements for the reform of town governments and for a greater measure of democracy, they found it expedient to support and lead such movements, and so the cause of the parliamentary opposition to the crown came to be identified with opposition to the urban oligarchies and with a movement for a wider franchise.

In the countryside, there was agitation over tenures and enclosures directed against landlords of whom, of course, the Crown was the largest.

> It was natural that the aggrieved peasants should have identified themselves with the Commons against crown and peers ... Thus the unpopularity of landlords and the decline of loyalty to landlords affected the king in the civil war more adversely than parliament, because he depended far more than parliament on the loyalty of peasants to their lords; and the erosion or disappearance of that

loyalty in many parts of the countryside restricted the amount of support and resources the king and the royalist nobility and gentry could command.[61]

Above all, it was popular intervention which transformed the whole character of events of the 1640s by introducing a growing note of social rebellion.

> The mere fact of the involvement of the people changed political conflicts and religious antagonisms into social conflicts and class antagonisms ... As the war went on, parliamentarians increasingly came to see the conflict, not so much as a struggle against the king, but as a struggle against the aristocracy.

With puritanism as their ideology, the middle ranks were a force to be reckoned with.

> Puritanism taught the middle sort of people to think for themselves and to assert their independence against King, lords and bishops. Godliness gave them status and the ability to express their identity as a separate class; and it enabled them to formulate and dignify their hostility towards the ruling class.[62]

As all restraints broke down, the English Revolution came to express basic social conflicts, which were articulated most clearly by the Levellers in their assault on the combination of wealth, power and privilege and in their demands for decentralization. To see the Levellers as in some way 'ahead of their time', as an older school of historians once argued, largely misses the point. The Levellers were very much a part of their time and can only be properly understood in relation to it. Moreover, the impact and failure of such groups explain a great deal about the English Revolution as a whole. The views from the top and from the centre might be more breathtaking but they are none the less limited. It is an encouraging sign that modern historians of the politics of this period, as the books by Dr Hirst and Dr Manning make abundantly clear, are not now concerned solely with the winners. As Barrington Moore (see p.148) has written,

> For all students of human society, sympathy with the victims of historical processes and scepticism about the victor's claims provide essential safeguards against being taken in by the dominant mythology. A scholar who tries to be objective needs these feelings as part of his ordinary working equipment.[63]

Chapter 9

The twentieth century: new perspectives and re-definitions

Before we explain why the English Revolution happened, we should ask again whether it ever did happen. (Conrad Russell, *Times Higher Education Supplement*, 8 March 1974.)

Recent writing on the seventeenth-century crisis in England has evinced a growing concern with *concepts* of revolution. This concern has taken several distinct forms in which historians have shown an increasing willingness to look at the events of the mid-seventeenth century from different angles and to avail themselves of the critical skills of other disciplines. At one level there has been an exploration of the ideologies, cyclical theories, and expectations of rebellion or resistance entertained by contemporaries themselves in the seventeenth century. Peter Laslett, for example, in his pre-historical demography days, pleaded for a re-examination of the meaning of the term *revolution* for men in the seventeenth century.[1] In a subsequent article on 'The Concept of Revolution in Seventeenth-Century England', Vernon Snow stressed the predominance of the scientific usage of the term in that period. Snow contended that 'political commentators and theorists were among the last to adopt the notion of revolution'. Hobbes, for instance, did not use the term in a political sense, preferring 'revolt', 'rebellion' or 'overturning'. John Locke made use of it only twice, and by 'revolution' in fact meant a complete cycle of political change including a restoration. 'He is confident that the majority of English people will take two looks backward before taking one step forward. Revolutions, therefore, are natural and justifiable, and need not be feared.'[2] G.M. Straka, like Snow, also emphasized the primacy of traditional and inherited principles as motivating forces in the seventeenth century, and warned that historians ran the risk of distorting the original reality in their 'search for nascent modernity'.[3]

Approaching the question of the concept of revolution from another direction, an attempt has been made to compare political and social development in England with what was happening elsewhere in Europe in that period. J.P. Cooper's interesting essay on 'Differences between English and continental governments in the early seventeenth century' was a case in point.[4] In particular, a macro-approach to the English Revolution has been attempted, locating it within the context of a general cisis of the seventeenth century, affecting countries such as France, Spain, the Netherlands, Sweden and Russia. R.B. Merriman's *Six Contemporaneous Revolutions* (1938) was the first instalment in the modern debate on the subject, and the theme was taken up again in the 1950s and early 60s in articles in *Past and Present*.[5] Eric Hobsbawm and H.R. Trevor-Roper, both historians with an indefatigable capacity for meaningful generalization, were the leading participants in this historical controversy, and they offered economic and political explanations respectively. Hobsbawm, in his articles published in 1954, suggested that:

> The European economy passed through a 'General Crisis' during the seventeenth century, the last phase of the general transition from a feudal to a capitalist economy ... The seventeenth-century crisis ... led to as fundamental a solution of the difficulties which had previously stood in the way of the triumph of capitalism as that system will permit.[6]

Trevor-Roper, on the other hand, argued that the General Crisis of the Seventeenth Century was a crisis — aggravated by war — in the relations between society and the parasitically bureaucratized Renaissance state. The crisis in England was so much more serious than in other countries because England had the 'most brittle, most overgrown, most rigid court of all', a political system untouched by antecedent partial reforms and one made intolerable by 'a fatal lack of political skill' in the country's rulers. 'Instead of the genius of Richelieu, the suppleness of Mazarin, there was the irresponsibility of Buckingham, the violence of Strafford, the undeviating universal pedantry of Laud.'[7] The provocative nature of the original articles as well as the intrinsic importance of the subject combined to attract further contributions to the debate which is still going on at the present time.[8] It must be admitted, however, that most historians of the English Revolution in this country still approach it in a fairly insular fashion. Membership of the European Economic Community has so far had limited historiographical consequences.

At yet another level, the seventeenth-century crisis in England has figured in a number of comparative studies of the major revolutions of the Western world. For example, the Harvard political scientist, Crane Brinton (1898-1968), looked at seventeenth-century England, eighteenth-century America and France, and twentieth-century Russia, with a view to tracing some of the obvious uniformities in the development and structure of revolutionary crises. The series of common features he identified in his book *The Anatomy of Revolution* were those of economic change, growing status and class antagonisms, the presence of groups of alienated intellectuals, inept and insecure ruling élites, and failures in government finance.[9]

Another American writer, the sociologist Barrington Moore Jnr (1913-   ) surveyed the English Revolution in connection with his work on the *Social Origins of Dictatorship and Democracy. Lord and Peasant in the Making of the Modern World.* Looking at seventeenth- and eighteenth-century England, the French Revolution, the American Civil War, and twentieth-century Asia, Moore's aims were 'to understand the role of the landed upper classes and the peasants in the bourgeois revolutions leading to capitalist democracy, the abortive bourgeois revolutions leading to fascism, and the peasant revolutions leading to communism'. These were the three main routes to the modern world identified by the author and, at a methodological level, he vigorously defended the value of the broad generalizations which resulted from such a wide-ranging survey.

> In the effort to understand the history of a specific country a comparative perspective can lead to asking very useful and some-times new questions. There are further advantages. Comparisons can serve as a rough negative check on accepted historical explana-tions. And a comparative approach may lead to new historical generalizations ... Generalizations that are sound resemble a large-scale map of an extended terrain, such as an airplane pilot might use in crossing a continent. Such maps are essential for some purposes just as more detailed maps are necessary for others.

Although, unavoidably in a work conceived on such a massive scale, labels and blanket descriptions were frequently used, Moore himself was ready to admit the deficiencies of such terminology.

The central difficulty is that such expressions as bourgeois revolution and peasant revolution lump together indiscriminately those who make the revolution and its beneficiaries. Likewise these terms confuse the legal and political results of revolution with social groups active in them.[10]

Barrington Moore's book provided evidence of the application of sociological models to the study of the English Revolution. Other works by the American political scientist Michael Walzer (1935-) and by Peter Laslett (1915-), of the Cambridge Group for the History of Population and Social Structure, were equally revealing from that point of view. The English edition of Walzer's volume on *The Revolution of the Saints. A study in the origins of radical politics* came out in 1966 and clearly owed much to the stimulus provided by the works of Max Weber. It attracted a great deal of attention on two fronts, firstly as a provocative reinterpretation of English puritanism, and secondly as a contribution to the sociology of revolution in general. Stressing the roles of the clergy (as intellectuals), and the gentry (as patrons) rather than Christopher Hill's 'middling sort of people', Walzer presented puritanism as a kind of politico-theological response to the neuroses of a sixteenth-century society bewildered by the consequences of population increase, inflation, the discovery of the New World, and by the Reformation break with the past.

Calvinism in its sixteenth- and seventeenth-century forms was not so much the cause of this or that modern economic, political, or administrative system as it was an agent of modernization, an ideology of the transition period. And as the conditions of crisis and upheaval in which Calvinism was conceived and developed did not persist, so Calvinism as an integral and creative force did not endure ... The very existence and spread of Puritanism in the years before the revolution surely suggest the presence in English society of an acute fear of disorder and 'wickedness' — a fear ... attendant upon the transformation of the old political and social order. The [later] triumph of Lockeian ideas, on the other hand, suggests the overcoming of anxiety, the appearance of saints and citizens for whom sin is no longer a problem.

Walzer's conclusion was a model of radical politics that easily lent itself, so he believed, to comparison with the French and Russian Revolutions. Ideological equivalents of English puritanism — and by that (in the context of the Civil War itself) it is clear that Walzer meant Independency — were thrust up by the logic of later revolutionary situations, similar in many respects to that in seventeenth-century England.

> All forms of radical politics make their appearance at moments of rapid and decisive change, moments when customary status is in doubt and character (or 'identity') is itself a problem. Before Puritans, Jacobins, or Bolsheviks attempt the creation of a new order, they must create new men ... There is a point in the modernization process when large numbers of men, suddenly masterless, seek a rigid self-control; when they discover new purposes, dream of a new order, organize their lives for disciplined and methodical activity. These men are prospective saints and citizens; for them Puritanism, Jacobinism, and Bolshevism are appropriate options. At this point in time, they are likely options.[11]

The range and purpose of Peter Laslett's *The World We Have Lost* (1965; 2nd ed. 1971) were very different, and it would probably be true to say that no other recent study of seventeenth-century society has received such a mixed reception. The main concern of Laslett's enquiry was with social organization and social relationships (especially in the family), and the book itself was designed as a manifesto announcing a new kind of sociological history and as a counterblast to the blinkered preoccupations of traditional historians. [12] To help him in this daunting task Laslett availed himself of the work of a number of distinguished sociologists, Dahrendorf, Durkheim, Runciman and Weber, together with that of the anthropologist Gluckman. The major part of Laslett's book dealt with historical demography and so falls outside the present study. But *The World We Have Lost* has a place in the recent historiography of the English Revolution by virtue first of Laslett's notion of a 'one class society', and second his reappraisal of the seventeenth-century crisis in the light of long-term trends in English social development.

By a 'one-class society' Laslett meant that only the élite was 'capable of concerted action over a whole area of society'. 'To exercise power, then, to be free of the society of England, to count at all as an active agent in the record we call historical, you had to be a gentleman ... *England* in the pre-industrial era meant a small minority of the English, small, select, and special.'[13] It was to this idea of a 'one-class society' that Christopher Hill took strongest exception.

Sir Lewis Namier used to speak of Mr Laslett's 'ruling minority' in eighteenth-century England as 'the political nation'. But that great historian would never have made the mistake of denying existence to those excluded from politics. Mr Laslett is simply succumbing to the illusion of the epoch which he is describing. That 'the minority lived for all the rest' (p.52) is no doubt what they themselves believed. It has needed a lot of hard work by historians to demonstrate that the 'subsumption' of the lower orders in their betters was not a 'fact' but a piece of ideological propaganda.[14]

Hill was no more impressed with Laslett's argument that the English Revolution, in the conventional sense, was largely a figment of historians' imaginations. The notion, Laslett contended, rested on the unproven assumption that great events must have had great causes. The reviewer in the *Times Literary Supplement* reacted in the same way as Hill to that part of Laslett's book.

Mr Laslett's great hypothesis appears to be that the English Revolution did not take place, because no mention of it can be found in the parish registers. The only kind of change which merits the term 'revolution' is one which effects substantial change in familial and social structure: and only industrialization has done this.[15]

Certainly Laslett played down the *social* significance of the English Revolution and dealt directly with the history of these years only in a kind of optional chapter (chapter 7) which readers could safely skip if they so wished. So far as Laslett was concerned there was no question of the English Revolution rotating around any form of class struggle, although there was social mobility in the seventeenth century.

The truth is that changes in English society between the reign of Elizabeth and the reign of Anne were not revolutionary ... Once it is recognized that the rise-of-a-capitalist-class interpretation can be misleading as well as informative, and that social mobility was present in the traditional world, then the idea of a social revolution however occasioned becomes an embarrassment rather than a help towards understanding political breakdown.[16]

In one sense, therefore, 'the world we have lost', in Laslett's view, was a world obscured by historians.

To Christopher Hill, *The World We Have Lost* was an unconvincing advertisement for the marriage of history with sociology. Other historians, however, have continued to emphasize the potential benefits to historians of looking beyond the methodological frontiers of their own discipline. Lawrence Stone, for example, has argued strongly that:

> In attacking the problem of revolution, as most others of major significance in history, we historians should think twice before we spurn the help offered by our colleagues in the social sciences, who have, as it happens, been particularly active in the last few years in theorizing about the typology, causes, and evolutionary patterns of this particular phenomenon.

The quotation comes from Stone's book *The Causes of the English Revolution*. The route taken in this study to the seventeenth-century crisis in England was by way of a general exploration of theories of revolution, in which the six-fold typology of Chalmers Johnson's *Revolution and the Social System* (1964) and *Social Change* (1966) was given an important place. 'This is much the most satisfactory classification we have so far,' Stone wrote. 'It is one that working historians can recognize and use with profit.' Stone's own approach to the English Revolution, involving a classified model of presuppositions, preconditions, precipitants, and triggers, clearly owed much to Johnson's work and to that of other political sociologists such as Eckstein, Olson, and Davies.[17]

> The history of history, as well as of science, shows that advances depend partly on the accumulation of factual information, but rather more on the formulation of hypotheses that reveal the hidden relationships and common properties of apparently distinct phenomena. For all their faults, social scientists can supply a corrective to the antiquarian fact-grubbing to which historians are so prone; they can direct attention to problems of general relevance, and away from the sterile triviality of so much historical research; they can ask new questions and suggest new ways of looking at old ones; they can supply new categories, and as a result may suggest new ideas.[18]

The vitality of history, as Tawney constantly emphasized, depends above all on its questioning approach to the past. From this stem both the research and the debates without which the study of history would lose its essential momentum and be exposed to the dangers of dogmatism, unfounded hypotheses or to the tyranny of established 'facts'. Fortunately, the debate on the English Revolution, already three centuries old, shows no sign of subsiding. The period remains almost as controversial today as it was in the seventeenth century, though of course for different reasons. Since the study of history is inseparably connected with social change, accepted definitions of the scope and possibilities of the subject have themselves altered enormously over time. Clarendon saw history as a route to political wisdom. Eighteenth-century Whigs and Tories used it as a weapon in their own contemporary political struggles. Gardiner tried (ultimately unsuccessfully) to take history out of the noise of current controversies into the secluded calm of academic detachment. Tawney proclaimed the need for a new kind of present-mindedness and urged the relevance of the humane concerns of social history. The transformation of history still continues. As new evidence becomes available, as new techniques of analysis are developed, as monographs proliferate still further, as different assumptions come into play, and as changing contemporary preoccupations go on helping to shift historical emphasis, the debate on the English Revolution seems certain to be prolonged. New questions will be posed as historians critically assess their predecessors' answers and explanations. In the nature of things, historians will never produce interpretations that are valid for all time. As R.H. Tawney, one of the greatest of them, once remarked, 'all flesh is grass, and historians, poor things, wither more quickly than most'.

Notes

The following abbreviations are used in the notes:

A.H.R.   *American Historical Review*
B.I.H.R.   *Bulletin of the Institute of Historical Research*
Ec.H.R.   *Economic History Review*
E.H.R.   *English Historical Review*
Hist. Jnl.   *Historical Journal*
J.M.H.   *Journal of Modern History*
P.P.   *Past and Present*
T.H.E.S.   *Times Higher Education Supplement*
T.L.S.   *Times Literary Supplement*
T.R.H.S.   *Transactions of the Royal Historical Society*

Preface

1 E.H. Carr, *What is History?* (Harmondsworth, Penguin Books, 1964), pp. 23, 44.

2 D. Forbes (ed.), *David Hume: The History of Great Britain. The Reigns of James I and Charles I* (Harmondsworth, Penguin Books, 1970), p. 18.

3 Pieter Geyl, *Napoleon For and Against* (London, Cape, 1949), p. 15.

4 On the historiography of the Revolution of 1688 see J.R. Jones, *The Revolution of 1688 in England* (London, Weidenfeld, 1973) and M. Ashley, 'King James II and the Revolution of 1688: some reflections on the historiography', in H.E. Bell and R.L. Ollard (eds), *Historical Essays 1600-1750 Presented to David Ogg* (London, Black, 1963).

Chapter 1

1 Quoted in R. MacGillivray, *Restoration Historians and the English Civil War* (The Hague, Martinus Nijhoff, 1974), p. 19.
2 Quoted *ibid.*, p.41.
3 F.S. Fussner, *The Historical Revolution. English Historical Writing and Thought 1580-1640* (London, Routledge, 1962).
4 Ibid., *op cit.* esp. pp. 44-59; P. Burke, *The Renaissance Sense of the Past* (London, Arnold, 1969), *passim*; L.B. Wright, *Middle Class Culture in Elizabethan England* (1935; reissued London, Methuen, 1964), esp. pp. 297-338.
5 Fussner, *op. cit.*, pp. 253-74; M. McKisack, *Medieval History in the Tudor Age* (Oxford, Clarendon Press, 1971); P. Styles, 'Politics and historical research in the early seventeenth century', in L. Fox (ed.), *English Historical Scholarship in the Sixteenth and Seventeenth Centuries* (London, O.U.P. for the Dugdale Society, 1956); C.C.G. Tite, *Impeachment and Parliamentary Judicature in Early Stuart England* (London, Athlone Press, 1974), pp. 24-53.
6 J.G.A. Pocock, *The Ancient Constitution and the Feudal Law. A Study of Historical Thought in the Seventeenth Century* (Cambridge, C.U.P., 1957), *passim*.
7 See J.P.D. Dunbabin, 'Oliver Cromwell's popular image in the nineteenth century', in J.S. Bromley & E.H. Kossmann (eds), *Britain and the Netherlands*, vol. V (The Hague, Martinus Nijhoff, 1976).
8 See H. Butterfield, *The Whig Interpretation of History* (London, Bell, 1931).
9 Compare the reviews of Brian Manning's book on *The English People and the English Revolution* (1976) by John Miller in the T.H.E.S., 28 May 1976, p. 16, and by Christopher Hill in *The Spectator*, 3 July 1976, pp. 21-22.
10 Burckhardt, *Judgements on History and Historians* ed. H.R. Trevor-Roper (London, Allen & Unwin, 1959), p. 158.

Chapter 2

1 T. Fuller, *The Church History of Britain*, ed. J. Nicholls (London, 1842), vol. III, pp. 160, 150.
2 Quoted in Fuller, *An Appeal of Injured Innocence*, p. 46.
3 Puritanism continues to be a controversial subject in the twentieth

century. See C.H. George, 'Puritanism as history and historio-graphy', P.P., 41 (1968), and M.G. Finlayson, 'Puritanism and puritans: labels or libels?', *Canadian Jnl of History*, VIII (1973).

4 C.H. Firth in 'The development of the study of seventeenth-century history', *T.R.H.S.*, 3rd series, VII (1913) lists these early writers on the English Revolution. On the development of the Press in this period see J. Frank, *The Beginnings of the English Newspaper 1620-1660* (Cambridge, Mass., Harvard U.P., 1961).

5 Quoted in H.R. Trevor-Roper, *Clarendon and the Practice of History* (Los Angeles, William Andrews Clark Memorial Library, 1965), pp. 38-9.

6 T. May, *History of the Parliament of England*, ed. F. Maseres (London, 1812), pp. xvii, xix.

7 *Ibid.*, pp. 6, 4.

8 T. May, *A Breviary of the History of the Parliament of England* (London, 1650), p. 2.

9 T. May, *History of the Parliament of England, op. cit.*, p. 15.

10 See P. Styles, 'Politics and history in the early seventeenth century' in L. Fox (ed.), *English Historical Scholarship in the Sixteenth and Seventeenth Centuries* (London, O.U.P. for the Dugdale Society, 1956); J.G.A. Pocock, *The Ancient Constitution and the Feudal Law. A Study of English Historical Theory in the Seventeenth Century* (Cambridge, C.U.P. 1957); C. Hill, 'The Norman Yoke' in *Puritanism and Revolution* (London, Secker and Warburg, 1958), and Q. Skinner 'History and ideology in the English Revolution', *Hist. Jnl*, VIII (1965).

11 There is a modern facsimile reprint of Sprigge's scarce work edited by H.T. Moore (Gainsville, Florida, Scholars' Facsimiles and Reprints, 1960).

12 J. Vicars, *England's Parliamentarie Chronicle* (1644-6), pp. 31-2; C. Walker, *History of Independency* (1648) quoted in R. MacGillivray, *Restoration Historians and the English Civil War*, (The Hague, Martinus Nijhoff, 1974), p. 237.

13 S.B. Liljegren (ed.), *James Harrington's Oceana* (Lund and Heidelberg, Publications of the New Society of Letters at Lund, 1924), p. 135.

14 P. Zagorin, *History of Political Thought in the English Revolution* (London, Routledge, 1954), p. 145.

15 E. Bernstein, *Cromwell and Communism* (London, Allen & Unwin, 1930), pp. 192-211; A.L. Morton, *The English Utopia*

(London, Lawrence and Wishart, 1952), pp. 75-6; C.B. Macpherson, 'Harrington's Opportunity State', *P.P.*, 17 (1960); Pocock, *Ancient Constitution and the Feudal Law, op. cit.*, p. 141.

16 C. Hill, 'James Harrington and the People', *Puritanism and Revolution, op. cit.*, p. 300. See also F. Raab, *The English Face of Machiavelli* (London, Routledge, 1964), and J.G.A. Pocock, 'James Harrington and the Good Old Cause', *Jnl of British Studies*, IX (1970).

17 Published in *Proceedings of the British Academy*, XXVII (1941); reprinted in Lucy S. Sutherland, (ed.), *Studies in History. British Academy Lectures*, (London, O.U.P. 1966).

18 Liljegren (ed.), *Harrington's Oceana, op. cit.*, pp. 54-5, 53, 49-50.

19 See C. Blitzer, *An Immortal Commonwealth. The Political Thought of James Harrington* (New Haven, Conn., Yale U.P., 1960).

20 The dedication was later suppressed.

21 For a brief account of Rushworth's career as a bureaucrat see G.E. Aylmer, *The State's Servants. The Civil Service of the English Republic* (London, Routledge, 1973), p. 260.

22 J. Nalson, *Impartial Collection of the Great Affairs of State from the Beginning of the Scotch Rebellion in the Year 1639 to the Murder of King Charles I* (1682-3), pp. i-iii, iv, vi, xxii, xxv, lxxvii-viii.

23 See Pocock, *The Ancient Constitution and the Feudal Law, op. cit.*, ch. 8.

24 W. Dugdale, *Short View of the Late Troubles in England* (1681), preface.

25 *Ibid.*, pp. 391, preface, 62, 649-50.

26 F. Tonniës (ed.), *Behemoth or the Long Parliament*, 2nd edn, with an introduction by M.M. Goldsmith (London, Cass, 1969), p. 45.

27 *Ibid.*, p. xiv.

28 C.B. Macpherson, *The Political Theory of Possessive Individualism.* (London, O.U.P.). On Hobbes as a historian see R. MacGillivray, 'Thomas Hobbes's History of the English Civil War: a study of Behemoth', *Jnl of the History of Ideas*, XXXI (1970), and J.G.A. Pocock, 'Time, history and eschatology in the thought of Thomas Hobbes', *Politics, Language and Time. Essays on Political Thought and History* (London, Methuen, 1972).

29 Macpherson, *Political Theory, op. cit.*, p. 65; Tonniës (ed.), Hobbes *Behemoth, op. cit.*, pp. 4, 25, 110, 126.

30 Tonniës (ed.), *Behemoth, op. cit.*, pp. 77, 125, 112.
31 Quoted in M.M. Goldsmith, *Hobbes's Science of Politics* (New York, Columbia U.P.), p. 241.
32 Tonniës (ed.), *Behemoth, op. cit.*, pp. 95, 46, 49-50.
33 S.I. Mintz, *The Hunting of Leviathan* (Cambridge, C.U.P., 1962), p. 47.
34 Tonniës (ed.), *Behemoth, op. cit.*, p. 58.
35 *Ibid.*, p. 1.
36 On the opposition to Hobbes see J. Bowle, *Hobbes and His Critics,* (London, Cape, 1951).
37 A.J. Grant (ed.), *English Historians* (London, Blackie, 1906) p. xx.
38 C.H. Firth discussed the structure and composition of Clarendon's *History* in three articles in the *E.H.R.*, XX (1904), pp. 26-54, 246-62, 464-83. The most recent study of the historian is B.H.G. Wormald, *Clarendon, Politics, Historiography, and Religion, 1640-1660* (Cambridge, C.U.P., 1964).
39 C. Hill, 'Lord Clarendon and the Puritan Revolution', *Puritanism and Revolution* (London, Secker and Warburg, 1958), p. 214.
40 G. Huehns (ed.), *Selections from Clarendon* (Oxford, Clarendon Press. The World's Classics, 1955), pp. 2-3, 5-6. The standard edition of Clarendon is by W.D. Macray (six vols, Oxford, Clarendon Press, 1888), but for greater convenience all quotations from the *History of the Rebellion* in this chapter have been taken from the World's Classics volume of selections.
41 *Selections from Clarendon, op. cit.*, pp. 1-3.
42 *Ibid.*, pp. 6-7, 316-17.
43 *Ibid.*, pp. 100-1.
44 *Ibid.*, p. 147.
45 *Ibid.*, pp. 103, 115-16, 118.
46 *Ibid.*, pp. 49-50.
47 *Ibid.*, pp. 166, 167, 170.
48 *Ibid.*, pp. 305-6, 355-8.
49 *Ibid.*, pp. 123-4, 317, 358.
50 *Ibid.*, pp. 253-4.
51 C.H. Firth, *Essays Historical and Literary* (Oxford, Clarendon Press, 1938), p. 119.
52 H.R. Trevor-Roper, *Clarendon and the Practice of History* (Los Angeles, William Andrews Clark Memorial Library, 1965), p. 48.

Chapter 3

1 The *Reliquae Baxterianae* (in Sylvester's edition) appeared in 1696, while the memoirs of the republican Edmund Ludlow followed two years later.

2 Clarendon, *History of the Rebellion* (1702-4) III, dedication.

3 The Gibbon quotation appears in the introduction by Duncan Forbes to Hume, *History of Great Britain. The Reigns of James I and Charles I* (Harmondsworth, Penguin, 1970) p. 43. On the political background see G. Holmes, *British Politics in the Age of Anne* (London, Macmillan, 1967); G. Holmes (ed.), *Britain after the Glorious Revolution. 1689-1714* (London, Macmillan, 1969); and also R. Willman, 'The origins of "Whig" and "Tory" in English political language', *Hist. Jnl*, XVII (1974).

4 A.G. Matthews, *Calamy Revised* (Oxford, Clarendon Press, 1934) p. xix.

5 A.G. Matthews, *Walker Revised* (Oxford, Clarendon Press, 1948), p.xi. Walker's attack on Calamy continued in 1719 with the publication of *The Church and the Dissenters Compared as to Persecution*, to which Calamy replied in 1727 with his *Continuation of the Account*. Daniel Neal's *History of the Puritans* (1732-8) was similarly defensive.

6 L. Echard, *History of England* (1707-18), vol. I, p. 980.

7 *Ibid.*, vol. II, p. 8.

8 Calamy, *A Letter to Mr Archdeacon Echard upon Occasion of his History of England* (London, 1718), pp. 11, 66, 62.

9 J. Oldmixon, *Critical History of England* (London, 2 vols, 1724, 1730) vol. I, pp. iii-iv.

10 *Ibid.*, vol. I, pp. 170, 200.

11 *Ibid.*, vol. II, pp. ii, 128, 217-18.

12 Oldmixon, *History of England during the Reigns of the Royal House of Stuart* (1730) pp. iv. vii, viii.

13 *Ibid.*, p. vii.

14 Rapin, *Impartial History of England*, (London, 2 vols, 1784), vol. I, p. 464.

15 *Ibid.*, vol. I, pp. 599, 800.

16 T. Carte, *A General Account of the Necessary Materials for an History of England* (London, 1738), p. 2.

17 T. Carte, *General History of England* (London, 1747-55), vol. III, p. 703, vol. IV, p.1.

18 *Ibid.*, Vol. IV, pp. 383, 403.
19 Kennett was attacked for his Whiggery by Roger North in his *Examen or an Inquiry into the Credit and Veracity of a Pretended Complete History, viz Dr White Kennett's History of England* (London, 1740); G.V. Bennett, *White Kennett* (London, S.P.C.K., 1957), p. 173.
20 W. Kennett, *Complete History of England* (1706), pp. 85, 141.
21 *Ibid.*, pp. 1, 2.
22 *Ibid.*, pp. 16, 18, 20.
23 I. Kramnick, 'Augustan politics and English historiography: the debate on the English past, 1730-35', *History and Theory*, VI (1967) and the same author's *Bolingbroke and his Circle: the Politics of Nostalgia in the Age of Walpole* (Cambridge, Mass., Harvard U.P., 1968). See also W.A. Speck, 'Political propaganda in Augustan England', *T.R.H.S.*, 5th series, XXII (1972), esp. pp. 24-7.
24 *London Journal*, 740, (1 September 1733), quoted in Kramnick, 'Augustan politics'; *op. cit.*, p. 41.
25 Hume, *op. cit.*, (1793 edn), VIII, p. 321.
26 Quoted in M. Belgion, *David Hume* (London, Longmans for The British Council and the National Book League, 1965), p. 5.
27 Hume, *Essays, Moral, Political and Literary* (London, Grant Richards. The World's Classics, 1903), p. 611.
28 Introduction to Hume, *History of Great Britain. The Reigns of James I and Charles I* (Harmondsworth, Penguin, 1970), p. 33. The text in this reprint is that of the comparatively rare first edition of 1754, originally designed to stand by itself and only later integrated into a complete history. See also D. Forbes, *Hume's Philosophical Politics* (Cambridge, C.U.P., 1975) which contains a stimulating discussion of Hume's *History*.
29 Hume, *op. cit.*, (ed. Forbes), pp. 396, 391.
30 Hume, *op. cit.* (1793 ed.), VIII, p. 323; quoted by H.R. Trevor-Roper, 'Hume as a Historian' in D.F. Pears (ed.), *David Hume: A Symposium* (London, Macmillan, 1963), p. 90.
31 Hume, *op. cit.* (ed. Forbes), pp. 502-3.
32 *Ibid.*, pp. 328-9. J.B. Black in his useful book *The Art of History* (London, Methuen, 1926), p. 113, contrasted the abusive adjectives with which Hume described the Parliamentarians and puritans with his sympathetic treatment of the Royalists.
33 Caroline Robbins, *The Eighteenth-Century Commonwealthman*

(New York, Atheneum, 1968); J.G.A. Pocock, 'Machiavelli, Harrington and English Eighteenth-Century Ideologies' in *Politics, Language and Time* (London, Methuen, 1972).

34 'Catherine Macaulay and the Seventeenth Century', *Welsh History Review*, (*Essays presented to David Williams*), vol. III (1967).

35 Catherine Macaulay, *History of England from the Accession of James I to that of the Brunswick Line* (1763-83), vol. I, p. viii.

36 *Ibid.*, vol. I, pp. 267, 350, 365.

37 *Ibid.*, vol. II, pp. 481, 220.

38 *Ibid.*, vol. IV, pp. 433-4.

Chapter 4

1 See T.P. Peardon, *The Transition in English Historial Writing 1760-1830* (New York, Columbia U.P., 1933).

2 Besides the article in the *D.N.B.*, there is some discussion of one side of Rutt's work in R.V. Holt, *The Unitarian Contribution to Social Progress in England* (London, The Lindsey Press, 1952), pp. 79, 82, 135.

3 J.T. Rutt, (ed.), *The Diary of Thomas Burton* (London, 1828), preface. Rutt also issued, in 1829, an edition of Edmund Calamy's autobiography. The seventeenth-century volumes in Cobbett's *Parliamentary History of England* appeared between 1806 and 1808.

4 W. Godwin, *History of the Commonwealth of England* (1824-8), vol. I, p. vi.

5 *Ibid.*, p. ix.

6 *Ibid.*, vol. I, p. 9.

7 *Ibid.*, vol. II, pp. 689-92.

8 *Ibid.*, vol. IV, pp. vii, viii, 587, 597.

9 G. Brodie, *Constitutional History of the British Empire from the Accession of Charles I to the Restoration* (1822), new edn (London, 1866), pp. vii, viii.

10 *Ibid.*, vol. III, pp. 343-4.

11 *Ibid.*, vol. I, p. 239, vol. II, pp. 3-21, 113, 235-6.

12 H. Hallam, *Constitutional History of England* (1827), new edn (London, 1872), vol. III. p. 201.

13 *Ibid.*, vol. II, pp. 101, 98.

14 *Ibid.*, vol. II, p. 138.

15 *Ibid.*, vol. II, p. 79.

16 See *Ibid.*, vol. II, pp. 138-50. On Hallam, see P. Clark, 'Henry Hallam Reconsidered', *Quarterly Review*, CCV (1967).

17 P. Gay, *Style in History* (London, Cape, 1975), p. 97. Macaulay's move towards the Whigs is discussed in J. Clive, *Macaulay: the shaping of the historian* (London, Secker and Warburg, 1973).

18 Quoted in Jane Millgate, *Macaulay* (London, Routledge, 1973), p. 119.

19 *The Miscellaneous Writings and Speeches of Lord Macaulay*, popular edn. (London, 1889), p. 154.

20 Macaulay, 'A conversation between Mr Abraham Cowley and Mr John Milton touching the Great Civil War', *Knight's Quarterly Magazine* (1824).

21 *Critical and Historical Essays contributed to the Edinburgh Review* (London, 1852), pp. 14, 23-4.

22 Macaulay, *History of England*, (London, Dent. Everyman edn. 4 vols., 1953) vol. I, p. 63.

23 *The Miscellaneous Writings and Speeches of Lord Macaulay*, pp. 583-4.

24 Macaulay, *History of England*, vol. I, p. 2.

25 See J.C. Morison, *Macaulay* (London, 1882). For Gardiner's strictures on Macaulay, see p. 70.

26 See pp. 77-8 for some discussion of Sir Charles Firth's difficulties at Oxford.

27 Reprinted in F. Stern, *The Varieties of History*, 2nd edn (London, Macmillan 1970), pp. 209-26.

28 F. Jones, 'John Lingard and the Simancas Archives', *Hist. Jnl* X (1967); Peardon, *op. cit.*, pp. 280-3; Lingard, *History of England from the First Invasion of the Romans to the Accession of William and Mary* 6th edn, (London, 1855), vol. VIII, pp. 119-20.

29 Lingard, *op. cit.*, vol. I, p. 6.

30 *Ibid.*, p. 5.

31 A. Carlyle (ed.), *New Letters of Thomas Carlyle*, 2 vols. (London, The Bodley Head, 1904), vol. I, p. 244.

32 *Ibid.*, vol. II, pp. 10-11. See L.M. Young, *Thomas Carlyle and the Art of History* (Philadelphia, University of Philadelphia Press, 1939).

33 D. Johnson, *Guizot. Aspects of French History 1787-1874* (London, Routledge, 1963), p. 327.

34 *Ibid.*, p. 330.

35 *Ibid.*, p. 366.
36 Hallam, *Constitutional History of England*, new edn (London, 1872), vol. I, p. vii.
37 F. Guizot, *History of the English Revolution of 1640* (London, 1867), pp. xvi-xvii.
38 *Ibid.*, p. 8.
39 *Ibid.*, p. 3.
40 *Ibid.*, p. 5.
41 *Ibid.*, p. 15.
42 *Ibid.*, pp. 49, 78.
43 L. von Ranke, *History of England chiefly in the Seventeenth Century* (1860s), vol. I, pp. xi, xiv. See C.E. McClelland, *The German Historians and England* (Cambridge, C.U.P., 1971), ch. 6.
44 *Ibid.*, vol. II, p. 330.
45 *Ibid.*, vol. II, pp. 552-3.
46 J.R. Green, *A Short History of the English People* (London, 1889), pp. xiii, vi, 559.
47 D. Woodruff (ed.), *Essays on Church and State by Lord Acton*, (London, Hollis and Carter, 1952), pp. 438-9; C.H. Firth, 'Dr S.R. Gardiner', *Proceedings of the British Academy* (1903-4), p. 295.
48 G.P. Gooch, *History and Historians in the Nineteenth Century* (London, Longmans, 1952), p. 335. The book was first published in 1913.
49 H.B. Learned, 'Samuel Rawson Gardiner', *Yale Scientific Monthly* (June 1902)
50 S.R. Gardiner, *History of England 1624-28* (London, 1875), vol. I, preface. Gardiner, *History of England 1603-42*, new edn (London, 1893-6), vol. I, p. vi.
51 Gardiner, *History of England 1628-37* (London, 1877), vol. I, preface.
52 Gardiner, *What Gunpowder Plot Was* (London, 1897), p. 4.
53 Quoted in C.H. Firth, 'Samuel Rawson Gardiner', *Quarterly Review*, CXCV (1902), p. 550.
54 Usher, *A Critical Study of the Historical Method of S.R. Gardiner* (Washington University Studies vol. III, Pt 2, no. 1. 1915), p. 74.
55 Gardiner, *The First Two Stuarts and the Puritan Revolution 1603-1660*, Epochs of Modern History series. 8th edn (London, 1888), p. v.

56 Gardiner, *History of England 1603-42*, vol. II, p. 197.
57 *Ibid.*, vol. VIII, p. 84-5.
58 Gardiner, *History of the Great Civil War 1642-49* (London, 1893), vol. I, p. 9.

Chapter 5

1 *T.L.S.*, (25 September 1919), p. 515.
2 *Ibid.*, (9 October 1919), p. 549. I am indebted to Mr Arthur Crook, former editor of the *T.L.S.*, for his help in trying to establish the identity of the anonymous 'Historian'. Unfortunately this proved impossible.
3 S.R. Gardiner, *History of the Great Civil War* revised edition (1893), vol. I, p. vii.
4 As Firth had written Gardiner's so Davies wrote Firth's obituary for the *Proceedings of the British Academy* (vol. XXII) in 1937.
5 *American Historical Review*, LXIII (1957), p. 280.
6 Godfrey Davies published a selection of Firth's *Essays Historical and Literary* in 1938 (Oxford, Clarendon Press).
7 C.H. Firth, *Last Years of the Protectorate* (London, Longmans, 1909), p. vi.
8 Gardiner reviewed Firth's book in the *E.H.R.*, XV (1900), pp. 803-4.
9 *E.H.R.*, XXVI (1911), pp. 585-6.
10 *T.R.H.S.*, 3rd series, 7 (1913).
11 C.H. Firth, *Commentary on Macaulay's History of England*, ed. G. Davies (London, Macmillan 1938), p. vii.
12 C.H. Firth, *Cromwell's Army* (London, Methuen, 1902), p. vii. The military history of the Civil War — which this study chooses to pass over very quickly — has continued to be an active branch of the historiography of the subject since Firth's day. See, for example, A.H. Woolrych, *Battles of the English Civil War* (London, Batsford, 1961) and P. Young and R. Holmes, *The English Civil War. A military history of the three Civil Wars 1642-51* (London, Eyre-Methuen, 1974).
13 C.H. Firth, *A plea for the Historical Teaching of History* (1904), pp. 15, 19.
14 G. Davies, *The Early Stuarts 1603-1660* (London, O.U.P. 1937), p. xxii.

15 For an explicit statement of Gardiner's influence on Montague see, for example, p. 491 of his book.

16 J.A.R. Marriott, *The Crisis of English Liberty* (Oxford, Clarendon Press, 1930), pp. v-vi.

17 *Ibid.*, pp. 16, 18.

18 G.M. Trevelyan, *An Autobiography and Other Essays* (London, Longmans, 1949), p. 1.

19 *American Historical Review*, XI (1905-6), p. 378.

20 These and other quotations from Trevelyan's *England under the Stuarts* are taken from the 12th edn, revised, of 1925 (London, Methuen).

21 G.M. Trevelyan, *The Recreations of an Historian* (London, Nelson, 1919), p. 8.

22 G.M. Trevelyan, *The Present Position of History* (London, Longmans, 1927), pp. 16, 7. Trevelyan published an anthology of Carlyle's writings in 1953.

23 J.H. Plumb, *G.M. Trevelyan* (London, Longmans for The British Council, 1951), p. 17.

24 G.M. Trevelyan, 'Bias in history' in *An Autobiography and Other Essays* (London, Longmans, 1949), p. 77.

25 G.M. Trevelyan, *England under the Stuarts, op. cit.*, pp. 1, 516.

26 *Ibid.*, pp. 228, 229.

27 G.M. Trevelyan, *History of England* (London, Longmans, 1926), pp. 406, 407.

28 G.M. Trevelyan, *English Social History* (London, Longmans, 1944), pp. 234, 253.

Chapter 6

1 J.M. Winter and D.M. Joslin (eds), *R.H. Tawney's Commonplace Book* (Cambridge, 1972. *Ec.H.R. Supplement 5*) p. 72. See also J.M. Winter, 'R.H. Tawney's early political thought', *P.P.*, 47 (1970).

2 N.B. Harte (ed.), *The Study of Economic History* (London, Cass, 1970), pp. 89, 96-7.

3 *Ibid.*, p. 106.

4 See R. Terrill, *R.H. Tawney and His Times. Socialism as Fellowship* (London, Deutsch, 1974), pp. 39-40.

5 R.H. Tawney, *The Agrarian Problem in the Sixteenth Century* (1912), pp.399, 400. Tawney's conclusions have been modified,

for example, by E. Kerridge, *Agrarian Problems in the Sixteenth Century and After* (London, Allen & Unwin, 1969).

6 Winter and Joslin, *op. cit.*, p. 29.

7 W.H.B. Court, *Scarcity and Choice in History* (London, Arnold, 1970), p. 18.

8 R.H. Tawney, *Religion and the Rise of Capitalism* (1926), pp. 211, 212.

9 In the historical debate on the subject, opposing positions have been taken by Christoper Hill ('Protestantism and the rise of capitalism' in F.J. Fisher (ed.), *Essays in the Economic and Social History of Tudor and Stuart England* (Cambridge, C.U.P., 1961)) and H.R. Trevor-Roper ('Religion, the Reformation and Social Change' in the book of that name published in 1967 (London, Macmillan)). The economist's contribution is represented by K. Samuelsson, *Religion and Economic Action* (Stockholm, Svenska Bokförlaget, 1961).

10 Winter and Joslin, *op. cit.*, pp. 80, 81.

11 The Harrington essay was published in *Proceedings of the British Academy*, XXVII (reprinted in Lucy Sutherland (ed.), *Studies in History. British Academy Lectures* (London, O.U.P., 1966). 'The Rise of the Gentry' appeared in *Ec.H.R.*, XI (1941) and is reprinted (with the postscript) in E.M. Carus-Wilson, (ed.), *Essays in Economic History*. I (London, Arnold, 1954).

12 R.H. Tawney, *Business and Politics under James I: Lionel Cranfield as Merchant and Minister* (Cambridge, C.U.P., 1958), p. 83. Menna Prestwich, *Cranfield. Politics and profits under the early Stuarts. The Career of Lionel Cranfield Earl of Middlesex* (Oxford, Clarendon Press, 1966) supplements Tawney's volume.

13 T.S. Ashton, 'Richard Henry Tawney', *Proceedings of the British Academy* XLVIII (1963), p. 477.

14 Quoted in Terrill, *op. cit.*, p. 103.

15 Tawney, *Business and Politics, op. cit.*, pp. 140, 291.

16 Tawney, 'Harrington's Interpretation of His Age', *op. cit.*, p. 217.

17 Cf. S.B. Liljegren's *The Fall of the Monasteries and the Social Changes in England leading up to the Great Revolution* (Lund and Leipzig, 1924).

18 Tawney, *The Rise of the Gentry, op. cit.*, pp. 181, 183-4.

19 *Ec.H.R.*, XVIII (1948)

20 H.R. Trevor-Roper, *Archbishop Laud* (London, Macmillan, 1940).

21 Tawney, 'The Rise of the Gentry: a postscript' in Carus-Wilson (ed.), *op.cit.*, p.214. By using this metaphor, Christopher Hill has

written, Tawney 'is not making a theological allusion. He wants us to see Prof. Trevor-Roper as a barbarian killer from a primitive stage of Middle Eastern history'. (Review of Terrill's book on Tawney, *Balliol Parish Magazine* (1974), p.30). For Trevor-Roper's involvement in other historical controversies, with Arnold Toynbee and A.J.P. Taylor, see V. Mehta, *Fly and the Flybottle* (London, Weidenfeld, 1962).

22 *Ec.H.R.*, 2nd series, IV (1952).

23 *Ec.H.R. Supplement 1* (1953).

24 As a social group the yeomen were far better covered than most at the time Trevor-Roper was writing. See Mildred Campbell, *The English Yeoman under Elizabeth and the Early Stuarts* (1940; 2nd edn, London, Merlin Press, 1960).

25 C. Hill, 'Recent interpretations of the Civil War' in *Puritanism and Revolution* (London, Secker & Warburg, 1958); P. Zagorin, 'The social interpretation of the English Revolution', *Jnl of Economic History*, XIX (1959). For some discussion of Zagorin, see pp.130-2.

26 Trevor-Roper published some second thoughts on the Independents in his 'Oliver Cromwell and his Parliaments' in R. Pares and A.J.P. Taylor (eds), *Essays Presented to Sir Lewis Namier* (London, Macmillan, 1956).

27 Terrill, *op. cit.*, p. 101.

28 L. Stone, 'Social mobility in England 1500-1700', *P.P.*, 33 (1966); 'The Educational Revolution in England 1560-1640', *P.P.*, 28 (1964); 'Literacy and Education in England 1640-1900', *P.P.*, 42 (1969); *The University in Society* (Princeton, N.J., Princeton U.P., 1974).

29 In between the 1948 article and *Crisis*, Stone published 'The nobility in business 1540-1640', *Explorations in Entrepreneurial History* (1957), and 'The inflation of honours', *P.P.*, 14 (1958).

30 L. Stone, *The Crisis of the Aristocracy 1558-1640* (Oxford, Clarendon Press, 1965).

31 *Ibid.*, pp. 7-8.

32 A. Everitt, 'The peers and the provinces', *Agricultural History Review*, XVI (1968).

33 *The Listener* (4 October 1973), p. 450.

34 R. Ashton, 'The aristocracy in transition', *Ec.H.R.*, 2nd series, XXII (1969), p. 311.

35 'The Gentry Controversy and the aristocracy in crisis', *History*, LI (1966).

36 L. Stone, 'R.H. Tawney', *P.P.*, 21 (1962); J.D. Chambers, 'The Tawney Tradition', *Ec.H.R.*, 2nd series, XXIV (1971); N.B. Harte (ed.), *The Study of Economic History* (London, Cass. 1970), p. xxviii.

37 Its unwieldy title is best relegated to a footnote: F.J. Fisher (ed.), *Essays in the Economic and Social History of Tudor and Stuart England in Honour of R.H. Tawney...* (Cambridge, C.U.P., 1961).

38 'The development of the London food market 1540-1640' reprinted in E.M. Carus-Wilson (ed.), *Essays in Economic History*, 1 (1954); 'Commercial trends and policy in sixteenth-century England', reprinted in *ibid.*; 'The development of London as a centre of conspicuous consumption in the sixteenth and seventeenth centuries' reprinted in *Essays in Economic History*, II (London, Arnold 1962); 'The sixteenth and seventeenth centuries: the Dark Ages in English economic history?', *Economica*, n.s., XXIV 1957.

39 D.C. Coleman, *Sir John Banks, Baronet and Businessman: A study of business, politics and society in later Stuart England* (Oxford, Clarendon Press, 1963).

40 'The fantastical folly of fashion: the English stocking knitting industry 1500-1700' in N.B. Harte and K.G. Ponting (eds), *Textile History and Economic History. Essays in Honour of Miss Julia de Lacy Mann* (Manchester, M.U.P., 1973). Dr Thirsk's Ford Lectures on *Economic Policy, Economic Projects, Political Economy, 1540-1700* are to be published by the Clarendon Press.

41 *J.M.H.*, XXVI (1954); *Ec.H.R.*, 2nd series, V (1952).

42 *History*, LIV (1969); in Thirsk (ed.), *Land, Church and People. Essays presented to Professor H.P.R. Finberg.* Supplement to *Agricultural History Review*, XVIII (1970).

43 Hill in Fisher, *op. cit.*, pp. 35-6.

44 Quoted in Mehta, *Fly and the Fly Bottle, op. cit.*, pp. 163-4. In 1950, Hill was pleased to be able to record that 'Professor Tawney has himself advanced a long way from his early Fabianism in politics'. ('Historians and the rise of British capitalism', *Science and Society*, XIV (1950), pp. 312 n.10.)

45 Terrill, *op. cit.*, pp. 273-4. I am indebted to Mr Terrill for clarification on this point; Hill, *Balliol Parish Magazine* (1974), pp. 30-1.

46 Terrill *op. cit.*, p. 244; Hill, *Balliol Parish Magazine* (1974) p. 31.

47 Terrill, *op. cit.*, p. 235.

48 Orwell described the communism of the 1930s as 'the patriotism

of the deracinated' (quoted in Terrill, *op. cit.*, p. 238).

49 *A.H.R.*, LXXVIII (1973), p. 1054.

50 'Reflections upon Marxist historiography: the case of the English Civil War' in B. Chapman and A. Potter (eds), *W.J.M.M.: Political Questions* (Manchester, M.U.P. 1975).

51 *Ec.H.R.*, VIII (1938), pp. 159-67.

52 The narrative base of Savine's *Lectures on the English Revolution* (1924) was provided by Gardiner's work, but Gardiner would have been amazed at the result!

53 Hill, *Puritanism and Revolution, op. cit.*, p. 154 n. (The essay was reprinted there with some revisions.) Arkhangelsky's major work was never published in English translation. See, however, *Agrarian Legislation and the Agrarian Movement in England during the Revolution of the Seventeenth Century* (Moscow, 1955).

54 This (A.L. Morton, *A People's History of England*) was issued in a revised edition by Lawrence and Wishart in 1949. Henry Holorenshaw was the pseudonym chosen by the scientist Dr Joseph Needham. (J. Lewis, *The Left Book Club. An Historical Record* (London, Gollancz, 1970), p. 8.)

55 C. Hill, *Science and Society*, XIV (1950), p. 313; Morton, *op. cit.*, p. 222.

56 David Petegorsky (1915-56), a Canadian-born Jew, studied under Harold Laski at the L.S.E. in the late 1930s, and his doctoral thesis formed the basis of his book. This was his only publication in the field; after the war his work centred on Jewish affairs. (I am indebted to Prof. Morris Silverman of Yeshiva University, N.Y., for this information.)

57 C. Hill, *Science and Society*, XIV (1950), p. 315; R.H. Hilton, *Labour Monthly* (January 1947), pp. 29-30. The reviews indicate how incestuous the Marxist writers of this period could easily become. Both Hill and Hilton were thanked by Dobb in his preface 'for guidance concerning the Tudor and Stuart age'.

58 On the poet and critic Edgell Rickword, see his collected *Essays and Opinions, 1921-31* (Cheadle, Cheshire, Carcanet Press, 1974). Margaret James (1901-43) had moved steadily leftwards in politics towards Marxism in the 1930s.

59 C. Hill, *The English Revolution 1640* (London, Lawrence & Wishart, 1940), pp. 9, 27 n.1, 82.

60 C. Hill, *Science and Society*, XIV (1950), p. 317.

61 C. Hill, *Science and Society*, XII (1948), p. 133.

62 C. Hill, *Science and Society*, XIV (1950), pp. 309, 311.

63 *Ibid.*, pp. 309-10, 320-1.

64 *Ibid.*, p. 317.

65 C. Hill and E. Dell, *The Good Old Cause, The English Revolution of 1640-1660* (1949), pp. 19, 21. Hill wrote a new introduction for the second edition of 1969 with some apologies for youthful excesses in the original.

66 This paragraph is based on H. Pelling, *The British Communist Party. A Historical Profile* (London, Black, 1958).

67 A. Simpson in *J.on.H.*, XXIX (1957), p. 261.

68 *History* XLII (1957), pp. 236-8. The book was enthusiastically reviewed by the American historian W.K. Jordan in *A.H.R.* LXII (1957), pp. 613-4, and by Norman Sykes in the *E.H.R.*, LXXIII (1958), pp. 294-8, although he felt that the economic factor had been overplayed at the expense of the religious.

69 *T.L.S.* (28 November 1975), p. 1419.

70 The original article appeared in the *T.L.S.* on 29 November 1974, p.1330. For the debate, see the correspondence columns in the *T.L.S.* issues of 13 December 1974, 10, 24, 31 January, 7, 14, February, 7, 21 March, and 11 April 1975.

71 Elliot Rose in his *Cases of Conscience. Alternatives Open to Recusants and Puritans under Elizabeth I and James I* (Cambridge, C.U.P., 1975), p. 177 n.1 makes the extraordinary claim that Hill's work has *affirmed* the idea of the Puritan Revolution.

72 C. Hill, *God's Englishman* (London, Weidenfeld, 1970), p. 268; *The Century of Revolution 1603-1714* (Edinburgh, Nelson, 1961), p. 75; *God's Englishman*, p. 268; *Economic Problems of the Church* (Oxford, Clarendon Press, 1956), pp. x, xiii; *Change and Continuity in Seventeenth-Century England* (London, Weidenfeld, 1975), p. 279.

73 C. Hill, *Puritanism and Revolution, op. cit.*, p. vii.

74 *Society and Puritanism in Pre-Revolutionary England* (London, Secker & Warburg, 1964), p. 9.

75 The interpretation is outlined most clearly in *Reformation to Industrial Revolution* (1967).

76 *The Listener* (4 October, 1973), pp. 448-9. Contrast C. Wilson, 'Economics and politics in the seventeenth century' *Historical Jnl*, V (1962) and the same author's *England's Apprenticeship 1603-1763* (London, Longmans, 1965). Cf. Joan Thirsk and J.P.

Cooper *Seventeenth-Century Economic Documents* (Oxford, Clarendon Press, 1972), p. v.

77 C. Hill, *Society and Puritanism in Pre-Revolutionary England, op. cit.*, p. 13. He will have nothing to do with the school of thought which denies to puritanism any distinctive identity of its own. See C.H. and C.K. George, *The Protestant Mind of the English Reformation 1570-1640* (Princeton, Princeton U.P., 1961). See also I. Breward, 'The abolition of puritanism', *Jnl of Religious History*, VII (1974) and M.G. Finlayson, 'Puritanism and puritans: labels or libels?', *Canadian Jnl of History*, VIII (1973).

78 C. Hill, *Society and Puritanism in Pre-Revolutionary England, op. cit.*, p. 134. The phrase 'industrious sort of people' is Slingsby Bethel's (1617-97) and is in fact drawn from a *post-Restoration* tract. Hill's work on puritanism runs parallel at many points with that of the American historian William Haller. See *The Rise of Puritanism* (New York, Columbia U.P., 1938), and *Liberty and Reformation in the Puritan Revolution* (New York, Columbia U.P., 1955). See also L.J. Trinterud, 'William Haller, historian of puritanism', *Jnl of British Studies*, v (1966).

79 C. Hill, *Society and Puritanism in Pre-Revolutionary England*, op. cit., pp. 138, 135.

80 C. Hill, *Intellectual Origins, op. cit.*, p. 6. This area of intellectual history that Hill helped to open up has since attracted a growing amount of attention. See, for example, K.V. Thomas, *Religion and the Decline of Magic* (London, Weidenfeld, 1971); H. Kearney, *Science and Change 1500-1700* (London, Weidenfeld, 1972; and most recently C. Webster, *The Great Instauration: Science, Medicine and Reform 1626-1660* (London, Duckworth, 1975). Hill's own work needs to be seen in relation to R.K. Merton, *Science, Technology and Society in Seventeenth-Century England* (1936; 2nd edn New York, Harper and Row, 1970).

81 C. Hill, *Intellectual Origins, op. cit.*, pp. 5, 1-2.

82 *Ibid.*, pp. 291, 294, 314.

83 H.F. Kearney, 'Puritanism, capitalism and the Scientific Revolution', *P.P.*, 28 (1964) and Hill's rejoinder in *P.P.*, 29 (1964); Kearney, 'Puritanism and science: problems of definition' and T.K. Rabb, 'Religion and the rise of modern science', *P.P.*, 31 (1965); Hill, 'Science, religion and society in the sixteenth and seventeenth centuries', *P.P.*, 32 (1965). (*P.P.* essays on *The Intellectual Revolution of the Seventeenth Century*, ed. C. Webster

were published in book form by Routledge in 1974.) See also A.R. Hall, 'The Scientific Revolution and the Puritan Revolution' *History*, L (1965), and the reviews by H.R. Trevor-Roper in *History and Theory*, V (1966) and G.E. Aylmer in *E.H.R.* , LXXXI (1966).

84 C. Hill, *The World Turned Upside Down* (London, Temple-Smith, 1962), p. 15.
85 C. Hill, *Intellectual Origins, op. cit.*, p. 3.
86 See also B.S. Capp, *The Fifth Monarchy Men* (London, Faber, 1972); P. Toon (ed.), *Puritans, the Millenium and the Future of Israel* (Cambridge, Clarke, 1970); A.L. Morton, *The World of the Ranters* (London, Lawrence & Wishart, 1970); B.S. Capp, 'Godly rule and English Millenarianism', *P.P.*, 52 (1971); and W.M. Lamont, 'Richard Baxter, the Apocalypse and the Mad Major', *P.P.*, 55 (1972), and the same author's *Godly Rule. Politics and Religion. 1603-1660* (London, Macmillan, 1969).
87 C. Hill, *Intellectual Origins, op. cit.*, pp. 2, vii: *Puritanism and Revolution, op. cit.*, p. 230.
88 H.R. Trevor-Roper, *History and Theory*, V (1966), p. 73. Cf. Blair Worden reviewing *Change and Continuity in Seventeenth-Century England, New Statesman* (24 January 1975), p. 113. Hexter, *T.L.S.* (24 October 1975), p. 1252. See also *T.L.S.* (28 November 1975). For some of Hexter's earlier forays into the demolition business see *Reappraisals in History* (London, Longmans, 1961).
89 John Miller, *T.H.E.S.* (7 March 1975).
90 C. Hill, *T.L.S.* (7 November 1975), p. 1333.

Chapter 7

1 J. Washbourn (ed.), *Bibliotecha Gloucestrensis* (Gloucester, 1825), pp. 4, 9.
2 Broxap's book — still extremely useful — was reissued by Manchester University Press, its original publisher, in 1974, with a new introduction by R.N. Dore. Cf. G.H. Tupling, 'The causes of the Civil War in Lancashire', *Trans. Lancs. & Ches. Antiquarian Soc.*, 65 (1955). B.G. Blackwood, 'The Lancashire Cavaliers and their tenants', *Trans. Historic Soc. Lancs. & Ches.*, 117 (1965), and 'The Cavalier and Roundhead Gentry of Lancashire', *Trans. Lancs. & Ches. Antiquarian Soc.*, 77 for 1967 (1974).
3 Mary Coate, *Cornwall in the Great Civil War and Interregnum*

1642-1660 (1933) pp. 1, 351-2. Mary Coate taught history at Oxford from 1918 to 1947 and was subsequently connected with the Extra-Mural Department at the University of Exeter. (I am indebted to the college secretary at Lady Margaret Hall, Oxford, for this information.)

4 A.C. Wood, *Nottinghamshire in the Civil War* (1937), p. ix. The book was published, like Mary Coate's study, by O.U.P. Wood, an Oxford-trained historian, spent his entire academic career at the University college (later University) of Nottingham, eventually becoming Professor of History in 1951.

5 The device suggests that in neither case did the author entirely succeed in integrating this aspect into his county study.

6 See, for example, the traditional studies by R.W. Ketton-Cremer, *Norfolk and the Civil War* (London, Faber, 1969), E.A. Andriette, *Devon and Exeter during the Civil War* (Newton Abbot, David & Charles, 1972), and R.E. Sherwood, *Civil Strife in the Midlands 1642-1651* (Chichester, Phillimore, 1974). The *Victoria County History* continues to pursue its ponderous way.

7 A. Simpson, *The Wealth of the Gentry 1540-1660. East Anglian Studies* (1961) p.2. The book was jointly published by C.U.P. and University of Chicago Press. Simpson also wrote *Puritanism in Old and New England* (Chicago, 1955).

8 Simpson, *Wealth of the Gentry*, pp. 20, 107-8.

9 *Ibid.*, p. 216.

10 M. Finch, *The Wealth of Five Northamptonshire Families 1540-1640* (Northants Record Society, XIX, 1956), pp. 165-70.

11 J.T. Cliffe, *The Yorkshire Gentry from the Reformation to the Civil War* (London, Athlone Press, 1969), p. 162.

12 *Ibid.*, p. 118.

13 H.A. Lloyd, *The Gentry of South-West Wales 1540-1640* (Cardiff, University of Wales Press, 1968).

14 Willcox's book was published by Yale U.P. (New Haven), and Barnes's study appeared under the imprint of O.U.P. (London). M.U.P. published the book on Staffordshire, while Everitt's work was published by the Suffolk Records Society (Ipswich), III, (1961).

15 A. Everitt, *The Community of Kent and the Great Rebellion 1640-1660*, Leicester, Leicester U.P., 1966).

16 Cf. Everitt's chapter headings: :The Community of Kent in 1640' / 'The Community in Opposition 1640' / 'The Community

Divides 1640-42' / 'The Community at War 1642-7' / 'The Community in Revolt 1647-8' / 'The Community in Eclipse 1649-59' / 'The Community of Kent and the Restoration 1659-60'.

17 Everitt, *op. cit.*, p. 13.

18 *Ibid.*, p. 23.

19 *Ibid.*, pp. 327, 326.

20 *Ibid.*, pp. 36, 44, 45-55.

21 The first was published as no.1 in the second series of Occasional Papers by the Department of English Local History at Leicester; the second was a Historical Association pamphlet. Cf. Everitt's chapter on 'The County Community' in E.W. Ives (ed.), *The English Revolution* (London, Arnold, 1968), and also the chapters there by Ivan Roots on 'The Central Government and the Local Community' and by D.H. Pennington on 'The County Community at War'.

22 See also Everitt's essays on 'Social mobility in early modern England', *P.P.*, 33 (1966), 'The English urban inn 1560-1760' in A. Everitt (ed.), *Perspectives in English Urban History* (London Macmillan, 1973), and 'Kentish Family Portrait: an aspect of the rise of the pseudo-gentry' in C.W. Chalklin and M.A. Havinden (eds), *Rural Change and Urban Growth 1500-1800. Essays in English regional history in honour of W.G. Hoskins* (London, Longmans, 1974).

23 A. Everitt, *Change in the Provinces*, p. 48 (see n.21 above).

24 A. Everitt, *Local Community and the Great Rebellion*, pp. 29 n.37, 26-27 (see n.21 above).

25 A. Fletcher, *A Country Community in Peace and War: Sussex 1600-1660*, (London, Longmans, 1975).

26 Underdown's book *Somerset in the Civil War and Interregnum* was published by David & Charles (Newton Abbot) in 1973. Professor Underdown contributed an essay on 'Settlement in the Counties 1653-1658' to G.E. Aylmer (ed.), *The Interregnum: The Quest for Settlement* (London, Macmillan 1972).

27 C. Holmes, *The Eastern Association in the English Civil War*; A. Everitt, *Suffolk and the Great Rebellion*, (Suffolk Records Society 1961), p. 21.

28 A. Everitt, *Suffolk and the Great Rebellion*, (Suffolk Records Society, 1961), p. 21.

29 Holmes, *op. cit.*, pp. 15, 20, 34.

30 J.S. Morrill, *Cheshire 1630-1660* published by O.U.P. (London) in

1974. Cf. R.N. Dore, *The Civil Wars in Cheshire* (Chester, Cheshire Community Council, 1966).

31 Morrill, *op. cit.*, p. 330.

32 Johnson's essay comprised part of P. Clark and P. Slack (eds), *Crisis and order in English Towns 1500-1700* (London, Routledge, 1972). Howell's book was published by the Clarendon Press (Oxford).

33 V. Pearl, *London and the Outbreak of the Puritan Revolution* published by O.U.P. (London) in 1961. See also Valerie Pearl's essays on 'London puritans and Scotch Fifth columnists: a mid-seventeenth-century phenomenon' in A.E.J. Hollaender and W. Kellaway (eds), *Studies in London History presented to Philip Edmund Jones* (London, Hodder & Stoughton, 1969), and 'London's Counter-Revolution' in G.E. Aylmer (ed.), *The Interregnum: the quest for settlement 1640-1660* (London, Macmillan, 1972). Brian Manning's book on *The English People and the English Revolution 1640-1649* (London, Heinemann, 1976) in some ways complements Pearl's book by viewing the London politics of these years from a different angle.

34 Pearl, *London and the Outbreak ...*, *op. cit.*, p. 284.

35 R.A. Marchant's book *the Puritans and the Church Courts in the Diocese of York 1560-1642* was published by Longmans (London) in 1960. See also his study of *The Church under the Law* (Cambridge, C.U.P., 1969).

36 R.C. Richardson, *Puritanism in North West England* appeared under the imprint of Manchester U.P. in 1972. See also, by the same author, 'Puritanism and the ecclesiastical authorities' in B. Manning (ed.), *Politics, Religion and the English Civil War* (London, Arnold, 1973).

37 J. Bossy, *The English Catholic Community* (London, Darton, Longman and Todd, 1976); K. Lindley, 'The Lay Catholics of England in the reign of Charles I', *Jnl of Ecclesiastical History*, XXII (1971), and 'The part played by the Catholics' in B. Manning (ed.), *Politics, Religion and the English Civil War* (London, Arnold, 1973); M.J. Havran, *The Catholics in Caroline England* (London, O.U.P., 1962); H. Aveling, *Post-Reformation Catholicism in East Yorkshire 1558-1790* (York, East Yorks Local Hist. Soc., 1960), 'The Catholic Recusants of the West Riding of Yorkshire 1558-1790', *Proceedings of the Leeds Philosophical and Literary Soc.*, X pt. vi (1963), *Northern Catholics: the Catholic Recusants of the North Riding of Yorkshire 1558-1790* (London Chapman, 1966).

Chapter 8

1 Wedgwood's books on European history include *The Thirty Years War* (London, Cape, 1938), *William the Silent* (London, Cape, 1964), and *Richelieu and the French Monarchy* (London, English Universities Press, 1949).

2 V. Mehta, *Fly and the Fly Bottle* (London, Weidenfeld, 1962), p. 159.

3 The books were published in 1955, 1958 and 1964 respectively by Collins (London).

4 Mehta, *op. cit.*, p. 155.

5 *The Spectator*, 12 December 1958.

6 C.V. Wedgwood, *Velvet Studies* (London, Cape, 1946) p. 157.

7 C.V. Wedgwood, *The King's Peace 1637-1641* (London, Collins, 1955), pp. 16, 15, 17.

8 Both versions were published by Cape (London). The appearance of H.F. Kearney's *Strafford in Ireland* (Manchester, M.U.P., 1957) and of J.P. Cooper, 'The fortunes of Thomas Wentworth, Earl of Strafford', *Ec.H.R.*, 2nd series, xi (1958) made necessary a fundamental revision of Wedgwood's original study.

9 H.R. Trevor-Roper, *Archbishop Laud* (London, Macmillan, 1940; 2nd edn, 1962).

10 M.J. Havran, *Caroline Courtier: the life of Lord Cottington* (London, Macmillan, 1973); M. van C. Alexander, *Charles I's Lord Treasurer. Sir Richard Weston, Earl of Portland, 1577-1635* (London, Macmillan, 1975).

11 Ashley's book was published by Hodder and Stoughton (London 1957) and Hill's by Weidenfeld (London, 1970). See also Antonia Fraser, *Cromwell. Our Chief of Men* (London, Weidenfeld, 1973). Cf. W.C. Abbott, *A Bibliography of Oliver Cromwell* (Cambridge, Mass., Harvard U.P., 1929) and P.H. Hardacre, 'Writings on Oliver Cromwell since 1929', *J.M.H.*, XXXIII (1963).

12 Gregg's book was published by Harrap (London), Lamont's by Routledge (London), Rowe's by The Athlone Press (London), and Spalding's by Faber (London).

13 Allen's book was published by Methuen (London), and the 1971 reprint of Judson's study was published by Octagon Books (N.Y.) Routledge (London) published Zagorin's book. Filmer's *Patriarcha and other Political Works* was edited by Peter Laslett (Oxford, Clarendon Press, 1949). See also G.J. Schochet, *Patriarchalism in Political Thought* (Oxford, Blackwell, 1975).

14 Gough's and Macpherson's books were published by the Clarendon Press (Oxford), and Pocock's by C.U.P. (Cambridge). For Macpherson's economic interpretation of Hobbes's political thought, see p. 22 above.

15 Q. Skinner, 'Hobbes's *Leviathan*', *Hist. Jnl.*, VII (1964); 'History and ideology in the English Revolution', *Hist. Jnl.*, VIII (1965); 'The ideological context of Hobbes's political thought', *Hist. Jnl*, IX (1966); 'Conquest and consent: Thomas Hobbes and the Engagement controversy' in G.E. Aylmer (ed.), *The Interregnum: the quest for settlement* (London, Macmillan, 1972).

16 J.A.W. Gunn, *Politics and the Public Interest in the Seventeenth Century* (London, Routledge, 1969); A. Pallister, *Magna Carta: the heritage of liberty* (London, O.U.P., 1971); H. Butterfield, *Magna Carta in the Historiography of the Sixteenth and Seventeenth Centuries* (Reading, The University, 1969). See also F. Thompson, *Magna Carta 1300-1629* (Minneapolis, University of Minnesota, 1945).

17 P. Zagorin. *The Court and the Country* (London, Routledge, 1969). See, for example, Zagorin's review of Hill's *Intellectual Origins of the English Revolution* in *A.H.R.*, LXXI (1966), pp. 951-2.

18 Zagorin, *op. cit.*, pp. 22, 13, 16, 32.

19 *Ibid.*, pp. 74, 90.

20 *Ibid.*, pp. 329-51.

21 For example, Zagorin's comments on the basic similarities of Royalist and opposition peers (pp. 95, 333) are not borne out by G.F. Trevallyn Jones, *Saw Pit Wharton. The political career from 1640 to 1691 of Philip, fourth Lord Wharton* (Sydney, Sydney U.P., 1967). The latter argues (p. 31) that not all Stuart-created peers became Royalists but only those who owed their titles to Charles I himself.

22 Hardacre's book, *The Royalists during the Puritan Revolution* was published by Martinus Nijhoff (The Hague, 1956), Underdown's *Royalist Conspiracy in England, 1649-1660* by Yale U.P. (New Haven, 1960). See Underdown, *op. cit.*, pp. 331, 324-8.

23 No adequate study of neutralism has so far appeared in print. On the virulence of anti-Catholicism in seventeenth-century England see Carol Z. Ziener, 'The beleaguered isle. A study of Elizabethan and early Jacobean anti-catholicism', *P.P.*, 51 (1971); R. Clifton, 'The popular fear of Catholics during the English Revolution',

P.P., 52 (1971); B. Manning, *The English People and the English Revolution*, pp. 21-45. On Catholic neutralism and the opposition pressures which forced many into alignment with the Royalists see K. Lindley, 'The part played by the Catholics' in B. Manning (ed.), *Politics, Religion and the English Civil War* (London, Arnold, 1973).

24 C. Russell in Russell (ed.), *The Origins of the English Civil War* (London, Macmillan, 1973), p. 23; N. Tyacke, 'Puritanism, Arminianism and Counter-Revolution' in *ibid.*

25 See, for example, W.K. Jordan, *The Development of Religious Toleration in England* (London, Allen and Unwin, 1932-40); W. Haller, *Liberty and Reformation in the Puritan Revolution* (N.Y., Columbia U.P., 1955); R. Schlatter, *Richard Baxter and Puritan Politics* (New Brunswick, N.H., Rutgers U.P., 1957); J.F. Wilson, *Pulpit in Parliament. Puritanism during the English Civil War 1640-1648* (Princeton, N.J., Princeton U.P., 1969); C. Russell (ed.), *The Origins of the English Civil War* (London, Macmillan 1973) and *The Crisis of Parliaments. English history 1509-1660* (London, O.U.P., 1971); R.H. Parry (ed.), *The English Civil War and After 1642-58* (London, Macmillan, 1970); B. Manning (ed.), *Politics, Religion and the English Civil War* (London, Arnold, 1973); and M. Walzer, *The Revolution of the Saints. A study in the origins of radical politics* (London, Weidenfeld, 1966).

26 J.H. Hexter, *The Reign of King Pym* (Cambridge, Mass., Harvard U.P., 1941). See also Valerie Pearl, 'Oliver St John and the 'Middle Group, in the Long Parliament, August 1643-May 1644', *E.H.R.*, LXXXI (1966). A more lengthy genealogy of the middle group, going back to the 1620s, has been suggested by C. Thompson in 'The origins of the politics of the parliamentary middle group', *T.R.H.S.*, 5th series, 22 (1972).

27 Hexter, *op. cit.*, pp. 200, 115, 15, 14.

28 *T.L.S.*, 28 November 1975, p. 1419. Hexter's article was first published in *A.H.R.*, XLIV (1938) and was reprinted with revisions in his *Reappraisals in History* (London, Longmans 1961).

29 George Yule, *The Independents in the English Civil War* (Cambridge, C.U.P., 1958).

30 D. Brunton and D.H. Pennington, *Members of the Long Parliament* (London, Allen and Unwin, 1954); D. Underdown, 'The Independents reconsidered', *Jnl of Brit. Studies*, III (1964) and 'The Independents again', *Jnl of Brit. Studies*, VIII (1968);

V. Pearl, 'The Royal Independents in the English Civil War', *T.R.H.S.*, 5th series, 18 (1968); L. Glow, 'Political affiliations in the House of Commons after Pym's death', *Bull. Inst. of Hist. Res.*, XXXVIII (1965).

31 S. Foster, 'The Presbyterian Independents Exorcised. A ghost story for historians', *P.P.*, 44 (1969). 'Presbyterians, Independents and Puritans', *P.P.*, 47 (1970). The contributors were Blair Worden, Valerie Pearl, David Underdown, George Yule and J.H. Hexter. Foster supplied a rejoinder.

32 The first work (in collaboration with F.H. Relf) was published by the University of Minnesota Press (Minneapolis), the second (with F.H. Relf and H. Simpson) appeared under the imprint of Yale U.P. (New Haven).

33 Published by Yale U.P. (New Haven), the edition carried the diary to the trial of Strafford. It was continued in W. Coates (ed.), *The Journal of Sir Simonds D'Ewes from the First Recess of the Long Parliament to the Withdrawal of King Charles from London* (New Haven, Yale U.P., 1942). That other historians have not completed the work which Notestein began has been described as 'a scandal to Anglo-American scholarship'. (Zagorin, *The Court and the Country*, p. x.)

34 The first was originally published in the *Proceedings of the British Academy* (1924-5). The second appeared under the imprint of Yale U.P. (New Haven). Notestein's other publications included *The English People on the Eve of Colonization* (New York, Harper and Row, 1954). See also W.A. Aiken and B.D. Henning (eds), *Conflict in Stuart England. Essays in honour of Wallace Notestein* (London, Cape, 1960), and T.K. Rabb, 'Parliament and society in early Stuart England: the legacy of Wallace Notestein', *A.H.R.*, LXXVII (1972).

35 Willson's book was published by the University of Minnesota Press (Minneapolis), Zaller's by the University of California Press (Berkeley, L.A.), Moir's by Clarendon Press (Oxford), Ruigh's by Harvard U.P. (Cambridge, Mass.), Mitchell's by Columbia U.P. (N.Y.), and Tite's by The Athlone Press (London).

36 In 1932 Notestein collaborated with other members of the Committee in producing an *Interim Report of the Committee on House of Commons Personnel and Politics, 1264-1832*. Cf. H. Butterfield, 'The history of Parliament', *The Listener*, 8 October 1964, pp. 535-7.

37 D. Brunton and D.H. Pennington, *Members of the Long Parliament*, published by Allen and Unwin (London, 1954). Reprinted in 1968 by Archon (N.Y.). 'To Sir Lewis Namier we owe even more gratitude than do most students of parliamentary history,' (p. viii). R.H. Tawney, however, supplied the introduction.

38 M.F. Keeler, *The Long Parliament 1640-1641. A biographical study of its members*, p.5. The book was published as vol. 36 of the Memoirs of the American Philosophical Society (Philadelphia).

39 Manning, *P.P.*, 5 (1954), pp. 71-6.

40 See, for example, H. Butterfield, 'George III and the Namier School' in *George III and the Historians* (London, Collins, 1957).

41 C. Hill, 'Recent interpretations of the Civil War' in *Puritanism and Revolution* (London, Secker and Warburg, 1958), first published in *History*, XLI (1956). See also S.D. Antler, 'Quantitative analysis of the Long Parliament', *P.P.*, 56 (1972) and the ensuing debate in *P.P.*, 68 (1975).

42 Brunton and Pennington, *op. cit.*, pp. 184, 176-7, 10, 185.

43 MacCormack's book was published by Harvard U.P. (Cambridge, Mass.)

44 D. Underdown, *Pride's Purge. Politics in the English Revolution* (Oxford, Clarendon Press, 1971), pp. 2-3. For Underdown's work on regional history see p. 00 above. *ibid.*, pp. 354, 358, 337, 336. See also H.R. Trevor-Roper, 'Oliver Cromwell and his parliaments', in R. Pares and A.J.P. Taylor (eds), *Essays Presented to Sir Lewis Namier* (London, Macmillan, 1956).

45 B. Worden, *The Rump Parliament 1648-1653* (Cambridge, C.U.P., 1974), pp. 17, 56, 58.

46 I. Roots, *The Great Rebellion 1642-1660* (London, Batsford, 1966), p. vii. 'Cromwell's Ordinances: the early legislation of the Protectorate' in G.E. Aylmer (ed.), *The Interregnum: the quest for settlement 1646-1660* (London, Macmillan, 1972); 'Swordsmen and Decimators: Cromwell's Major-Generals' in R.H. Parry (ed.), *The English Civil War and After 1642-1658* (London, Macmillan, 1970).

47 A. Woolrych, 'The calling of Barebone's Parliament', *E.H.R.*, LXXX (1965), 'Oliver Cromwell and the rule of the saints', in Parry, *op. cit.*, 'Last quests for a settlement' in Aylmer, *op. cit.*

48 *'No Standing Armies!'* was published by Johns Hopkins U.P. (Baltimore, Maryland), Barnard's book by the Clarendon Press

(Oxford), Korr's by University of California Press (Berkeley, L.A.), Thirsk's by Longmans (London) and Aylmer's by Macmillan (London).

49 G. Aylmer, *The King's Servants: the Civil Service of Charles I 1625-1642*, p. 6. Like *The State's Servants* the book was published by Routledge (London), who issued a revised edition in 1974.

50 Aylmer, *The State's Servants, op. cit.*, p. 3.

51 Prest's book was published by Longmans (London), Eusden's by Yale U.P. (New Haven), Levack's by the Clarendon Press (Oxford), Jones's by Allen and Unwin (London). Prall's study was entitled *The Agitation for Law Reform during the Puritan Revolution 1640-1660* (The Hague, Martinus Nijhoff, 1966). Veall's book was *The Popular Movement for Law Reform 1640-1660* (Oxford, Clarendon Press, 1970).

52 Aylmer, *The State's Servants, op. cit.*, p. 5.

53 Thompson's book was published by Routledge (London). Keith Thomas's article was originally published in *P.P.* 13 (1958) and is reprinted in T. Aston (ed.), *Crisis in Europe 1560-1660* (London, Routledge, 1965). The essay by Miss Higgins is part of B. Manning (ed.), *Politics, Religion and the English Civil War* (London, Arnold, 1973).

54 Morton's book was published by Lawrence and Wishart (London), Barbour's by Yale U.P. (New Haven). Cole's article is reprinted in Aston, *op. cit.*

55 See G.E. Aylmer (ed.), *The Levellers in the English Revolution* (London, Thames and Hudson, 1975) and its critical bibliography. There is an excellent discussion of the Levellers in Brian Manning, *The English People and the English Revolution* (London, Heinemann, 1976).

56 J.H. Plumb, 'The Growth of the electorate in England from 1600 to 1715', *P.P.*, 45 (1969). D. Hirst's book, *The Representative of the People? Voters and Voting in England under the Early Stuarts*, was published by C.U.P. (Cambridge). Dr Hirst is now on the staff of Washington University.

57 Hirst, *op. cit.*, p. 193.

58 *Ibid.*, pp. 31, 44-64, 95, 105.

59 *Ibid.*, pp. 148, 149, 152, 176.

60 B. Manning, *The English People and the English Revolution 1640-1649* (1976), pp. v, 2, 20, 70.

61 *Ibid.*, pp. 96, 98, 197, 148, 137, 184. The small farmers and

craftsmen, however, were not mutually exclusive categories. The proto-industrialization of parts of the countryside meant that large numbers with dual occupations shared the grievances of both groups.

62 *Ibid.*, pp. 102, 234, 162.
63 B. Moore, *Social Origins of Dictatorship and Democracy* (Harmondsworth, Penguin University Books, 1973), p. 523.

Chapter 9

1 P. Laslett (ed.), *John Locke: Two Treatises of Government* (Cambridge, C.U.P., 1960).
2 V. Snow, 'The Concept of Revolution in Seventeenth-Century England', *Hist. Jnl.*, V (1962), pp. 169, 174.
3 G.M. Straka, 'Revolutionary ideology in Stuart England' in P.J. Korshin (ed.), *Studies in Change and Revolution. Aspects of English intellectual history 1640-1800* (Menston, Yorks., Scolar Press, 1972), p. 15.
4 Cooper's essay appeared in J.S. Bromley and E.H. Kossman (eds), *Britain and the Netherlands* (London, Chatto & Windus, 1960).
5 Merriman's book was published by the Clarendon Press (Oxford). The *P.P.* articles on this subject were collected together in T. Aston (ed.), *Crisis in Europe 1560-1660* (London, Routledge, 1965).
6 Aston, *op. cit.*, pp. 5-6. The 'General Crisis' thesis was explored simultaneously in R. Mousnier, *Les XVIe et XVIIe Siècles* (Paris, Presses Universitaires de France, 1954).
7 Aston, *op. cit.*, p. 95.
8 *Past and Present* has published further articles on this theme since the appearance of *Crisis in Europe* in 1965. See, for example, J.V. Polisensky, 'The Thirty Years' War and the Crises and Revolutions of Seventeenth-Century Europe', and H. Kamen, 'The economic and social consequences of the Thirty Years' War', *P.P.*, 39 (1968); J.H. Elliott, 'Revolution and continuity in early modern Europe', *P.P.*, 42 (1969); A. Clarke, 'Ireland and the General Crisis', *P.P.*, 48 (1970); and J.I. Israel, 'Mexico and the General Crisis of the Seventeenth Century', *P.P.*, 63 (1974). See also A.D. Lublinskaya, *French Absolutism: the crucial phase, 1620-1629* (Cambridge, C.U.P., 1968); N. Steensgaard, 'The economic and political crisis of the seventeenth century', *Thirteenth International Congress of Historical Sciences* (Moscow, 1970); J.H. Elliott,

184 *The debate on the English revolution*

'England and Europe: a common malady?' in C. Russell (ed.), *The Origins of the English Civil War* (London Macmillan, 1973); D. Stevenson, *The Scottish Revolution, 1637-1644. The Triumph of the Covenanters* (Newton Abbot, David & Charles, 1973); R. Foster and J.P. Greene (eds), *Preconditions of Revolution in Early Modern Europe* (Baltimore, Johns Hopkins University Press, 1970); and D. Parker, *Europe's Seventeenth-century Crisis: a marxist review* (London, History Group of the Communist Party, 'Our History' pamphlet series, no. 56, 1973).

9 Brinton's book was first published in 1938 (Prentice-Hall, N.Y.) with revised editions 1952, 1965.

10 B. Moore, *Social Origins of Dictatorship and Democracy* (Harmondsworth, Penguin University Books, 1973), pp. xiv, x, xi, 428.

11 Walzer's book was published by Weidenfeld (London). *See* pp. 300, 303, 315. Cf. G. Lewy, *Religion and Revolution* (N.Y., O.U.P. 1974).

12 In fact, from a methodological point of view Laslett's book was much less original than it appeared since it was clearly indebted to the work of French historians such as Ariès, Goubert and Henry. P. Laslett's book *The World We Have Lost* was published by Methuen (London, 1965; 1971).

13 Laslett, *op. cit.*, pp. 24, 28, 29.

14 C. Hill, *Change and Continuity in Seventeenth-Century England* (London, Weidenfeld, 1975), pp. 213-14.

15 *T.L.S.* (9 December, 1965).

16 Laslett, *op. cit.*, p. 167.

17 L. Stone, *The Causes of the English Revolution*, pp. 3, 7. The book was published by Routledge (London) in 1972. H. Eckstein (ed.), *Internal War* (London, Collier-Macmillan, 1964); M. Olson, 'Rapid growth as a destabilizing force', *Jnl of Economic Hist.*, XXIII (1963); J.C. Davies, 'Toward a theory of revolution', *American Sociological Review*, XXVII (1962).

18 Stone, *op. cit.*, p. 22.

Further reading

The real bibliography of this book lies in its notes. What follows is simply a selection of some of the most important and easily accessible items.

General

C.H. Firth, 'The development of the study of seventeenth-century history', *T.R.H.S.*, 3rd series, VII (1913).

C.H. George, 'Puritanism as history and historiography', *P.P.*, 41 (1968).

C. Hill, *Puritanism and Revolution* (London, Secker and Warburg 1958).

J.R. Hale, *The Evolution of British Historiography* (London, Macmillan, 1967).

F. Stern (ed.), *The Varieties of History from Voltaire to the Present*. 2nd edn (London, Macmillan, 1970).

L. Stone, *Social Change and Revolution in England 1540-1640* (London, Longmans, 1965).

_____, *The Causes of the English Revolution 1529-1642* (London, Routledge, 1972).

P.A.M. Taylor, *The Origins of the English Civil War* (Lexington Mass., Heath, 1960).

Joan Thirsk, *The Restoration* (London, Longmans, 1976).

The Seventeenth Century

Edward Hyde, Earl of Clarendon, *History of the Rebellion and Civil Wars in England*, ed. W.D. Macray (Oxford, Clarendon Press 1888).

James Harrington, *Oceana*, ed. S.B. Liljegren (Lund and Heidelberg, 1924).

Thomas Hobbes, *Behemoth, or the Long Parliament*, ed. F. Tonniës, 2nd edn, with a new introduction by M.M. Goldsmith (London Cass, 1969).

R. MacGillivray, *Restoration Historians and the English Civil War* (The Hague, Martinus Nijhoff, 1974).

J.G.A. Pocock, *The Ancient Constitution and the Feudal Law. A study of English historical theory in the seventeenth century* (Cambridge, C.U.P., 1957).

H.R. Tevor-Roper, *Clarendon and the Practice of History* (Los Angeles, William Andrews Clark Memorial Library, 1965).

B.H.G. Wormald, *Clarendon. Politics, historiography and religion 1640-1660* (Cambridge, C.U.P., 1964).

P. Zagorin, *A History of Political Thought in the English Revolution* (London, Routledge, 1954).

The Eighteenth Century

J.B. Black, *The Art of History* (London, Methuen, 1926).

Bridget and C. Hill, 'Catherine Macaulay and the Seventeenth Century', *Welsh Hist. Rev.*, III, (1967).

David Hume, *History of Great Britain. The reigns of James I and Charles I,* ed. D. Forbes. (Harmondsworth, Penguin, 1970).

T.P. Peardon, *The Transition in English Historical Writing 1760-1830* (N.Y., Columbia U.P., 1933).

Caroline Robbins, *The Eighteenth-Century Commonwealthman* (N.Y., Atheneum, 1968).

The Nineteenth Century

C.H. Firth, *A Commentary on Macaulay's History of England* (London, Macmillan, 1938).

S.R. Gardiner, *History of the Great Civil War* (1893).

G.P. Gooch, *History and Historians in the Nineteenth Century* 2nd edn (London, Longmans, 1952).

C.E. McClelland, *The German Historians and England* (Cambridge, C.U.P., 1971).

The Twentieth Century

1) *The Gardiner Tradition*
C.H. Firth, *Essays Historical and Literary* (Oxford, Clarendon Press, 1938).

_____, *Oliver Cromwell and the Rule of the Puritans in England* (1900, World's Classics edn, 1953).

G.M. Trevelyan, *England under the Stuarts* (London, Methuen, 1904, 21st edn, 1957).

2) *Society and Revolution*
C. Hill, *The English Revolution 1640* (London, Lawrence and Wishart, 1940).

_____, *Intellectual Origins of the English Revolution* (Oxford, Clarendon Press, 1965).

_____, *The World Turned Upside Down, Radical ideas during the English Revolution* (London, Temple-Smith, 1972).

_____, *Change and Continuity in Seventeenth-Century England* (London, Weidenfeld, 1975).

L. Stone, *The Crisis of the Aristocracy 1558-1641* (Oxford, Clarendon Press, 1965).

R. Terrill, *R.H. Tawney and His Times. Socialism as Fellowship* (London, Deutsch, 1974).

R.H. Tawney, *Religion and the Rise of Capitalism* (London, Murray, 1926).

_____, 'Harrington's Interpretation of His Age', in Lucy Sutherland (ed.), *Studies in History. British Academy Lectures* (London, O.U.P., 1966).

_____, 'The Rise of the Gentry' in E.M. Carus-Wilson (ed.), *Essays in Economic History*, vol. I (London, Arnold, 1954).

3) *Local and Regional*
Mary Coate, *Cornwall in the Great Civil War and Interregnum 1642-1660* (Oxford, Clarendon Press, 1933).

A.M. Everitt, *The Community of Kent and the Great Rebellion* (Leicester, Leicester U.P., 1966).

_____, *The Local Community and the Great Rebellion* (London, Historical Association, 1969).

J.S. Morrill, *Cheshire 1630-1660. County government and society during the 'English Revolution'* (Oxford, Clarendon Press, 1974).

Valerie Pearl, *London and the Outbreak of the Puritan Revolution* (London, O.U.P., 1961).

R.C. Richardson, *Puritanism in North-West England. A regional study of the diocese of Chester to 1642* (Manchester, Manchester U.P., 1972).

4) *Political Studies*

G.E. Aylmer, *The King's Servants. The civil service of Charles I, 1625-42* (London, Routledge, 1961, 2nd edn, 1974).

———, *The State's Servants. The civil service of the English Republic 1649-1660* (London, Routledge, 1973).

D. Brunton and D.H. Pennington, *Members of the Long Parliament* (London, Allen and Unwin, 1954).

D. Hirst, *The Representative of the People? Voters and Voting in England under the early Stuarts* (Cambridge, C.U.P., 1975).

B. Manning, *The English People and the English Revolution 1640-49* (London, Heinemann, 1976).

D. Underdown, *Pride's Purge. Politics in the English Revolution* (Oxford, Clarendon Press, 1971).

C.V. Wedgwood, *The King's Peace 1637-41* (London, Collins, 1955).

———, *The King's War 1641-47* (London, Collins, 1958).

B. Worden, *The Rump Parliament 1648-53* (Cambridge, C.U.P., 1974).

5) *New Perspectives*

T. Aston (ed.), *Crisis in Europe 1560-1660* (London, Routledge, 1965).

C. Brinton, *The Anatomy of Revolution* (N.Y., Prentice-Hall, 1938. revised eds, 1952, 1965).

P. Laslett, *The World We Have Lost* (London, Methuen, 1965, 2nd edn 1971).

B. Moore Jnr, *Social Origins of Dictatorship and Democracy. Lord and peasant in the making of the modern world* (Harmondsworth, Penguin University Books, 1973).

V. Snow, 'The concept of revolution in seventeenth-century England', *Hist. Jnl*, V (1962).

M. Walzer, *The Revolution of the Saints. A study in the origins of radical politics* (London, Weidenfeld, 1966).

Index